MW00345322

White Picket Fences

A Mennonite Boy's Global Adventures

By Doug Gehman

Copyright © 2014
J. Douglas Gehman
All Rights Reserved

All rights reserved. No part of this book may be reproduced in any form, except for the inclusion of brief quotations, without permission in writing from the author or publisher.

Library of Congress
Control Number:

ISBN 978-0-9765168-3-5

First printing 2014 (b)

Published by:
Globe Publishing
PO Box 3040
Pensacola, FL 32516-3040

ENDORSEMENTS

Readers, young and old, will enjoy Doug Gehman's newest book, *White Picket Fences*. Stories about his Mennonite childhood, his prodigal youth, his journey back to God, his family's rigorous evangelistic experiences in Southeast Asia and his angst and recovery in personal tragedies will evoke laughter, tears, pondering and historical and political insight. These are told in an authentic way that will keep your rapt attention from beginning to end. Throughout his life's tapestry, you will discern a golden thread, pulled by the needle of the Holy Spirit, of God-given desire and its sometimes unusual fulfillment. The book holds much to amuse us and stir our emotions. You will be inspired to seek God for your own lives. *White Picket Fences* might get on the best-seller list! It is that good. Doug's gift is literary genius – a MUST READ!

- *Beth Bishop, wife of J. Robert Bishop, Founding Director of Globe International. Richmond, Virginia*

White Picket Fences is a special book and a great read. Doug Gehman is a gifted communicator. He is poignantly honest about life's highs and lows, but more so from a unique life – Mennonite background, teen rebellion, radical conversion, Charismatic ups and downs and heart-wrenching struggles as a missionary family in Southeast Asia. The chapters lamenting the suicide of his dear brother left me in meaningful tears; Our family too has had to walk out the tragic aftermath of suicide. Doug's writing is redemptive yet not preachy, helpful without clichéd answers. I have known Doug for decades as a friend and a pastor. He is the real thing, and I am honored to recommend his artful writing.

- *Doug Holmes, Sr. Pastor, Christian Life Church. Milton, Florida*

A well-written trip down memory lane: One man's journey from a young Mennonite boy to a global world missionary. *White Picket Fences* is a great resource for understanding Mennonite culture and how your origins help shape your character and determine your destiny.

- *Jim Britnell, President, Reconciled Ministries. Pensacola, Florida*

3

What a great story of what God can do when religious foundations align with a sincere pursuit of God's will and purpose in our lives. Having known and worked closely with Doug Gehman as friend and colleague over many years I can heartily recommend *White Picket Fences*. May it inspire you as it has me in our journey from where we came from to that place where God is taking us.

- *Buford Lipscomb, Sr. Pastor Liberty Church, President of Liberty Network International, Pensacola, Florida*

White Picket Fences is an inspiring and absorbing adventure into a life story that for most would only be experienced through a Hollywood picture. Travel with Doug Gehman from the cornfields of Lancaster, Pennsylvania to the battlefields of South Asia; all the while being directed on a path set by his Savior. If you have ever asked yourself, "Can my simple life ever make a difference," Doug Gehman's *White Picket Fences* will prove to you that if God be your partner, make your plans large.

- *Scott Brown, author of "Baseball in Pensacola" and co-author of "Three Finger, The Mordecai Brown Story." Pensacola, Florida*

White Picket Fences will be an inspiration to parents and grandparents because it reaffirms one thing: that the example we set for our children will endure. Doug is living the legacy, on a global scale, that his grandparents and parents gave to him... and now passes it to his children and grandchildren. *White Picket Fences* offers rare insights into the Mennonite community! A delightful read!

- *Sandy Carter-Britnell, Director, Children of Destiny Children's Home. Los Cedros, Nicaragua*

TABLE OF CONTENTS

ACKNOWLEDGEMENTS

This book could not have been written without the support of my family, especially my wife. Our children, my parents and grandparents, my siblings, and the aunts and uncles from the Gehman and Stoltzfus branches of the tree that is my progeny not only provided the content for this book, but, more importantly, they contributed to the experiences that still live in my memories, and the subsequent happy nostalgia I will cherish to my dying day. Those experiences, and their memories, made these words worth writing down.

I am thankful for my Mennonite community, the church where I grew up in Neffsville, my college experience and the introduction to Zion Chapel, now called Harvest Community Church, the church that propelled my family toward our ultimate destiny.

I am also deeply indebted to my friends on the mission field where we served for fifteen years. John Whalen, one of my dearest friends, inspired so many stories and made me laugh so heartily – even when life was tough – that I still grin when I think about him and those intrepid adventures. I am forever indebted to him for being a part of my life. Wayne Crooke, who nurtured our early years, gave us a chance to serve and preach, and showed us the power of faith and determination; Ray Jennings and his team who led us into some of the most powerful experiences in ministry we have ever known. All our colleagues and friends – Bill and Mitzi Katz, Randy Matsumoto, Pastor and Sheila Yoganathan, who so encouraged us through the years and have remained lifelong friends, and so many others – you have enriched our lives by sharing with us in a great legacy of service, risk, and adventure on our common journey around the world.

I am so thankful for my pastor friends, specifically Sam and Nancy Webb (Honolulu) and Doug Holmes (Pensacola) who insisted this story be told.

Finally, I am indebted to my current community of friends and family in Pensacola Florida who helped me bring this book to the publisher. They are too many to mention, but a few made significant contributions to the process. First of all, my wife listened to my ideas and told me when I got too wordy (my chronic malady). Josh Britnell read the first draft and offered helpful suggestions. Our son Trevor noted the stories that made him laugh, and made me share them with others. And finally, my Staff were exceedingly supportive and encouraging – with special thanks to Kristiana Hardy, who helped design the cover and finalize the manuscript. I greatly appreciate all of you for your friendship and assistance!

FOREWARD

Some of my friends have asked me why I wrote *White Picket Fences*. A good question, considering every author ostensibly has a compelling reason for engaging the discipline of writing. Arranging thoughts into a stream of words that become paragraphs and then chapters all of which eventually emerges as an organized thing we call a "book" is serious work. It is not for the faint of heart or the sporadically inspired. I've been at this book, my third, for nearly two decades. So, my *reason* for writing would seem to be self-evident.

Why then did I write? Honestly, I had to think about the answer. The project started as nostalgia, a huge pile-up of memories that crowded into my consciousness when our family moved back to Lancaster County after nearly twenty years in another galaxy called South East Asia. The nostalgia needed to flow somewhere. So, out came the computer. I sat for hours, happily tap-tap-tapping words and paragraphs and chapters. But stories about a man's childhood are not a compelling purpose for writing a book, unless of course the guy has lived an extraordinary life, or simply wants to give his children a commemorative of their pedigree. As it could be compared to most of my relatives and friends in Lancaster County, one could say my life has been extraordinary. But frankly, my kids and grandkids are reason enough for me to write stuff down. Simply put, I wanted *them* to know.

But, as the stories transferred from sentiment to computer, I realized I was writing for another reason. I wanted to share with a larger audience the story about where I came from. I am not talking about Lancaster County or Mennonite culture per se. Where I came from is defined by something more specific. I came from Aaron F. and Katie Stoltzfus, and Eli H. and Mary Gehman, and James Robert Gehman and Fannie Arlene Stoltzfus Gehman. These are my grandparents and parents. More than anything else, these *people*, and their values defined the person I am today. Their influence has had a profound effect on my perspective, identity, and choices.

It is difficult to make a case for family influence in Western culture. We have become too individualistic. Our worldview, our private and professional lives, our educational systems, even our religious beliefs are deeply influenced by a paradigm of individualism. The framework is so ubiquitous that most of us are not even aware of it. Western culture is the most advanced expression of human existence the planet has ever known, so we aren't inclined to critique its worldview and paradigms, not with our surpassing knowledge, scientific advancements and sophisticated technology. We can eradicate once-deadly infections with simple drugs, we can fly around the globe in less than twenty-four hours, and we can talk to almost any other human being on the planet within minutes. So, we Westerners tend to be self-absorbed, even arrogant.

But for all of our learning, for all our wealth and sophistication, for all our advancements in technology, science, and medicine, we can't seem to love each other. We simply do not know how to sustain long-term intimacy. Our primary relationships, the ones that should provide us with the most meaning, safety and stability, seem impossible after the honeymoon wears off and real life happens.

I wrote this book to expose the root of that problem. I could just crow about my accomplishments. I suppose I have enough of them about which to brag, and will provide a few examples along the way to keep this book interesting. But I wrote to tell another human story, namely about why, after nearly forty years, I'm still married to the same woman. That didn't happen by accident; in fact, in today's world that is quite an accomplishment. It is a gift my wife and I have given to each other. We have given the gift *back* to our parents and grandparents, forward to our children, and now it goes forward *again* to their spouses and children.

We weren't simply lucky. My wife and I didn't – in our very human yearning to find someone to love, marry, and have sex with – miraculously meet our one true soul mate, the perfect partnership that Destiny arranged and through which everything came together in unshakeable cosmic harmony. This naïve idea, and its underlying worldview – which makes billions of dollars for the movie and publishing industries – is a big, fat lie.

Okay, we married for romantic love, but we stayed together for love of another kind. In truth, for about a decade in the middle of our journey, we didn't like each other very much. Sometimes we even hated each other. And, in all that alienation and loneliness, I didn't like God much either. I certainly couldn't figure Him out, or understand why He was allowing me to suffer. I didn't want to worship Him, not in the way we define worship – as a euphoric expression of gratitude and affection toward God who made my life complete and meaningful. The emotional side of my worship experience in those years was better defined by bewilderment and indifference. When your primary relationships are going to hell, nothing else makes much sense.

But worship is more than passion. It is ascribing *worth* to God, and we do that by aligning ourselves with His character and *living* His way. The reasons I survived those years are based squarely upon the stuff I learned from my Lancaster County family. My wife would add that her contribution to our success was the result of similar influences gleaned from her Methodist upbringing in rural Indiana. Our parents taught us how to live, how to love, and how to make life work, even when it isn't easy.

Their values were plowed into the fertile soil of my childhood; I carried them forward into adulthood. Unfortunately, those values have almost disappeared from western culture. Duty, covenant, patience, and perseverance have been replaced – even in our practice of faith – by a pre-occupation with passion, personal fulfillment, and fun. The latter has almost eradicated the former. And now we wonder why we are so lonely and can't make life work.

That these principles work in primary relationships proves their power, and illustrates why they are the only sensible way to live on the planet. All other endeavors, all other human pursuits, even spiritual ones, amount to nothing in comparison to the fruit those qualities produce.

I'm preaching when I meant to tell a story. Why did I write *White Picket Fences*? Well, now you have a hint....

PROLOGUE

We drive through barren, sun-burned flat landscape up to the entrance of an unmarked military base, tires crunching on broken asphalt, and stop in front of a dilapidated guard post bunker. The "Base" is farther down a dirt road, viewable in the shimmering heat, mostly unimpressive rows of faded green tents and a smattering of similarly faded vehicles. My driver, Anthony, and I emerge from our sweltering van into the scorching tropical sunlight, pouring sweat. Perspiration is a constant and aggravating part of existence in South Asia. So too is a feeling, burned on my psyche after only a week, that everything on this Indian Ocean faded green patch of sand and rock is dirty, old and tired. The van we drive is falling apart, the roads are worn out, the electric grid provides power sporadically, water comes and goes in odd colors from the faucets, and nothing ever happens on time. Even the parched landscape seems grim in the relentless heat. I wipe my brow and squint at the bunker. A guard's eyes glow from the shadows, and the tip of his AK-47 sticks out into the sunlight, aimed at my chest. Fat sandbags protect the front and sides of the bunker, the rusty tin roof is covered with a double layer, but the guard is taking no chances. His gaze shifts between the two odd-looking civilians, one white, the other brown. We walk slowly towards him twenty feet away. The guard eyes my briefcase suspiciously. It is now an annoying burden that prevents me from doing what I really want to do: reach for the sky. I think about dropping the briefcase, but decide against it. With the guard's testy demeanor and that weapon, any sudden move could be fatal. To demonstrate submission, I spread my arms like wings, a maneuver that leans me to the left under the briefcase's weight. Beside me, Anthony, who has *his* hands in the air, starts talking, explaining, I presume, in his native Tamil language, our reasons for being here. We are close enough to see the guard's finger on the trigger of that assault rifle.

The base is located at "Elephant Pass," a narrow, flat, sandy sun-scorched isthmus separating the mainland from Jaffna Peninsula. It is one of many makeshift military installations in the north and east of this island nation, set up and populated by combat-ready soldiers, the government's hasty response to insurgency. Sri Lanka has been fighting a civil war between races, Tamils against Singhalese, for several years. Tens of thousands have died, including officers and soldiers by bombings and surprise attacks on military bases, and by roadside bombs, bus bombs and nail-laced bombs in the public market at the busiest time of day. The conflict has imposed appalling trauma on a weary and victimized, but not wholly innocent, civilian population. Life is tough in this former island paradise, especially around military installations.

I don't like the weapon, but can empathize with the poor guy pointing it at us. He is just obeying orders and trying to stay alive. The guard is Singhalese, of this I am sure, because Tamil separatists don't maintain public military posts. The Tamil Tigers, a name the separatists have adopted for themselves, fight the Singhalese government mostly from secret bases, attacking by surprise and disappearing back into the jungle. My white skin distinguishes me as a non-combatant, obviously not local, but it hasn't removed the tension in the air. The stupid briefcase in my hand is the guard's clear concern.

With normal skin-tone variations, the Tamils and Singhalese are coffee-colored people, and although different in

14

every other way – language, culture, and religion – their physical features make them veritable racial twins. To distinguish themselves, even from each other, native-born Sri Lankan's must speak. Language differences or, for the bilingual, accent nuances, help clarify race and make the determination about which side of the conflict they are on. ("Say 'Shibboleth!'") It is an awkward complication of war, when the enemy isn't easily identifiable. Right now, my Caucasian appearance helps me a little – it might even be keeping us alive – not so my despised companion who is still jabbering away in Tamil. Unfortunately, neither my foreignness nor his ethnicity is persuading the guard to lower the working end of that Kalashnikov. The guard looks confused (what is this foreigner doing here?!) but, trained to trust no one, the gun remains pointed at us, and the guard's finger doesn't move. As we approach the bunker, with me still leaning to the left (this stupid BRIEFCASE!), Anthony reaches down and slowly pulls his Sri Lanka ID card from a shirt pocket, an obviously practiced move. An order is barked from the bunker. Anthony stops and asks me to open the briefcase. I carefully comply. Finally, with preliminary clearance, the guard lowers his weapon and an officer emerges from the shadows of the bunker to examine our documents.

"What do you want?" he asks in heavily accented English, through a wisp of musty cigarette smoke and body odor. His bloodshot eyes shift between Anthony, me, and our documents.

"I'm a local pastor at Jaffna New Life Church," Anthony offers hopefully. "We are planning an open air meeting, and need a permit from the Base Commander. The Kilinochchi Police told us to come here."

I am not new to Asia – our family has been wandering around the sub-continent for over six years working with various teams – but I am new to the island and to this war. I have come here on a mission, braving the dangers and the naysayers, to preach the Good News of Jesus to the nation's eighteen million people. Friends ask me why go to a war-torn country when there are many other peaceful places to preach. I reply that even in war women have babies, and children get up for breakfast and march off to school. If Sri Lanka is safe enough for them, it is safe enough for me.

I have a grandiose goal (eighteen million Sri Lankans!) – a dream I'll pursue by conducting open-air meetings wherever churches will invite me. I haven't yet figured out the other details. I'm building my team, some of whom are with me on this trip, and others like John Whalen and Bill Katz, whom I met when we worked together in India, will come later. I hope within a few years I will spawn a massive move of God on the island. I'm starting small (what grand idea doesn't?) which is not as much a decision of intent as a limitation of budget and experience. I'm young, only twenty-eight, and have dreams of expansive adventures through unchartered waters, and at this age have an abundance of one great commodity: time.

Every young man wants to make a mark on the planet. The fact that my untested vision is God-oriented and Christ-centered doesn't completely expunge the youthful ambition. A proverb says, "The glory of young men is their strength; the gray hair of experience is the splendor of the old." As I write this, now in middle age, I more fully appreciate Solomon's wise observation. Only young people are too ignorant to know what can't be done and what won't work. Every generation produces a bumper crop of youthful souls whose hearts beat with unrealistic dreams to change the world. Naïve maybe, but thank God for them! If the wisdom of old men, learned from a lifetime of too many failures and too few successes, were foisted onto the young, the knowledge would destroy their ambition to try. So, I say, "More power to youthful naiveté! May millions of young adults foolishly reach for the impossible!" Time and again throughout history, and against all odds, many such young people made an impact, changed a paradigm, and pushed the world an inch or two farther away from catastrophe. God knows we need the push.

Human beings are way too predisposed to live at the edge of disaster.

Besides vision, I have little else. I don't even own a vehicle on this island, and can hardly afford transportation – hence the broke-down rental. For the first year we will drag our equipment – a heavy, wooden crate containing a sound system, and lights and wires – into buses, trains, and taxis. We will stay in cheap or free accommodations, unwilling to waste our limited resources on creature comforts. Not that Elephant Pass and Kilinochchi offer such indulgences. We take what we find, mostly decrepit guest houses, and spend our cash on the Goal. Making the sacrifices, while inconvenient, is a part of the Dream. Young volunteers who travel with me happily adjust to the inconveniences, schlepping personal stuff and team equipment over deteriorating roads and squeaking rail lines in arduous tropical heat to obscure destinations like Ratnapura, Pusselawa, Kilinochchi, and Mullaitivu.

We get the permit – I presume the base commander was a humanitarian or libertarian – and a few days later conduct the meeting outside Kilinochchi. It goes off without interruption – five continuous nights – which for me is an incredible victory on this first trip to Sri Lanka. I will spend a decade working in this country. In that time living conditions will improve, and the original dream will mature exponentially. Time and experience has a way of pruning and proving vision. In my case, it was not a reduction. We reached a lot of people in that decade, at least ten thousand souls. I dreamed of preaching to multitudes; God helped me plant scores of churches, and in the planting the multitudes were reached. Plus, we built something permanent – church families – who continue to grow and multiply.

The word catalytic comes to mind. With a supply of oxygen and a source of fuel, a little flame, started by a simple strike of a match, will become an inferno. In our case, the fuel was hungry people and a message of hope. People gathered, sometimes by hundreds and sometimes by thousands, mostly in remote villages. Churches emerged, little gatherings of people, and each grew as a local presence of Jesus in a community. It started with a dream and a few bold steps by an idealistic group of young American men and a Sri Lankan who we affectionately called Pastor Yoga. We joined hands, started a fire and God fanned it into a flame. At the beginning, it was only a dream that struggled at first, but then it grabbed hold and grew and in time made an impact on the nation. Today thirty-five thousand people trace the roots of their faith to the foundations we put down, one patient day at a time.

Thank God, when I first traveled to Sri Lanka and walked up to that guard bunker with a Sri Lankan friend, I was too stupid to know what could not be done. Through history, countless young people have done similar things and lit similar fires. Early church leaders – they were all young men and women – turned the world upside down in a few decades. They had a Message, a Mandate, and a super-empowering Force called the Holy Spirit. Compared to what we enjoy today, the infrastructure called the Roman Empire, with its road systems and shipping lines, their support system was pitiful. But they had vision, they were determined, and they loved not their lives to the death!

But this book is about more than our successes in Asia. It is equally about the people who brought me into this world and, by their nurture, made it easier for me to get where God wanted me to go. The older I get the more I appreciate patience and determination, and where I got mine. It came from God; He ultimately gets the credit. He set me on fire when I was eighteen, at Jesus '73. But God also gave me determination through the people of my heritage. During my formative years, my parents and grandparents deposited something into me that made the fire burn stronger and longer. The Pentateuch speaks about "The Blessing," an ephemeral goodness or empowerment or identity that flows through a family line from parent to child and onward to the third and fourth generation. My Mennonite heritage, and the specific family into which I was born, handed me some of those foundational tools. The Blessing traveled to me through the lives of Eli H. Gehman and Aaron F. Stoltzfus, my grandfathers, and James Robert and Fannie Arlene Gehman, my parents. They gave me determination, and a lot of other things, not as gifts, but an example, a life well lived based on duty, commitment, and finishing well. I am the product of their influence, and that is the essence of this story.

WHITE PICKET FENCES

1 Nostalgia

It's summertime, 1993. We just arrived in Pennsylvania after a year in Honolulu, and are at this moment settling into a new life in Lancaster County, the place of my birth. Hawaii was twelve months of delightful paradise living that followed twenty-four other months of *un*-delightful transitions: three major moves in two years, from Thailand to Indiana to Hawaii. This fourth move to Lancaster County is I hope the last one. We are unpacking a mountain of luggage intending to settle permanently among the people of my heritage.

For the fifteen years preceding these recent global "transitions," our existence is best described as a meandering family-on-mission journey through tropical South and East Asia. Fifteen years! It was not wasted time. But, I am glad it is over, or at least in a lull. World travel is over-romanticized. Absence from home does produce one alluring commodity: nostalgia. I now have an overflowing cauldron of it, hence these words on these pages.

After twenty years and with nearly thirty countries under my travel belt, from Taiwan in the China Sea to the western coasts of Holland, I have finally come home. Home is the quintessential land of the Amish and Mennonites. I left these roots in the summer of 1973, an eager high school graduate, with long hair and a hopeful mustache, just newly in love with Jesus, and ready to go out and conquer the world. Except for a rather cacophonous mixture of emotions about everything I've done and everywhere I've been these past two decades, it feels pretty good to be back. One thing is certain in my mind: it is time to build a white picket fence.

Why? Because this white linear marker on the property line is the undisputed symbol of American nostalgia. And I want some of my own. Lancaster County's ambiance is not Bangkok or London, a comparison lost to residents who have lived in folksy nostalgia all their lives, but in my current state of mind, overrun as it is with world vision and international stimulation, Lancaster's homey atmosphere is absolutely soothing. Besides, on the salary I've accepted as pay for my contribution to this struggling planet, our family's choices are limited. But we'll survive here, and even enjoy a few creature comforts. Anyway – and frankly this might be the real reason I'm writing all this stuff about my origins – everyone who hasn't actually lived here thinks Amish culture is quaint.

Most of the locals simply do not understand why anyone would leave Lancaster County. My mother pointed out this fact recently when I tried to explain my angst. We were talking over cups of steaming coffee at a local supermarket cum restaurant. Such combinations actually exist here. The place was filled with farmers, construction workers, a few professionals, and the requisite number of conservative Mennonites. The women wearing plain dresses and head coverings make the last distinction easy. The restaurant was buzzing. Everyone had come during the noon hour for the bountiful buffet offerings of Lancaster County cooking. Mother and I sat at our little table, covered with a red-and-white-checkered tablecloth, while servers and guests browsed the four buffet islands. I went on and on about world travel, exotic cultures, money problems and fatigue. The woman who brought me into this world nearly forty years before and who reluctantly accepted my departure after high school, sipped her cup of coffee and stared at me. When I paused to take a breath she said, "Well, you could have stayed here. Nobody forced you to go traipsing all over the world."

We'll get to back to my mother, but first the angst. There's a lot of it, revolving mostly around the absence of roots, a terrible by-product of too much travel. Of all the feelings wrestling for position inside of me right now, getting settled has most ardently prevailed. I feel so strongly about having a home of my own that once I get it – and go up to my eyeballs in debt for the privilege – I think I will go out in the front yard, build a picket fence along the property line, and paint it Tom Sawyer white-wash white so I can gaze at it each morning.

Benjamin Franklin once said, "Variety is the spice of life!" With his philandering reputation, I rather think old Ben was referring to a different kind of variety than has been my experience, but the sentiment conveys. However, musings about variety appeal primarily to bored people who have been sitting at the same breakfast table, gazing out the same picture window at the same white picket fence for twenty years. Not so a distraught world traveler such as myself, over-extended as I am by airports, hotels, hostile immigration officials, unstable governments, strange customs and dim restaurants serving pungent-smelling foods that require prayer for more fundamental reasons than gratitude.

I'm actually looking forward to being bored to death for a while. I have had such a kaleidoscope of variety these past twenty years that I am ready to puke. Like the kid who pays for ONE ride on the Ferris Wheel, and then the controller goes out for lunch, leaving the poor soul going around and around and around forever, I'm plum worn out. Stimulation is meant to be temporary, served up in small, manageable doses.

"Spice" is having a vacation every year, or a glass of fine wine at a wedding. The annual county fair only lasts a week, for heaven's sake! Life, on the other hand, is defined by the spaces in between. Yard maintenance, including trimming around white picket fences, is the stuff that makes life real… and stable. It also makes nostalgia so appealing. There's a reason movies end with the guy and his girl driving peacefully into the sunset along a lonely Nevada highway. We long for boring tranquility. Contrary to pop-culture's reinterpreting history in film, with torrents of adventure, conflict, and impassioned romance, America was built on dull routine. Routine is the essence of everyday life – not the aberration – and now it's my turn to have good dose of it.

Lancaster does boring really well. So, this book starts with Lancaster County and her people, with me at the center. What you're going to get is eastern Pennsylvania and beyond, all the way to the ends of the earth, through the eyes and ears of a Mennonite boy who left his home but never his roots. This is not a history lesson about the Mennonite Church. My reflections will be limited to the observations and experiences of an Anabaptist boy from Rothsville, Pennsylvania in the 1950s and 1960s who, now as an adult, is struggling with an overflowing pot of nostalgia and too much time on his hands. Writing is a satisfying way to pour off the contents.

After twenty years, I'm back in the neighborhood. Our high school twenty-year class reunion is this Friday night. I wonder if I'll run into old Del Miller and his basketball, a childhood experience that has shaped me perhaps more than I care to admit. I'm not looking for a fight with Del. After all these years, I doubt he even remembers me... or the incident. Maybe writing about him will be my revenge. If this book gets published, I'll change everyone's name but his. But right now I just want to build a white picket fence.

2 The Mennonites and Amish

Pennsylvania's Anabaptist community where I started my life – the bearded men in black hats and clothing and the women in head coverings and modesty aprons – makes for great storytelling but isn't representative of most of the Mennonites in Lancaster County. Even our immediate family, my mother especially, adorned in plain dress and head covering before she married, dispensed with the stereotype soon after I was born. My dad never grew a beard, and he rarely wore black, except maybe to a funeral. Pertaining to the faith and its biblical disciplines, they held the line, but abandoned the rigorous dress code as soon as they left home. My paternal and maternal grandparents, on the other hand, fit the Mennonite mold flawlessly, and in public life never deviated from the role. Black trousers, jackets and hats for the men, and head coverings and plain dresses with modesty aprons for the women – all symbols of holiness, austerity, and dedication to God – were a public responsibility they would not relinquish.

Conservative Mennonite and Amish folk are on display in Lancaster County for anyone who wishes to come and observe them. They don't mean to be on display, they don't even *want* to be on display, but their appearance in fact puts them on display... the clothing and head coverings sort of stand out. Black attire is couture de rigueur for public appearances. The color black also applies to cars and other forms of transportation that conservative Mennonites use. The big tractors, for use in their fields, somehow slipped through the color requirement probably because Allis Chalmers only sells orange-colored products. Farm-All offers only red, and of course John Deere is famous for its green line of farm equipment. What's a good Mennonite to do? We're too frugal to spend money on a paint job for a field tractor.

Every morning, upon rising from bed, my two grandmothers gathered their copious locks of hair (unbounded, it flowed down their backs to their waist-lines) into a bun, pinned the bun to the back of their heads, and tucked the bundle under a linen head covering. They rarely ventured from their bedrooms before this necessity of dress was completed. The tied-in-a-bun hair, tucked neatly under a head covering, is forever a part of my memories of my grandmothers, as unchanging as the calendar and as predictable as a sunrise. The modesty apron, that loose piece of cloth worn over the chest to minimize the curves, was another unchanging staple of these matrons. At home, Katie and Mary – to their faces I would never call them by those names, "Grandma" was the only name I ever used – sometimes wore breezy cotton pattern dresses, with the modesty apron. But for church, it was formal black every Sunday. Aaron and Eli wore black trousers with gray or blue shirts at home, but for formal occasions, mostly church services, they were covered in black from toes to crown. A white shirt peaked out around the neckline, hidden behind a tightly buttoned black jacket.

My immediate family – Dad and Mom and sister Judy and brother Dale, and a wider circle that included most of the members at Neffsville Mennonite Church – simply were not so conservative. My mother dispensed with the head covering early in married life when she started selling Avon products. Her piety remained, but except for Sunday mornings, the symbol was gone. In dress, we pretty much looked like everyone else. But we were very different, very conservative, and very sheltered. From early childhood it was quietly drilled into all Mennonite boys and girls that there are two kinds of people in the world: Us and Them. The "Us" group were Mennonites - Bible believing, modestly dressed, community conscious, puritanical pacifists. The "Them" group was pretty much everyone else, that is, anyone who wasn't a Mennonite or Amish. A few magnanimous Mennonites widened the circle to include other churches in the Anabaptist tradition.

Social exclusivity aside, Mennonites are some of the most sincere, hard-working, honest, caring, fair-minded, fun loving, family-oriented religious people I have ever met. To this day I hold great admiration for Mennonites. The men work hard and the women are great cooks, especially when any excuse for a special occasion provides opportunity for all of them to out-do each other in volume and flavor.

Jake: "Hey Amoos! How many Mennonites does it take to change a light bulb, vonst?"

Amos: "Vell, I don't know, Chake. How many, nah?"

Jake: "Von hundred, you know. Von to change the light bulb, and ninety-nine to cook the meal after!"

Mennonites aren't bad people. We are just pretty sure everyone else is. Not beyond redemption, but desperately in need of it, and certainly a bad influence to be avoided. Being constantly on guard lest the worldly ways of outsiders corrupt us is a compulsory Mennonite bearing. Of course, there is *much* to be avoided: worldly places, worldly activities, worldly clothes, worldly music, worldly cars, worldly media. Mennonites and Amish share this general cosmo-phobia. The Amish simply have a longer list of sins and maintain a greater distance from the temptations.

Most Mennonite communities, including Lancaster County, have a strong Amish presence nearby. Generally speaking, Amish are farmers. Other vocations, like carpentry and construction, are options, with cautious approval from overseeing Bishops, and more Amish men are delving into them to provide for their families. The Amish worldview believes that a simple rural lifestyle, with ample separation by farmland and occupation, offers its own protection against worldly influences. Most people think the Amish came first, and then through the gradual influences of the secular community, less strict Mennonites somehow emerged and broke away. Not so. Menno Simons started the movement. He was a Catholic priest who broke from the Church of Rome in the early 1500s over the issue of infant baptism. Baptism is for believers, he contended, and babies can't believe. So, the Mennonite Church emerged over an issue of timing: a question of when the human conscience develops and a person becomes morally responsible. Baptism was the catalyst. A hundred years later Jakob Ammann got into a dispute with Mennonite leadership over unacceptable social compromises pertaining to lifestyle. He broke with the Mennonites and the Amish Church (hence the name) was born.

Today, Amish communities quietly temper their Mennonite neighbors. In Lancaster County, and other such communities, the two faiths generally co-exist. There is no outward conflict, except when an Amish person leaves the faith and joins the Mennonites. The resultant Amish "shunning" of the departing soul and his welcome into the Mennonite Church produces an institutional form of passive-aggressive behavior. Nobody is really upset, but protocols must be followed. The rebel is excommunicated and no Amish person will ever talk with him or eat with him again. Generally, however, Amish and Mennonite communities get along. It's a good thing too, since pacifism is a cardinal tenet of both faiths; it is sincerely observed. And, anyway, fighting over social or theological issues wouldn't bode well for the community's witness to the outside. Most outsiders aren't big on the idea of pacifism, but they admire its qualities.

The followers of Jakob Ammann stubbornly resist anything too modern or too dependent on the world's systems. Eschewing dependence on the world is the root of the issue. To a lesser degree, the followers of Menno Simons adhere to the same value. Jesus taught that His followers should be "in the world but not of the world." Mennonites and Amish take Jesus seriously. The question, of course, is: What is "of the world?" I remember when our church debated for a year over buying a piano for worship in the sanctuary! For many congregants and leaders, musical instruments were worldly. The Amish have codified Jesus' admonition into church policy and require all members to live almost wholly disconnected from dependence on the outside world.

For example, the wheel is OK, and the cart and wagon are acceptable, but where does the Bible authorize the use of rubber tires (a replaceable component you will need to buy again, hence dependence on the world)? Equally taboo is neo-fire called electricity and the neo-horse called an internal combustion engine! Clothing styles are utterly simple. Clothes are to be worn, thus eliminating the nakedness problem of original sin. What else, really, is the point? Minimalistic function prevails over vain fashion. Amish culture has evolved, but it is always defined by simplicity and austerity. Conservative Mennonite and Amish communities are not evangelistic about these aspects of their faith, but the traits are an integral part of the message, and an expected expression of one's faith.

Martha, as the story goes, is a conservative Mennonite missionary woman serving in rural Africa. She is back home in Lancaster County for a visit and goes to see her friend Mary. Mary asks, "Martha, are you teaching ze women ze doctrine of ze plain clothes?"

"Vell, Mary," Martha replies, "Vee are chust glad if vee can get them to vare any clothes at all, you know!"

Once Jacob Ammann went down the moral road of protest, there was no turning back. The Amish decided anything introduced after 1700 was evil. God simply refused to allow technical progress past December 31, 1699. So clothes with buttons were out too.

Question: How do you distinguish an Amish baby from a heathen baby?

Answer: Heathen babies have belly buttons; Amish babies have a hook and eye.

It all gets rather complicated, even for the Amish. They can ride in an automobile, but never own one. They can talk on the telephone, but never have one installed in their home. They can be electrocuted, but not inside their house or on their property, because they don't buy electricity, not from the grid at least. My sister Judy pointed out this detail when we were discussing the subject. The Amish are not against electricity per se, she said. Some branches of the church allow for generators for essential tasks like keeping fresh milk cold before it is sold to the wholesaler. The Amish objection is the connection to the grid, that is, to become dependent on the world. This would deviate from the teachings of Jesus and the Apostle Paul who taught that Christians should not become "unequally yoked" to the world. Paul was referring to marriage outside the faith. The Amish have stretched Paul's intent to include every kind of interaction with the outside world.

The Amish avoid the world's grid, but they still have to get around. So symbiotic relationships have emerged, compromises with the surrounding world. Whole industries have arisen around Amish communities to cater to their unique needs to be "in the world but not of the world" and not be unequally yoked. Mennonites and entrepreneurial members of the "English" (i.e. outside) community make a good living off the Amish, providing transportation and other modern services to their Amish friends and neighbors. They haul Amish men and women around in their vans, and receive payment, ironically, in U.S. dollars, another worldly system with which the Amish have had to compromise. Telephone companies install phone booths at the end of the Amish farmer's lane, just over the property line so Jacob Stoltzfus can make telephone calls. Don't ask me whom he is calling. By allowing the use of the some of the world's conveniences but avoiding dependence on them, the Amish stay at least partially compliant with their tenets.

I rather think Paul's and Jesus' admonitions were referring more to a state of mind than a specific policy about telephone or electric service. But, every faith defines itself in part by prohibitions. My church frowned upon dancing, card playing, movies and the use of alcohol, even though, except for drunkenness, the Scripture is silent on these activities. Prohibitions aren't a bad thing. The Ten Commandments have eight "Thou Shalt Not's!" The other two, "Remember the Sabbath to keep it holy," and "Honor your Father and Mother" are written in the affirmative. I admire the list for its simplicity. God was very gracious to give us only ten rules, considering human propensities. If the IRS were in charge of our eternal souls, one hundred volumes could not contain the list of prohibitions. God kept it simple: Don't mess around with false gods, or His Name and His Image, take a break every week, and be nice to your neighbor. Don't kill your neighbor, don't sleep with his wife, don't steal his stuff, don't tell lies about him, and don't be envious over his successes. Basically, the Ten Commandments are good common sense ideas.

The Amish lifestyle is for the Mennonite Community a subtle and visible reference to our Anabaptist root values, sort of like a cultural leash. Unfortunately, in recent decades controversies circulating through the Mennonite and Amish communities have put the leash under incredible strain. For example, not many years ago a group of young Amish men were arrested for drug trafficking. They were helping a motorcycle gang distribute cocaine to Amish youth. It was a huge embarrassment to everyone. But such hullabaloos are rare. The Amish generally are well-behaved people who live under the radar and out of the news. Good thing, because the "quaint Amish lifestyle" attracts droves of curious outsiders to the County. Their tourist dollars are a huge boost to the local economy. So everybody wants the Amish to remain untainted.

Every summer ten million tourists come to Lancaster County to briefly experience Amish culture. The irony of Anabaptist objection to worldliness is nowhere more glaring than in the local tourist industry. Millions visit Lancaster County every summer to briefly experience a refreshing diversion from urban living. Most never stay long enough to notice the ironies. They rush around to the tourist traps for a few days and then return home to a more stimulating existence near Wall Street or Capitol Hill. But, they come, they spend a couple of billion dollars, and in the great tradition of Mennonite hospitality and the human love of money, Lancaster County welcomes them. On any given summer day the booming tourist industry chokes traffic to a stand-still along sections of Route 30, Route 340 and Route 896, where the locals – Mennonite, Methodist, Catholic, heathen, even a few resourceful Amish – clamor over each other to sell symbols of the quiet Anabaptist life-style.

Tourists buy Amish buggy rides and spend the day at mock-up Amish farms. They eat "authentic" Amish food served family-style by Amish costume-attired waitresses at Amish-style tables. They buy Amish hats, Amish dolls, Amish sayings carved on plaques, and Amish good-luck charms, etc. Tourists send home post cards, printed with Amish memorabilia. The crowds get so thick shopping for Amish stuff and site-seeing in Amish communities like Bird-In-Hand and Intercourse (the name originated from the intersection of two highways; it had absolutely nothing to do with the Seventh Commandment) that it is difficult to find the Amish sometimes. Indeed, if every "authentic Amish" retail item were genuine, the Amish would have become naked, homeless vagrants a long time ago. Truth is: many Amish families, frustrated with all the bustle, have thrown in the towel, sold their valuable Lancaster County real estate and moved to future tourist traps in Lebanon and Dauphin Counties. Some have even gone west to Ohio and Iowa.

Frankly, I can't blame them for leaving. Lancaster County has gotten too crowded. One story illustrates the point well: a tourist couple from New York came upon an Amish man working in his field along Route 30. They stopped the car to take a few quaint Amish photographs for friends back home in the city. The woman asked the Amish man to stop working so she could take his picture. Being a good Amish man, and believing that a photograph was a graven image ("Thou Shalt Not" Number Three), he refused. So the New Yorker, being from New York, ordered him to, "Stand up straight and let me take your picture!" Again he refused and turned his back on her. The couple drove off in a huff and reported to the Bird-in-Hand Sheriff, "You should go fire that Amish man!" they demanded. "He wouldn't let us take his picture!" The sheriff kindly informed the city slickers that the gentleman in the field was a real Amish farmer working in his field, and it was his constitutional right to snub them. They were dumbfounded. They believed the whole county was a big tourist park and that all the Amish folk in their houses and barns and fields were normal heathen like themselves, dressed up in Amish costumes and working for the County Tourist Board!

For me, immersed for a lifetime in the plainness, Anabaptist culture was suffocating boredom. That covering on the top of my Mother's head, well, how do I describe youthful embarrassment? Some of my high school friends disparaged the head covering as a "tilly cap." Mennonites and Amish were "tillys," a derisive commentary about our agricultural connections, i.e. we tilled of the soil. Except for my Dad's vegetable garden, our family members weren't farmers. Dad worked as a technician at RCA and by the time I entered high school my mother hadn't worn a head covering or plain clothes in years, but the insult cut into me as sharply as if I had a picture of her stenciled on the front of my t-shirt with the subtitle, "My Mom's a Mennonite... and so am I!" Years after Mother dispensed with the head covering, I was sure everyone could still see through the façade of my modern clothes and *smell* the Mennonite on me. I grew up with a nagging voice in my head: "YOU'RE DIFFERENT!" In those days, this was not a distinction to which one aspired. The modern idea of "individualism" is of course an aberration. Even in today's highly individualized culture, people continue to act and dress surprisingly the same. Except for occasional forays into zany behavior to get attention, most people prefer to look and act like their friends. Nobody *really* wants to be different.

Early in life I set out to prove, to US and THEM, that I was NOT different! My first venture toward the outside happened a month before my tenth birthday. I begged and begged until my parents capitulated to my emerging worldliness and bought me an A.M. radio. The "Amplitude Modulation" radio band contained the only pop broadcast frequencies going. F.M. (Frequency Modulation) radio existed, but no cool teenager ever tuned in to public radio programs and symphony music. A.M. radio broadcast rock 'n roll, folk and Americana hits all day and all night.

With that pocket-sized A.M. radio I was "With It!" I was COOL. I took my A.M. radio to school, put my mono ear plug into my right ear, and listened to Simon and Garfunkel at recess: "I am a rock, I am an iiiiiiisland. And a rock feels no pain, and an island never cries." I had no idea what Simon and Garfunkel meant by those lyrics, but they were from New York City so it had to be cool! Unfortunately, a little pocket radio cannot drown out generations of tradition even with the volume turned all the way up. I soon discovered that the journey to the outside was a long trip. The Beatles had rocked New York City the year before and long hair was definitely IN. So, I started letting my hair grow. Bangs, as long as possible, became my statement to the world. "I am NOT different! Look at me, I have bangs in my eyes!"

Mother did not understand the symbolism on my forehead. Most parents don't grasp youthful angst nor the parent-child gap that widens in adolescence. At this age, children have not yet developed the courage to talk about what is on their minds, and adults, in the busyness of keeping house and making a living, have forgotten the struggles of

36

that age and aren't paying attention to the yearnings rattling around in the heads and hearts of their pre-pubescent children.

In my Mother's estimation, Child Number Two's hair was getting too long, so she added "Get Dougie a haircut" to her weekly "To Do" list. One June day, right after school dismissed for the summer, and just before we left for a long weekend at the shore in Ocean City, New Jersey, Mother took me to a barber. Mother's choice of a barber was no normal heathen hair-cutting professional. He was probably a "jerked-over" Amish. I knew this because he acted like an Amish... with a clean-shaven face. Married Amish men always wear a beard. Young, unmarried Amish men are clean-shaven. This guy was an old fart of a man, wrinkled, shaking, and bent-over, so I knew he was married, or *had* been married at some point in distant history. His clean-shaven status therefore meant he had left the Amish community and shaved his beard. His hair-cutting equipment consisted of a comb and a scissors and nothing else, which bolstered my belief about his past. All heathen barbers use electric trimmers. This guy left the Amish but he kept some of the equipment.

The term "jerked-over" is a crude description of Amish folk who leave the Amish church. The Amish church classifies them as apostates. Most of these rebels join the Mennonites because just going fully heathen is too big a leap. They haven't necessarily abandoned their faith in God, but they want out of the rigors of the Amish religion. I am making a case for incremental backsliding here. Backsliding is scary business; it takes time and is usually done in small steps. I know this, having lived among highly dedicated people for most of my life. I also know it because I made my own teenaged forays out of the nest. When one determines to leave the tradition that has defined oneself for a lifetime, a quick disconnect is not easy. The psychological toll is heavy, whether the issue is one of theological belief or of lifestyle change. A teenage girl who has never gone dancing before, because her parents and the church said it was wrong, will have some serious internal struggles on her way to the first party. Coming to faith is the same journey, in reverse. Converts to faith always test the waters in small steps. Missiologists and anthropologists have studied the process of conversion and note there are ten or twelve very specific steps on the journey to faith. Backsliders are simply going in the opposite direction.

Amish don't hate rebels who leave the fold. That would be a sin. The Amish will not hate anyone. But they won't talk to an apostate, or even eat with him either. Mothers may weep for a straying son, and a father may have a tender heart for his offspring, but shunning is the rule. The rebel left the faith and is therefore an outcast, and anathema. The community must be protected, and its integrity maintained.

My Mom liked the barber, not because he was jerked-over, but because he was cheap. Frugality is the Mother of All Virtue in both Amish and Mennonite communities. Economy trumps style every time. For my penny-pinching Mennonite Mother, cheapness was an irresistible quality.

So, I obediently sat down in the barber chair while the old gentleman squinted at me. He had bad eyesight too! And his hands are shaking! This was not going to turn out well. But, in truth, his dimmed eyesight and quivering hands did not worry me as much as his philosophy about a boy's hair. The moment our eyes met I knew his thoughts: "This boy NEEDS a haircut." I pleaded with him to spare the bangs, don't cut the bangs, anything but the bangs! Pointless futility. He snipped and clipped my treasured bangs, squinting his eyes and snipping away with that quivering scissors, trying over and over to cut a straight line across my forehead. In the end I was left with nothing. No bangs remained, except what had drifted to the shop floor. The hair on my forehead was so short it wouldn't even lie down anymore. That awful Gehman cowlick on the left side of my now exposed dome, the one I had trained for months to lie down and behave, was now standing up and waving like a hairy flag. My Mom paid the jerked-over Amish man his fifty cents and off we went to Ocean City, New Jersey with my self-esteem gone forever, scattered on the wooden floor of a Pennsylvania barbershop. At the boardwalk I bought some sunglasses to compensate and kept my baseball cap on the whole weekend, even in the shower.

But, these are my people, and this is my county. For family origins, one could do much worse. Which brings us to our next chapter.

3 Aaron F. Stoltzfus

To understand this story, we must go back a couple of generations, to the early life of Aaron F. Stoltzfus. It's an important trip. It won't take much time because Grandpa Stoltzfus never wrote a book, his peers are long gone, and his daughter, my Mother, who is a primary source of information about her father, is seventy-five years old. The only other source, my uncle Mel, is not available since he and Aunt Nancy relocated to Sarasota and rarely come north. Mother, who has been an enthusiastic fountain of Grandpa stories for many years, now repeats the same anecdotes over and over, so we are left with her reruns and my memories.

That I owe my existence to this man is obvious. If not for the intersection of two young people, Aaron F. Stoltzfus and Katie Lapp, who got married and produced my mother, well, I wouldn't now be sitting in a Starbucks on a sunny afternoon pecking happily away on a laptop, transferring nostalgia from brain and watery eyes to a computer screen. Such peculiarities are the stuff of everyone's legacy. I would not exist if...

- Aaron F. Stoltzfus had *not* been born,
- He had *not* met his second wife, my grandmother, Katie Lapp, and

- They had *not* produced two more children, the first being my mother.

The human race obsesses over such factoids, and their accompanying musings about existence and relationships. Writers and philosophers love to ponder these existential staples. Knowing our origins helps us understand who we are and where we're going. It isn't a bad way to pass the time.

My existence is of course more than a result of a physical transaction between Aaron and Katie Stoltzfus and Mom and Dad. I also *exist* because of the influence and example of these people. Abraham Maslow asserts that humans aspire to loftier goals than finding shelter and food. Finding purpose and meaning motivates us powerfully. My grandfather worked hard all his life to provide his family with the necessities – food, shelter, and safety – but Grandpa also *lived*! He existed in the rarified air of loving relationships and ultimate purposes. For that, I am forever indebted to him.

A black and white photograph of Aaron and Katie hangs on the wall behind my desk. It's a great source of inspiration. They were married for nearly six decades. He died in 1986, ninety-one years old, a wealthy man in every way that matters. Grandma died in 2003 at the age of ninety-five; she was thirteen years younger than him. I hung their picture on my wall after her funeral. Having them look over my shoulder every day keeps me centered. My life has not been a difficult one. Oh, like everyone, I have had to walk down a few bumpy roads. But, the journey was easier because Aaron and Katie Stoltzfus paved the way and guided me along. I navigated life's uncertainties better because they and my parents showed me how. In these days of the self-made man, of go it alone and have-it-your-own-way narcissism, it is no wonder people are lost, lonely and have a tough time. Meaning and purpose is not something we do well alone. Our individualistic "Do it yourself" paradigm is antithetical to community. Meaningful existence can only be experienced in community! We are not designed to go it alone, and most of us make a mess of things when we try! We *need* lifelong connections with people, starting with parents, grandparents, and siblings. The nuclear family is God's idea, and when it is done right life is good!

Any fertile male can impregnate a woman and produce another human being who "exists." The creative process – and I hesitate to say this because pregnancy and childbirth (having participated in four) is for me absolutely miraculous – is the easy part (said with all due respect to the woman's larger role). Men are doing it all the time all over the planet – way too casually in my opinion – and then expecting their inseminated partner to terminate the pregnancy because the eventual arrival of a baby will create an intolerable inconvenience. Don't get me wrong, I'm all for choice, one hundred percent. I can even make the case that God is pro-choice: He gave human beings free will. We can do it whenever we like. However, when two people climb into the sack and engage in the act of pro-creation, the choice has been made. At this most delightful point of intimacy, two very aroused human beings have decided to take a chance at creating new life. The fact that God made it fun is in my view an indication of His joy in the creative process. Our participation, through sexual intercourse, is utterly profound. That we want to have the fun but not the responsibility is ultimate human selfishness.

Don't get me started on existential debates about creation and design, because even the most ardent atheist believes implicitly that he or she is on this planet for a greater purpose than eating, sleeping, defecating, and propagating the species. When atheists argue with creationists about meaning and design, their animation just proves my point. Atheists would be bored out of their minds if they had no religious freaks with whom to argue. Humans are the only species in the solar system who engage debate. We love this stuff! These purposeful connections define life and connect us with others. We will do almost anything to avoid isolation. But *healthy* relationships are harder to come by, and we need all the help we can get. Children need selfless, nurturing role models who are nearby for a lifetime. Aaron F. Stoltzfus was one of those people to me and I am forever grateful for his influence.

So off we go to a farm near Quarryville, where Aaron started his life in an Amish family.

******

Aaron F. Stoltzfus was born in 1895. He grew up immersed in the time-tested Amish values of hard work, simplicity and faith in God. The Amish lived this way intentionally, resisting culture's ruthless drive toward modernization, convenience, gadgetry, and wealth. As a culture, the Amish and Mennonites are far from perfect, but they have discovered one immutable truth about human existence. The Apostle Paul summed it up with these words: "Godliness with contentment is great gain." There simply is no substitute for simplicity. It has its own rewards.

In 1916 Aaron, having just turned twenty-one, married a young Amish girl named Katie Hertzog. Before long, she gave birth to their first child, a son. Their life plan, common for most young Amish couples in those days, was to buy a dairy farm and raise a family with many children. The family would help them buy the farm, because the Amish don't borrow money from banks. Aaron's dairy farm would have fifty to seventy cows, possibly Guernsey and Jersey varieties for their rich butter and cream, or Holsteins because they produce higher volumes of milk. Milk sales to local retailers would become their primary source of income. To supplement their income, Aaron also planned to raise tobacco. He had lots of choices, because Lancaster County's dark rich soil and favorable weather patterns produce bountiful crops. Tobacco was a quick-cash crop, and being newly married, Aaron needed to make money quickly.

Time has stolen the story of how Aaron and Katie first met, of their courtship and early married life, but there was never any doubt in anyone's mind, including his second wife and the children he produced with her, my Mother being one,

44

that Aaron loved Katie Hertzog Stoltzfus. Years later, my Mother, grown and married with her own children and grandchildren, asked her father to tell her about his life's most difficult experience. His immediate reply was, "Losing my first wife and baby."

So now you know the end of Act I in the grand story about Aaron F. Stoltzfus.

In 1918 his beloved Katie and their son – even his name has been lost to history – were struck down by the influenza virus that ravished the United States. Alone and grief stricken, Aaron tried to make sense of his life and move on. For ten years he lived as a single widower, working at odd jobs in the area and then joining a transient team of laborers to follow the wheat harvest across the mid-west.

During this time the Amish religion of his heritage became too strict and legalistic for Aaron. It contradicted what he read in Scripture and what he observed from the life and teachings of Jesus. And, to his grieving, lonely heart, the Amish faith lacked the renewing grace of God. Jesus, by contrast, offered a refreshing example of defiance against meaningless religiosity. Amish tradition, with its emphasis on appearances, codes of conduct and strict dogma, began to look like the Pharisees of the New Testament who resisted Jesus. After agonizing reflection, he decided to leave the Amish church. When he returned to Lancaster County he joined the Mennonites. Aaron was immediately ex-communicated. The entire Amish community, including his parents and siblings, "shunned" him. He was ignored, abandoned, cast out... the shunning lasted for the rest of his life. Aaron left the Amish church before he turned thirty; until his death at ninety-one, most of his family never spoke to him again.

After Aaron returned to Lancaster County he met a beautiful young Mennonite girl named Katie Lapp. The woman who was to become his second wife, my grandmother, was also named Katie. Katie Lapp was thirteen years younger than Aaron, all of eighteen years old when they met. Many years later Aaron told my Mother, "I had to wait for her to grow up so I could marry her." Mother never was quite sure if that meant Aaron knew her earlier in life or if he was speaking hypothetically. Her parents agreed to let her date this thirty-year-old jerked over Amish man, who might have been a distant cousin.

Mennonite dating of that time was nothing like the interactions between young men and women today. Besides visits to the home of one or the other, church was the de rigueur activity. Spending time alone was limited, if not forbidden, and usually happened during horse and buggy rides between church and home. Aaron enjoyed such outings not only because it afforded solitude with his girl, but also because of the long quiet country rides home during which a man develops a special bond with his steed. The rhythm of the horse's breathing and gate, the sounds and smells of the leather rigging as the reins and harnesses rub and jingle against each other, even the squeak of buggy wheels, are soothing music to the soul. Experiences like these are almost unknown to modern culture. My Grandpa often talked about falling asleep while driving home from church or a date with Katie, and being awakened by the horse's hastened cadence as they neared the farm and the changed clatter of hoofs when they entered the drive.

This was quintessential Lancaster County in the early 1900s. Compared to today's unabated cacophony of distractions, force-fed to the public in city *and* country via television, radio, satellite, billboards, cell phones, and the internet, the world at that time was pretty simple. Single room schools, homes with the bathroom outside and no running water inside, wood burning fireplaces for heat, iceboxes for refrigeration, and the horse as primary transportation were the norm for most people.

The entire world did not, however, live in this serendipity. Changes, big ones were coming rapidly to the cities and the heartland. The complexity that defines us today simply wasn't as pervasive. The front page of our local paper recently commemorated the history of Naval aviation. It

46

featured a photograph taken in 1915 of Lt. Commander Henry C. Mustin being launched in a bi-plane from the USS North Carolina in Pensacola Bay. This was the first aircraft catapult launch by the United States Navy, a historic event that happened more than ten years before Aaron F. Stoltzfus fell asleep in his horse-drawn carriage on the way home from a date with Katie Lapp.

And, a decade *before that*, on an obscure September day in 1903, about the same time eight-year-old Aaron was learning from his father how to do barn chores and control a team of plow horses, two bicycle mechanic brothers from Dayton, Ohio – five hundred miles to the west – were boarding an east-bound train carrying a few tools, some funny looking pieces of wood and fabric, and a dream that would change the world. Their destination was Kill Devil Hills, North Carolina where they would construct and test a bi-wing flying contraption. The railroad line that took them on their eastward journey to a paradigm-shifting destiny at Kitty Hawk probably passed near Lancaster County.

For three years the Wright brothers had been experimenting with heavier than air flying machine proto-types, constructed around a wing warp idea. They built models and made trips to Kill Devil Hills for test flights, because North Carolina's Outer Banks offered perfect wind conditions for such things. The forays to North Carolina had to be spaced between their obligations to repair and sell bicycles in Dayton.

By the time young Aaron mastered the team of horses on his father's farm, Orrville and Wilbur Wright had unlocked the key to controlled flight. On a historic day in 1903 at Kitty Hawk, North Carolina their wood and fabric flying machine got airborne for twelve seconds. The bi-plane glider traveled one hundred twenty feet over the ground from launch to landing, a single event that proved controlled flight was possible. A short time later they successfully flew a motorized version of their airplane. The Wright Brothers became world famous almost immediately and launched the era of human aviation.

Ten years later, while teenaged Aaron dozed on sleepy rides along tree-lined country roads ambling through bucolic southeastern Pennsylvania Amish farmland, the United States Navy had begun catapulting new aircraft designs from floating steel behemoths, transforming the world's biggest and most powerful ships into first generation aircraft carriers. Like I said, a little perspective.

Aaron and Katie Number Two would in time, and by Providence, become my grandparents. But first, Aaron F. Stoltzfus had to fall in love with Katie Lapp and convince her to marry him. When that time came, she said yes and the family agreed, so the two were married in a local Mennonite church at a service officiated by Katie's pastor and attended by the Lapp family and their friends (his family refused to participate). A short time later, and with a little assistance from the Lapp clan, Aaron and Katie bought an eighty-five-acre dairy farm near Quarryville, Pennsylvania, for which they paid $16,500! In the years following, they had two children, a daughter Fannie, who would become my mother, and a son, my Uncle Melvin.

Aaron's faith in God and his agricultural acumen grew. In addition to the standard crops – corn, alfalfa, and hay that was harvested and fed to the livestock, primarily the dairy cows – Aaron grew tobacco because of its value as a quick cash crop. In later years, God told him to stop growing tobacco. I never learned how my grandpa heard God's voice on this subject, but it was clear enough. I'm certain it involved his knowledge of the health issues associated with tobacco use, but the decision came years before those dangers were widely known. The only detail he ever related to us was that God told him to stop.

He was active in his home church and became recognized as a leader with an exceptional combination of grace, patience, tolerance, and vision. I can't help but believe that this defining style of leadership developed in the crucible of personal pain and rejection. He first served as an elder, and then eventually, while still farming his land, became pastor. Over the years, his influence grew until he was recognized as a Mennonite Bishop with leadership responsibilities over churches in Pennsylvania, Delaware and Maryland. The appointment process for becoming an elder was made by casting lots. A piece of paper was inserted into one of several Bibles that were then lined up on a table at the front of the church sanctuary. Five candidates, one at a time, walked to the table and chose one Bible. Many years later, Grandpa told us God led him to the correct Bible; he knew he would be chosen! During the course of his career, he helped plant and lead twelve different Mennonite churches.

Aaron was known and respected all over Lancaster County. His positive, outgoing, happy demeanor were not qualities of character that I appreciated as a child – kids are experts at taking adults for granted – but later in life, when my family and I visited Lancaster County and spent time with Grandpa, I was struck time and again by the huge impact he had made on others over a lifetime of consistent living. Invariably, when we visited local restaurants with Grandpa and Grandma, someone would approach the table to greet them. Everybody seemed to know Aaron and Katie! Of course, after an exchange of pleasantries, he would proudly introduce his grandson's family and brag about the work we were doing all over the world. In my adult life I came to admire my grandfather and what he stood for, defined more by the respect others gave him than by what he said about himself.

4

The Name Change

Aaron M. and Katie Stoltzfus endowed their firstborn with the name Fannie Arlene. The infant debuted on Lancaster County's small corner of the world stage on a cold November day in 1931, just after Thanksgiving, arriving as most babies did in those days, at her parent's home with the help of a midwife. Fannie was the first child for Katie, and of course the second for Aaron, who had lost his first wife and baby a decade earlier.

My mother's name was commonly given to Amish and Mennonite girls, so, for her entire life – at least until an event, that we will get to shortly, changed everything – my mother was Fannie. Many people are familiar with the namesake, made famous by Fanny Crosby the songwriter (1820 – 1915) and Fannie Mae the mortgage fund among others. The name was charming in the 1800s and, for today's mature crowd, still conjures nostalgic warmth, trust and goodness. However, except for its lingering representation among Amish, Mennonites and the mortgage industry, the name long ago has dropped off the list of pop culture's names for girls.

Mennonite and Amish communities around Lancaster County still have relatives and friends named Fannie. Among these conservative people my mother benefitted from its familiarity. It helped that her identity was tied to a well-

51

known local pastor-leader, Aaron Stoltzfus. During our early teenage years, Mother drove one day to her parent's house for a visit. Aaron and Katie still lived in Paradise. From Landis Valley Road the drive takes about forty-five minutes. Mother took a different-than-normal route that day, winding along country roads through farmlands south of Leola and Smoketown. She made a wrong turn and got lost. It may seem odd that Mother could get lost only a few miles from where she grew up. But, if you have ever driven down the country roads of Lancaster County, winding as they do over rolling hills, through green meadows or grain-rich fields set amid patches of woods and quaint farmsteads, you get the idea. Without an intersection or a road sign, everything quickly blends together, including orientation toward east-west and north-south.

After they sold the farm to my Uncle Melvin, Grandpa and Grandma Stoltzfus built a simple ranch house on a half-acre of country land outside Paradise, Pennsylvania. Paradise is not far from Strasburg, another reference to German roots, a quaint town famous for the Strasburg Railroad Museum and its impressive collection of antique trains. The list of these idyllic Mennonite communities – Smoketown, Bird-in-Hand, Intercourse, and of course Strasburg – all charming Pennsylvania Dutch settlements nestled between expansive stretches of rich-earth rolling Appalachian farmland – is for me the essence of nostalgia.

In late summer, these country roads are tightly bordered pathways that meander through very tall green forests of corn. Mother soon became disoriented. She drove onward, looking for something familiar. Eventually, up ahead "a piece," she saw an Amish woman walking toward her on the roadside. The middle-aged woman was clothed from neck to toes in black, including black stockings and black shoes that peeked out below the long mid-calf dress. A gray bonnet covered her entire head; she was carrying a cardboard box. Mother pulled along side and asked, "Can you tell me how to

---

get to Route 741? I'm trying to get to my mother's house and don't want to be late."

The Amish lady pointed down the road and said, "Oh yes, Seven Forty Von is right dahn this vay."

"Are you walking home?" Mother asked, curious.

"Yes," came the answer. The Amish woman eyed Mother tentatively.

"Why don't you hop in the car and I'll take you home. It's on my way," Mother offered.

"Oh, noah. I'll chust valk." Amish women aren't in the habit of accepting rides from English strangers.

"Really, it's no trouble. I'll be glad to give you a ride."

"Noah, I'll chust valk."

Not to be dissuaded, Mother tried again. "You might know my Father and Mother, Aaron and Katie Stoltzfus."

The woman brightened instantly. "Oh, bish du de Fannie Arlene?!" With that she gathered her long skirts, jumped into the passenger seat and slammed the door. On arrival to her home she asked Mother to please wait a moment, whereupon she entered the house and quickly returned with a dozen eggs, an Amish thank you for the ride home from a neighborly friend.

The Fannie familiarity didn't translate as nicely to the outside. For a few years during my upbringing in the 1960s, Mother worked for Good 'N Plenty Restaurant, one of several famous Mennonite and Amish family restaurants that served Pennsylvania Dutch cooking to the tourist hordes from New York. Good 'N Plenty was located along a part of the tourist strip on Route 896. During summer months hungry guests waited for hours to eat an Amish family-style meal, served in Amish family-style tradition at a table set for twelve. Unless you arrived with your own large group, you shared your meal with total strangers, passing the heaping dishes down the line. Dinner always started with a drink order (no alcohol) followed by unlimited supplies of warm, freshly baked bread, with mounds of creamy whipped butter, rich dark apple butter, succulent home made jellies and jams, and golden clover honey.

If there was any room after this introduction – and by design the owners hoped guests would stuff themselves with cheap carbohydrates – plentiful Amish delicacies followed. Mashed potatoes, sweet potatoes, boiled new potatoes, succotash (a corn and lima beans combination), green beans, carrots and peas, and lavish quantities of meat loaf (a ground beef preparation), pork chops, and fried-chicken arrived, on overflowing platters and plates. Ample offerings of dessert – mostly fruit pies – completed the meal, and always included one famous Pennsylvania Dutch favorite, Shoo-Fly Pie. The name adequately defines the concoction. Brown sugar, vegetable lard, corn syrup, flour, dark and light molasses are mixed together and baked into a piecrust. Negligible nutritional value, and off the caloric index charts, but YUM!

My mother was one of the servers, assigned to several tables during her eight or nine hour shift that began at 10:30am. During her employment at Good "N Plenty she wore a name tag, identifying her simply as "Fannie," perhaps a quaint Amish addition to the restaurant ambience. For outsiders, however, the name was, well, odd. Mother received regular commentary, usually in for the form of friendly curiosity, about the name.

"Fannie? Is that really your name?" to which Mother replied, "Yes, it is."

"Oh. That's, uh, an interesting name."

"Well, Fannie is a common name in Lancaster County."

Mother took it in positive stride at first, but later wearied of the attention and commentary and offered a more truncated, tight-lipped, reply: "Yes. (pause) THAT is my name." (Stare down. I'm picturing a stony-faced waitress tapping a pencil on her pad waiting for a nonplussed customer to move on to the drink order). Most people let it go, perhaps satisfied, or put off by the tension in the air. The customers' curiosity has some merit. Among a large portion of the outside world the word Fannie (or Fanny) is not actually a name for humans. It rather refers to that particular part of the human anatomy on which one sits. It's a nice enough term, like derriere, more polite than "backside" or "butt," and nowhere near the vulgarity of "ass."

In the UK, however, apologies to the reader (and eventually my Mother when she reads this) for this embarrassing fact, Fannie means something else entirely. It is not a nice word at all. In truth the word is a crudity, and I mean a most explicitly vulgar one. But I'll stop at this point. Really prudent of me. Thankfully for Mother, there is nothing in memory about British tourists choosing to eat at Good 'N Plenty Restaurant during the years of Fannie's employment. If they were served, they either were not seated at Fannie's table or they had the wisdom to keep their mouths shut. To my knowledge that unimaginable encounter never happened.

This story has, however, stimulated my memory about another anecdote from Mother's experiences at Good 'N Plenty. Nostalgic musings such as these have a terrible tendency to drift me off into mental side streets. I therefore digress yet again. Mother shielded this particular story from us kids for a very long time, allowing it to emerge long after we had reached adulthood. Like I said, we were sheltered. Good 'N Plenty Restaurant, as I said, did not serve alcohol, which to some naïve visitors, accustomed as they were to wine, beer and spirits at mealtime, was a big surprise and to some an almost intolerable inconvenience. One man, after waiting in line for an hour, complained about this deficit on the menu as my mother offered, from memory, the drink selections – water, lemonade, ice tea, hot coffee and soft drinks – and took the order. Glaring unhappily at this cute thirty-something server name Fannie he declared, "What!? No beer! No wine! NO GO-GO GIRLS!"

Not to be outdone – and here, for good or bad, and in my lifetime I have experienced both, is where my Mother shines – she immediately retorted, "You're right! We don't have beer or wine. But we DO have Go-Go Girls! I'm your Go-Go Girl! I go-go-go from the time I arrive here until I quit and

I go-go home." The man was mollified. He dropped the complaint, ordered lemonade, and turned his attention to decadent portions of Pennsylvania Dutch cooking, without the alcohol.

I should add here that my mother was a beautiful woman. The pictures that still exist in frayed photo albums of my teenaged Mother and her girl friends, of a twenty-something newlywed in a plain white wedding dress and head covering, and of Mother and Dad in early family years, provide ample proof of her country beauty. The Good 'N Plenty Amish style restaurant uniform, while not flattering to her figure, and ill-suited for the preoccupations of a certain thirsty and lusty New Yorker, did not hide the fact that the German and Swiss, from which many Mennonite families descended, have produced beautiful women.

As is true for all oddities, including names that require repeated explanation, the issue eventually grinds down to a sore nub. So, Mother grew tired of her name.

"Can you move your Fannie over here and pour me another glass of lemonade, please?"

"Get your Fannie back to the kitchen and bring me some more meat loaf."

On it went, ad nauseam, until Mother had enough.

One auspicious day, just another in the grand scheme of food service flowing out of the kitchens of Good 'N Plenty Restaurant, but D-Day in the history of one Fannie Arlene Gehman, a group of New Yorkers (and perhaps a Brit or two) were seated at Mother's table. As she was taking the drink order, one distinguished, blue-haired lady glanced at Mother's nametag and with an ill-timed air of incredulity said, "That really isn't your name is it?" to which my Mother (again!) gave a tight-lipped reply: "Yes. It is." What followed can only be described as a pregnant pause. Calm before the storm. The six little words that next flowed from the tourist's mouth became the catalyst that forever altered my mother's identity.

"You have got to be kidding!"

No one will ever know who this woman was, whether she was British or just another outspoken New Yorker. But she changed my mother's life. It is a testimony to Mennonite pacifism that my mother didn't deck the blue-haired dim wit on the spot. What a great story that would have been! My high-strung Mother was not violent, and for the most part, she wasn't mean-spirited either. When it suited her, she *could* give a tongue-lashing that would set your hair on fire. But on this day, in this pregnant moment, Mother held her tongue. She graciously finished the round of service for the guests and returned through the double-hinged doors to the safety of the kitchen. Wounded, outraged, and fighting back tears, she tore off the contentious Fannie nametag and tossed it into the trash bin. That evening, she called her parents and declared to my Grandma Stoltzfus, "Mother, I do not want to dishonor you and Dad, because you gave me my name, but I am no longer your Fannie! Never call me that again. I am changing my name. From now on, I am Fran."

Mother was obviously hesitant to disrespect her parents, even at this juncture, as a fully-grown, married-with-children adult. Our contemporary culture of independence and empowerment of youth is largely unfamiliar with the principal of *showing* respect for one's parents. Mother feared her father in the most godly and honorable way. It was unthinkable that Aaron F. Stoltzfus would ever abuse – even verbally – anyone in his family, or any other person for that matter. But he commanded respect. He was no fool, and he wasn't to be trifled with. He was unwaveringly kind and gracious, but also represented a life of steadfast commitment to the Bible and its principles. I never knew my Grandpa Stoltzfus to be anything but a gentleman, but his kindliness was built upon an unshakable adherence to God and His Word. He lived by the tenets of the faith, and expected the same from family members.

Mother learned this as a child and carried it forward into marriage, through child raising years – handing down the same values to us – and to a D-Day decision at Good 'N Plenty

Restaurant. She sometimes reminisced about a moment in childhood when she learned the principal of respect for parental authority, and of integrity. All of twelve years old, little Fannie Arlene was out in the fields driving the family's Farm-All tractor, pulling a disc to cultivate the soil for planting. It might seem odd to you, Dear Reader, that a girl of twelve would drive a tractor alone in the fields. The practice was not uncommon in those days. If growing up is defined in part by the ability to take responsibility, children grew up earlier in the 1940s. Mother remembers the day as one of her first opportunities to drive the tractor. It was a coveted chore for an enthusiastic child and she was extremely excited. Her father Aaron instructed her how to drive the tractor in a straight line down the field, and how to make a safe U-turn at the end, and then head back.

The tractor engine was a crank type, which means it had no battery and no starter motor. Aaron had to insert a crank handle into the engine at the front of the tractor and give it a good stiff turn. This was a man's job; Mother had not strength or the stature to do it. Aaron gave her these instructions: "If the tractor stalls, don't try to start it. You could break your arm. I'll be watching from the barn, and I'll hear if the engine stalls. Just wait for me and I'll come out to restart it for you."

Grandpa always kept candy in his desk in the house – nonpareils and licorice – and another kind called Good 'N Plenty hard candy on a shelf in the closet. During these years on the farm – and I remember this because he owned and worked this same farm until I was ten, and we would find the candy treasure when we were playing in the barn – he also kept "barn candy." Barn candy, a pink, round, pill shaped hard candy, satisfied Grandpa's "sweet-tooth" cravings during the day. Grandpa's sweet tooth dated all the way back to Mother's childhood. It's nice that some things don't change. Fannie and Melvin had permission to eat the house and barn candy, within reason, so they'd help themselves from time to time when they were playing in the house or working in the

58

barn. The unspoken rule was that you only took a couple of pieces at a time.

On the day Mother got the tractor driver job, she decided to take extra candy with her. She secretly emptied a matchbox and filled the box with Good 'N Plenty candy and then tucked the box into her sweater and carried it with her out to the field. She sucked on the sweet bits while driving the tractor. The savory taste eventually gave way to a guilty conscience for taking more than her share. Each stolen piece began to taste more and more bitter as she tilled the straight rows. Finally, in the middle of the field, and only half way through the box of candy, guilt overcame her and she threw the sinful box and its contents as far as she could. It landed in the freshly plowed dirt.

A little later the tractor stalled, so, following her Dad's instructions, she sat and waited. Soon, Aaron came walking through the acres of plowed soil toward my Mother. On the way, and by an almost miraculous coincidence, he found the box of candy. Arriving at the tractor he presented it open-handed to Mother with only three words: "What is this?"

Mother tearfully confessed what she had done. Grandpa nodded and that was the end of it. Nothing more was ever said or done, but Mother learned a precious truth: It wasn't the candy. There was always plenty of candy. It was the deception. "Thou shalt not steal" and "Thou shalt not lie," the Eighth and Ninth Commandments of Moses, were serious business in the Stoltzfus home. In her childish yearning for a little extra, she had violated both.

Contemporary readers may balk at such strict austerity. A small box of candy? Conditioned as we are with prosperity and conventional wisdom about how discipline and restraint of children can damage their emerging psyche, stories like these sound harsh. Perhaps the standards were severe. Perhaps the Stoltzfus family teetered off the pinnacle of grace into legalism. But, compared to today's tolerance for unruly and disrespectful children, and the rampant juvenile delinquency we accept as the norm, we cannot point a judging finger. We've descended into a quagmire. The vagaries of the 1960s – the free thinking and relativism, the aversion to discipline, boundaries, saying "no," and imposing beliefs on anyone, including children – has after fifty years finally born its untenable fruit. From my perspective, it is difficult to make a case for social progress. My mother turned out okay, even better than okay. By any measure, she is a model citizen.

Mother's name-change to Fran happened forty years ago. Family and friends eventually accepted it and Fran perfectly served Mother's interaction with the outside English world too. Unfortunately, times change and a few decades later the interminable evolution of pop culture introduced new scandals associated with Fran Arlene Gehman. Earlier in life Fannie Arlene Stoltzfus agreed to another name change, when, on a now forgotten day in 1950 a young man named James Robert Gehman made a marriage proposal. A year later, in July 1951, Miss Stoltzfus became Mrs. Gehman. It was a simple enough transaction, made official at a wedding and the signing of a marriage certificate.

Mother recently reminded me that, as either Fannie or Fran, her initials spell FAG. In 1950, the term was a benign slang reference to cigarettes. But in this new century even a seventy-five-year-old great grandmother knows current renderings. To add to the conundrum, the GEH in Gehman is now problematic. It should be pronounced like the word GET, with a slight clearing of the throat, but is mostly mispronounced "GAY." A generation ago that word meant nothing more than a happy state of existence. Today the meaning is a little more, uh, nuanced. Much has changed in the United States of America. My sons – one an Officer in the Air Force and another an engineer – now occasionally discuss changing their names to their Mother's maiden name, Wolfe. Wolfe has a manly ring to it. It is certainly easier to spell… and pronounce. I don't think they are kidding.

The subject is prickly. Johnny Cash bemoaned the struggles of a misnamed hero in his song, "A Boy Named Sue." We don't get to choose our names, but we live with the

60

consequences. Given names are hard enough. Family names, handed down over generations, can be impossible. I regularly hear the hesitation when people try to pronounce my family name from its spelling. "Is it Mr. Gee... men? Or... German. Or, uh..." I want to shout at them, "IT'S GAYMEN, OK!!!"

Both my Mother and I – she is now the only remaining sage in our small branch of the Gehman family tree, and is closing in on her ninth decade on the planet – are resigned to some of life's uncomfortable, and unalterable, realities.

5 The Gehmans

My other grandfather, Eli H. Gehman, made important contributions to our hero that took a little longer to appreciate. In adolescence, I viewed Grandpa Gehman with a combination of endeared admiration and solemn respect. I knew he cared for his family, including wife Mary, son Robert, daughter Arlene, and the eight grandchildren. The respect, however, was serious, a godly kind for sure – no one ever questioned his character or staunch commitment to the Faith – but for a very frivolous seven-year-old boy, his stoic demeanor made him seem stern.

Grandpa Gehman was not one to display affection. No big hugs and broad smiles from this man. His affability was offered in another form, ice cream, provided after dinner every time we visited. It was an expensive commodity in those days, always in one flavor (vanilla), but Grandpa scooped up heaping dishes of it from a box he fetched from the old top-open freezer on the porch. We added Hershey's Chocolate Syrup, manufactured in a town by the same name only thirty miles from Lancaster County. After dinner and ice cream, summer evenings invariably included a hayride. Grandpa piled fresh green hay or yellow straw into a little two-wheeled cart and then hitched it to his little red two-wheel tractor. With him at the controls, sometimes sharing them with me or another grandchild who sat on his lap, we chugged through local fields and farm trails. He also invited us to accompany him on evening rounds to tend to the chickens. Thousands of them lived in the large two-story "chicken house" on his farm. I walked beside Grandpa, lugging an oversized egg basket through the pungent air. To this day I cannot pass a chicken farm and its ever-present stench without thinking about my paternal grandfather. We fed the chickens and collected their eggs, and then carried the burgeoning basket into a small basement room next to the garage. In this little basement "Egg Room" – it was naturally cooler below the ground – Grandpa cleaned, "candled" (examined under light) then gently packed each egg into wire-bound wood-lattice crates with the name "Humpty-Dumpty" stenciled on the side. After a few days, when all the crates were full, the egg wholesaler came and hauled them away.

For most of his adult life Grandpa Gehman also worked a few hours per week at the Gehman Feed Mill making small deliveries to local farmers. An uncle or cousin owned the mill and gave Grandpa a little extra work. On summer days when school was out I sometimes accompanied him, sitting in the passenger side of his old blue Chevy pickup. We'd drive to the mill, load a few bags of feed, some medicine or farm tools, and make deliveries out in the country, down dusty old farm lanes to dusty old farm houses and barns. We carried our lunches with us, packed in brown paper bags by Grandma Mary that morning. At noon we found a clump of shade trees or a quiet churchyard and parked the truck and ate our sandwiches in silence. Grandpa was not one for frivolous conversation either.

Besides chickens, Grandpa raised sheep. He gave the grandkids rides on the backs of the big ones, fetching one from the barn with a rope around its neck. Under the expansive shade of a big old apple tree in the yard, we'd grab a tuft of nappy wool and climb on for a slow ride around the property. A tire swing hung from the apple tree's massive branches, and while waiting our turn, my brother Dale and sister Judy and I would ride that too. Every year the apple tree produced a copious harvest of apples. The branches drooped low, straining under the weight of the pale green spheres. Hundreds of ripe apples dropped to the ground and covered the grass like a lumpy carpet. The sheep loved the apples, so getting out of the paddock, even to give rides to irritating children, was an irresistible opportunity to snack. We collected bushels of the tart fruit, climbing as high as we could to pick them from the branches, and collecting unblemished ones off the ground. Mother carried them home in the car trunk and then boiled them down into applesauce.

Religion flowed deeply in Grandpa Gehman's core, a faith bought and paid for by the blood of Jesus on Calvary, handed to him by his parents, grown into maturity by hard work, careful country living, and service to others. When he needed to correct a wayward grandchild's behavior – at the innocent age of seven, when I was eager to drive the two-wheel tractor and accidently tipped it onto its nose – he gently but firmly reprimanded me.

"I did not tell you to get the tractor out of the garage Dougie," he said, pulling the tractor upright. "I told you to wait for me."

"Sorry Grandpa."

Grandpa nodded and said no more. And I learned a valuable lesson: Grandpa was kind, and he never raised his voice, but he expected respect and obedience. Such austerity and reticence pretty much defines the conservative Mennonite and Amish culture I knew. In those days, my people demonstrated their faith and their love more by action than words. There was little interest in one's emotional condition. What relevance are feelings, really, when there is work to be done? The predilection never worked well for my mother. Her prima donna flair emerged during childhood; it delighted her father, grated her mother and her brother, endeared her to some friends, and outraged others. Now in old age, she has not changed. "I wish," she once confessed, "that Mother would ask me how I feel! She NEVER asks me how I feel. It's always, 'So, what are you *doing* today?' She has never asked me how I FEEL?'" Those were days when Mother wasn't feeling very well, and needed a little empathy. Apparently Grandma wasn't getting the message. In a million years, no one would ever doubt Katie Stoltzfus' love for her daughter, but she didn't think much about feelings or make such inquiries to others. The subject was simply outside of her Mennonite paradigm.

Culture today has drifted wholly to the other side of the axis. Now, it's all about feelings. Everybody is talking about his or her feelings, and people are taking each other's temperatures all the time. How do you feel? I'm not feeling the love! I don't feel fulfilled! If it feels good, do it. Etcetera and so forth ad nauseam. While I'm glad we have opened the emotional doors and are talking, I'm not sure the shift has improved the human condition. Sometimes the stage simply isn't big enough for all the drama. There is still work to be done regardless how one feels. Most of the time, we'd probably all feel better if we would just shut up and do something positive and helpful.

Again I have drifted off subject onto side roads.

On our evening rounds through the chicken houses during one summer afternoon, Grandpa Gehman found several dead or dying birds scattered about on the sawdust-covered floor of the henhouse. He collected the birds and carried them outside, then sat in his portable chair in the grass while a wide-eyed grandson watched. He picked up a dying chicken and with a quick flick of his hands, wrung the bird's neck. I asked him what he was doing. "I'm putting her to sleep," he replied. Before my shocked but insatiably curious eyes, he took a pocketknife and sliced the dead animal, from the breastbone to anus, and tore her open. She was sick, he said, and he was looking for the reason. Digging into the organs, he found the problem – worms in the digestive system – and held up the evidence before my popping eyes.

"See," he said, peeling open an organ. "Worms. That's why she was sick."

"Are you going to make her better?"

"No, she isn't going to get better."

"When is she going to wake back up?" I asked.

"Oh, she isn't going to wake up."

An incomplete but a satisfactory answer for eight-year-old sensitivities.

Earlier in his life, long before his son James Robert married Fannie Stoltzfus and gave birth to me, Grandpa Gehman carried heavier burdens than the farm and the family. Their third daughter Lucile, only six years old, the youngest of three, contracted stomach cancer. Lucille suffered for months before the disease took her life. Grandpa kept a journal, a heart-wrenching day-by-day account of her illness and death in their home. Our family still possesses the original handwritten pages. It is included, unedited, in the next chapter. Grandpa's agony, and his amazing fortitude in heart-rending circumstances, conveys powerfully and tenderly through the narrative.

I knew nothing about Lucile until I was an adult. Very little was ever said about her illness and death, which like other topics of a sensitive nature – the list includes sexual matters (puberty, libido, and the consummation of marriage) and other delicate human subjects – were rarely discussed in Mennonite homes, including ours until Mother abandoned the discretion.

After the birth of their three children, and the death of Lucille, Grandpa Gehman also lost his wife Elizabeth to leukemia. She died much later, a couple of years after both Arlene and Robert had married. My sister Judy was just an infant. Except for a few faded black and white pictures, I know nothing about Grandma Elizabeth. Grandpa remarried Mary Martin two years later, an older never-married spinster. She was the only Grandma Gehman I ever knew. My mother, who was the first in our family to break from the Mennonite proclivity to keep ones mouth shut, and tended to err on the other side of the scale, told me that Mary was never as sweet as Elizabeth. I have no point of comparison, so I'm taking Mother's word for it.

By the time I was born my father, James Robert Gehman, had long before settled into responsible adulthood. Stories remain about his refractory youth – stories, I might add, he did not share with me until I was beyond twenty, now also established and past teenage recalcitrance, and focused on adult responsibilities. I'm glad to know the stories. They paint a picture of an inquisitive, inventive, resourceful young man, driven to explore the boundaries of conservative Mennonite tradition, not to break them, mind you – Dad was never that rebellious – but to push them back a little.

Dad was an engineer and an inventor by nature. Born in 1927, my father entered the world at an opportune time for a technology-minded new generation, when the industrial revolution was well underway, two years before the stock market crash of 1929. He was too young to appreciate the ravages of that infamous economic crash and the Great Depression that followed, and by the time he entered his teenage years a decade later the industrial power of the United States was recovering and had begun gearing up to defend England against the ambitions of a little German/Austrian man with a mustache. Dad turned fourteen in 1941. That year, on the other side of the planet, the Japanese did a dirty deed to a U.S. island military base in the middle of the Pacific Ocean, a day that will live in infamy. The attack on Pearl Harbor, three months before Dad's fifteenth birthday, thrust the United States into World War Two.

Like millions of others in the "Builder" generation, Dad grew up at an incredible time in American history. This generation garnered the power of mathematics, physics, chemistry, and applied sciences, and laid the foundations for incredible technological advances and unprecedented prosperity. In time the Builder generation leveraged that knowledge to win wars on two continents, sacrificing hundreds of thousands of young men like my Dad to do it. Twenty years later, rising to a challenge this time from the

Soviet Union, that same generation put a man on the moon, made it possible for human beings to fly safely around the planet in a single day, to carry computers in our briefcases and telecommunication devices in our pockets. It is ironic that of the two things my Dad's generation gave us – the foundations of technology and solid family values – we seem to have enthusiastically retained only one.

When, later in adulthood, Dad returned to night school to take a writing class – a hunger for learning he cultivated throughout his life – he wrote a brief autobiography, appropriately entitled "My Education or Lack of It." Here is that story, written with more wit and self-awareness than I could ever muster...

> *I was born and raised in a Mennonite home among the plain people who felt that higher education, including high school, was not necessary. My father told me he wanted me to have more education then he had. I thought this meant college but after I was through the eighth grade he told me he only had six years of education and he wanted me to have eight.*

> *I wanted to go to high school even though it was not compulsory in our township at that time. My father said I may, but we would have to find a way. There was no bus service at that time, and he and my mother may not be able to help me with my homework. I needed a lot of help. Book and classroom learning wasn't easy for me. Reading and writing was a struggle. Every glitter outside the window caught my attention. I was good at art and doing things with my hands so the teacher gave me the job of decorating the interior of our one room country schoolhouse for Christmas. This I loved.*

> *I was left-handed but my first teacher insisted I write with my right hand, and my peers insisted I throw the ball right-handed so I worked at this until I mastered it. I got away with batting left-handed. I was probably a right-brained kid and nobody knew it. Recently I took a test to see which hemisphere of my brain I use most and it showed 52%*

right and 48% left. So maybe all the effort to conform helped to develop my whole brain.

In my religious community I often heard the Bible quoted, especially these words of Paul, "knowledge puffs up but love builds up." Taken out of context or overemphasized perhaps, but I can testify I got the love and support I needed.

We had fun times at school. One snowy winter day we heard sleigh bells approaching. The school and the teacher gave everyone permission to go to the windows after they began circling the schoolhouse, to see the meaning of the sounds. Then I knew what my cousin had been saying. (She was not one to keep a secret). My uncle, her father, and his neighbor each hitched up their two-horse sleighs and came to the West Stevens School to take the whole school out sleighing for the rest of the day. My uncle invited me to sit on the driver's seat with him and off we all went to circle other country schoolhouses and see the faces peering out the windows as we screamed at the top of our voices drowning out the sleigh bells. I'll never forget that day.

I passed all my grades but came close to flunking my fifth year. That scared me, so I studied harder the next years. In my seventh year West Stevens got their first Encyclopedia. It was the Britannica with a vocabulary that the kids could not handle, but even with the big words it stirred in me an interest in science, particularly electricity. A neighbor friend of mine who was a class ahead of me was interested in the same thing so with this reinforcement we started building a telephone between our two houses. We got the information from the book "Electrical Things Boys Can Make." Our two families, living about one hundred feet apart, used this telephone for years until they bought into the telephone system.

It was the encyclopedia and the reinforcement of my friend that helped me to decide I wanted more education. It was Vo–Tech that I needed but there was no Vo–Tech in the high school system in our area at that time. I was among the top of my high school class in science and math but among

70

the bottom in language and social studies. When I was through my senior year I took a general high school test to see where I was. I passed senior science and math but flunked sophomore language and social studies. I was discouraged and was developing emotional problems because of the pressures so I quit school and went to work as an apprentice electrician. This I enjoyed very much. I began taking a correspondence course on electricity and electronics but being a high school dropout disturbed me for many years. I tried to take language and social studies in evening courses several times but decided it wasn't worth the trouble. Furthermore, I wanted to get on with my interests.

I became an electrical apprentice and learned residential and commercial installation and some maintenance wiring. I looked forward to getting into the industrial maintenance, the subject of my correspondence course studies. By changing employers I was able to do this. After several years, April 1956 to be exact, I was hired at RCA as an apprentice electrician in maintenance. That's when I saw a real need for electronics. While still studying my correspondence course I signed up for electronics studies at Stevens Trade evening school. After five years as an RCA electrician I was offered a technician job. I then started taking RCA's in-plant courses in physics, chemistry, logic, computer, math, etc.

Now after thirty years with the company and almost thirty certificates of achievement I find I still can't do more than just sign my name on those darn enrollment cards.

For both my parents, formal education began in one-room schoolhouses within walking distance from home. During the entire *formal* education experience, my mother walked less than a mile to her country schoolhouse, a public institution, down the road from the farm. She dropped out after the eighth grade, more interested in farm work with her father, than in a high school education. Mother recently reflected about her decision to leave school, and although she could not fully remember details, she said that one influencing factor was the plain clothes her mother expected her to wear.

"In the world but not of the world" can be a huge burden for a teenager.

Dad's parents helped him get into Lancaster Mennonite High School. He wanted the "higher" education, but his parents were more concerned about ungodly influences in the public school system. At Lancaster Mennonite High, in addition to an excellent academic education, he was further subjected to the rigors of Mennonite conservatism. LMH enforced a strict dress code. For the guys the de rigueur uniform was black trousers, white shirt, bow or regular tie, and black shoes with laces. What my father did with this dress code provides poignant insight into the kind of person he was and helps me understand my own inclinations.

Formal education always focuses on two things: 1) what is known from the past, and 2) the teacher's correct answers. To progress through the system, and earn the right to be creative, students must demonstrate that they are adequately informed about both. Creativity, on the other hand, looks for *another* correct answer, the answer no one has thought of yet. Creativity is always outside the box. It is always a little rebellious.

So being both youthful and inventive, Dad explored the boundaries of the LMH dress code. He replaced the black laces in his shoes with colored ones – the brighter the better. A response came rapidly: the school authorities redefined the rules to codify black laces in the shoes. Next Dad applied his knowledge of electricity: He wired colored Christmas-tree-type lights into his bow tie, strung the wire under his shirt to a trouser pocket where he attached a battery pack and switch. Then, as he walked down the hallway or sat in Math Class, he pressed a switch in his pocket and the colored lights flashed on and off! It didn't take long for the activity to once again get Dad into trouble. In the eleventh grade, disillusioned with the educational system – the pressures of academia and the rigors of tradition – Dad dropped out and went to work.

Later in life Dad focused his creativity on more productive things than pressing the edges of the school dress code, but let's face it, young people rarely express their creativity in wholly productive activities. Creativity is in fact defined by breaking the rules. No creative idea ever emerges unless the creator challenges convention.

By the time I was born, Dad was well established at the Radio Corporation of America. A constant tinkerer, Dad played around with a basement full of old televisions, radios, and other odds and ends, including battery-powered (DC) and alternating current (AC) motors. He'd bring home discarded stuff from RCA, or collect equipment from friends, and tear the stuff apart in his workshop to make something useful or playful or just see what made it work. RCA was the first company to bring stereophonic sound to the market. Today, stereo is taken for granted, but at the time was a huge advancement in recorded sound. Dad got his hands on one of their first stereophonic cassette players. We set it up in our basement. The unit was the size of a microwave oven, and the cassette tape cartridge was a half-inch thick and as big as a shoebox lid. It fit onto spindles on the top of the machine. We hooked up the modular speakers and placed them on opposite sides of the room.

The Demo tape was electrifying! The narrator's deep voice came on first with "WELCOME TO STEREOPHONIC SOUND FROM RCA!" The narrator then proceeded to expound on RCA's wonderful new technology: "What if we put one speaker over here," he said, and his voice miraculously jumped to the right side of the room. "Then," he continued, "we put another speaker over here," and this time his voice jumped to the left side of the room. "If we could control the sound, and make it come from only one speaker at a time, or both, then we would have STEREOPHONIC SOUND FROM RCA!" As he spoke his voice followed his footsteps and walked across the room, from the left speaker back to the right! Moments later, racing cars roared through the room, from one side to the other, and people shouted to each other, one voice from this side, another from that side. The demo also took us poolside to a public swimming pool, with voices shouting and playing and water splashing, filling the room with such a richness of sound that we felt we were inside the scene. Next we traveled to a music hall where an entire orchestra was warming up. Percussion instruments played on the left while brass instruments played on the right, and the string section played from the center! The experience was spellbinding. We played the tape over and over. Every time guests came to visit, Dad took everyone down to the basement, set up the speakers, and played the demo tape. It was a sensation! Today's culture has become so accustomed to sophisticated technology that we are numbed to the simple pleasure of its greatness. I'll never forget those years, interpreted to me through the passions of my father, and the stuff he brought home from work.

Grandpa Gehman was never thrilled with Dad's involvement in technology, although he came to terms with it and was never contentious at family gatherings. To be sure, Grandpa used technology. He drove a car, always painted simple black. He drove a pickup truck on his delivery route for the Gehman Feed Mill. I think they had a radio, but, there never was a television in his house. Mother's parents never owned a television either. It was a big deal, therefore, when our family actually got our first *viewable* television. I say viewable because we owned televisions, all broken units Dad acquired and brought home. He worked on them in the basement for the simple joys of learning more about the technology. I don't remember him actually getting one to work, and now that I think about it, maybe that was by design.

In early years we had no television and weren't allowed to watch. When he finally capitulated to the family's demand – and I really don't remember who was the biggest influencer on this issue – Dad got a small black and white television and installed it in the basement family room right outside the door of the bedroom I shared with my brother.

Dad attached a makeshift antenna to the roof of the house. Television was another dangerous step toward the world.

It was an irony of Dad's personality that he loved technology – for its complexity and sophistication – while maintaining a cautionary posture about the content it channeled into our brains. Like his father, Dad preferred the simpler life, close to the soil. So besides his love for things complex, Dad enjoyed the great outdoors, working in his garden, cultivating fruit trees, and landscaping the property. Like his father, he was the consummate do-it-yourselfer. I hated such nonsense during my childhood and youth, simply because it required more work and time away from idle play including of course watching television and listening to my A.M. radio (two activities I enthusiastically adopted). But there was no getting out of chores at the Gehman house, so I mowed the yard, picked vegetables in the garden, helped Dad build something or other (like the stable in the garage for our first pony, Molly), and did general cleaning and maintenance around the house. In adulthood, I have come to appreciate the mandatory home duty. It was empowering! The experiences developed skills with tools, and instilled confidence and an eagerness to learn.

So, Grandpa Gehman and my father maintained a respectable relationship, with tension that comes from old ways fading slowly away and new ones pressing steadily in. No voices were ever raised – that was not their style – and there was never a hint of disrespect. But Grandpa had a way of voicing his objections.

6 Lucile Marie Gehman

We must briefly visit, on the Gehman side of our story, the life and untimely death of Lucile Marie Gehman. Hers was a short stay on the planet, only six years, but in that time, especially the months leading to her passing, Lucile made a lasting impact on her father. Grandpa Gehman wrote the account of his little girl's battle with cancer, a heart-wrenching journal detailing, in the matter-of-fact style typical of Mennonite pragmatism, the events as they unfolded – doctor visits, diagnosis, surgeries, suffering, prayers for healing, and final passing. No garnishments of false hope, unrealistic faith or super spiritual innuendo here. Only earthy realism, with humility and wrenching heartache, prayers to a trusted God, and a prevailing wish that a loved one would be okay while bravely bracing for another possible outcome.

Grandpa Gehman was not a writer, but in this narrative he was without peer. If good writing is defined by the telling of a compelling story, in the account of his precious Lucile's battle with cancer, Eli H. Gehman was world-class. I suppose the same could be true of anyone's account of a deeply personal journey. The records of our most painful or exultant experiences are always more compelling than fiction.

In "A Million Miles in A Thousand Years," Don Miller reflects about how every good story contains essential criteria.

A flawed hero with endearing qualities faces a challenge, usually an almost insurmountable one, and then, through struggles that stretch him to the breaking point, he comes face to face with his fears and flaws and ultimately overcomes the difficulty. We love these stories! We read them in books, we watch them in movies, we dream that our lives could be so meaningful. Through each drama we live, vicariously, in the characters. Miller challenges us to live such stories in real life.

While we resonate with the idea, none of us wish to experience the conflict and sometimes tragedy of difficult journeys. We call on God to protect us, and order our lives to avoid difficulty. Oddly, while we long for heroic adventure, we spend our lives seeking safety and comfort. Most advances in science, medicine, economics, and politics are motivated by this quest: to make life on this fragile planet a little easier, a little quieter, and a little safer for its inhabitants.

Through the drama of his daughter's death, my grandfather lived a heroic story. He didn't want to live it! He prayed for it to pass him by, for his daughter to be healed, and he did everything possible to make the path easier and better for little Lucile. But still, he had to walk the path, and this he did with grace and dignity. I hope, if such a dreaded shadow ever darkens my path, I will be as human, as godly, and as heroic as my grandfather.

Lucile Marie Gehman
Born: December 21, 1935
Passed away: January 25, 1942
Age: 6 years, 1 month, 4 days

Oh, how we miss her smiling face
Miss her in a thousand ways
Miss her footsteps and her prayer
Miss her always, everywhere.
Eli H. Gehman
February 2, 1942

It is with a heavy heart that I take my pen in hand to record a few of the sad and trying experiences which we passed through the last seven or eight months, for we have just last Thursday, January 29, 1942, buried our six-year-old daughter.

Last May 1941 Lucile developed severe pain in her abdomen. My wife called me home from the feed mill and when I came home, the doctor was there. He examined her and pronounced it appendicitis. We rushed her to the Ephrata Hospital. There, she was examined again by Dr. Riffort. He found it to be a fast growing tumor and told us very candidly that if they don't operate, she will surely die, and if they operate, she may die - it being a rare case and would be a very serious operation. With much crying and many protests, Lucile finally submitted. We left her at the hospital and after two days Dr. Riffort operated.

Our hearts were heavy, and with much prayer and fasting, we besought the Lord that He would bring her safely through the operation. On the morning of the operation, I was called to the hospital and Dr. Riffort took a pint of blood out of my arm just in case it was needed for Lucile. Thanks to the Lord and the skill of Dr. Riffort, the operation proved to be successful, however it was not without mishap, for one of the large arteries was punctured, and in no time, the opening filled with blood.

Dr. Roberts afterwards said that if the artery had not been closed immediately, she would have bled to death in half a minute. But it was closed successfully, and she recovered splendidly. It was with joyful hearts that we brought her home fourteen days later. In a month, she had completely recovered. She was her happy, hearty self again for about seven months, when alas, she developed abdominal pains again. Dr. Roberts warned us on the day of her operation that the disease would come back and would eventually take her but she had been so well that we felt the Lord's blessing was upon us and trusted she had been healed permanently. However our hopes and joys were short lived.

Well do I remember the night she came over to our bed softly crying, saying: "My belly hurts."

I took her into our bed, soothed her and she soon fell asleep. I then examined her abdomen gently and was alarmed to feel a hard lump or object on one side. Fear for the worst seized me, and I slept no more that night but planned to take her to the hospital as soon as possible.

In the meantime, Lucile was quite well again and complained only occasionally. On one occasion, she was all dressed to go over to a neighbor's house to play with their children. She was as happy as a lark when she started across the lot. It was only by chance I glanced across the lot from the chicken house and saw her kneeling down at the corner of the fence. She appeared to be hiding from someone I thought. But to make sure that everything was all right, I whistled and waved my hand, but no answer. Again I whistled and waved. Then I saw her hands go to her eyes. She was crying. I quickly went to her side, and she sobbingly said, "I fell and my belly hurts."

Oh that terrible thing in her belly. What will the end be?

We took her to the hospital the following Saturday. Dr. Riffort examined her thoroughly. Then while her mother was dressing her the doctor called me aside and said, "I am very sorry, but I am afraid you will have to lose Lucile, for I felt something on both sides. There is nothing we can do. I feel so sorry for her but we did all we could. We tried all the methods of science" (referring to the X-ray treatments she had received at Lancaster from Dr. Smoke, being two series of six treatments each with the series being three months apart).

He also called Mother aside and told her the same. There would be progressive pains and much suffering, and there was nothing we could do but give pain pills or injections to relieve the suffering. I asked how long the suffering might continue. He said about six weeks; this kind of tumor grows very fast.

—
80

We left the hospital brokenhearted. Then we stopped in the store for a few things, and there we met Mrs. Heffley, a neighbor who asked about Lucile. So in tears, we had to tell her the sad news. They had bought a book for Lucile's birthday, and they gave it to her right there so she would have more time to enjoy it. Next, we stopped in at Grandpa Gehmans' to tell them, and on Sunday, we went to Grandma Martin's house to tell them. Lucile was along, feeling quite well except for an occasional pain spell. She enjoyed herself very much, and said she wanted to stay with Mammy for supper.

The next Saturday we made ice cream for her birthday, and she had a party with Ivan and Mary Ellen Diem on the little table I made for her. On Sunday, December 21, 1941, we went to Indiantown Sunday School and church. Lucile received a Christmas gift from Sunday school - it was also her birthday and the last time that she was able to go to church. We came home and Lucile rested while I fed the chickens. Then we went to her Uncle Benje's for dinner. She seemed to enjoy the visit except for occasional pains again. On the way home from Benje's, we stopped off at her Uncle Amos Zimmerman's for a short time. There she got severe pains, and we hurried home.

From then on, she grew worse and worse. She developed pains more often and more severe day and night. She now slept either with her mother or myself. When the pain would waken her, we would rub her abdomen vigorously, and she would soon quiet down again.

On the night before Christmas, she had severe pain, so we thought we should call the doctor in, but it eased up a little, and by rocking her a great part of the night, she rested fairly well. On Christmas morning, we took her to Dr. Robert's. He gave us some pain pills to give her if the pain was too severe. The pain grew worse and worse, so that she would waken at night and scream and cry of pain until the medicine we then gave her would take effect.

One evening her pain was so severe that she screamed and cried at the top of her voice. She could not sit. She was dancing from one foot to the other when she suddenly stopped crying and said, "Why doesn't Jesus help?"

Oh my, the dear child had great faith in Jesus. We told her many stories of healing and miracles of Jesus as bedtime stories, and she also heard our prayers on her behalf. Three times before, we had experienced answers to our prayers on her behalf when she was younger, and we told her how we believed that Jesus had healed her before. But the poor child's faith was put to a severe test, for although we had many prayers within our hearts for her, there were times she would ask us to pray again when she said her bedtime prayer. We then prayed in her presence, laying her condition before the Lord, telling Him of her aches and pains and asking Him if it is not against His will that He would rebuke this thing that is causing her so much suffering and heal her completely.

However, it seemed it was not the Lord's will to heal her, for her pain grew more and more severe and it is with a troubled heart that I write the next few lines.

It was in one of her spells of extreme pain when she screamed and cried for about twenty minutes when she suddenly stopped and said brokenly, "Why doesn't Jesus heal me? If He doesn't heal me I won't love Him anymore."

Oh, what have we done? Have we built this child's faith up too high? Does she expect too much? Must we see her faith crumble in great disappointment? Oh, what shall I say? What can I say to comfort her? I knew only too well that if Jesus does not help, her time on earth would be very short. So these words came to my mouth, and with a lump in throat I said to her, "It won't be long anymore. We must just wait. Jesus knows best."

I now stayed home every day, for it was only three weeks after her examination at the Ephrata Hospital that she could not lie down anymore. Her abdomen was very full, causing her so much pressure. She could not lie down day or night, neither could she sit alone. We fetched Grandpa's large rocking chair. So day and night either her mother or I would hold her on our lap until the pain would drive her off, and she would walk back and forth until she was tired or the pain left her. Many times her mother would rock her, and the pain would come and annoy her. She would say, "Mamma sing," and her mother would sing. Sometimes I would hold her, and mother would lie down on the couch trying to get a little sleep, and the pain would come. She would say to me, "Rock faster so it won't hurt so much," and I would rock faster. Then she would call mother saying, "Mamma sing," and mother would sing until sleep overtook her. Oh, the soothing and comfort came from a singing mother, causing her to relax in peaceful rest.

The doctor came to see her every day, and one day he said if he would open her abdomen and drain it, it would relieve her of a lot of pressure. So he opened it, but it drained just a very little, and in about five days it was healed shut again, not giving much relief. And well do I remember the day when her pains were very severe, and she refused to take her medicine. Oh, how we pitied our dear child. We did not like to force her to take the medicine, for she dreaded it so much and cried saying, "I won't take it. It won't help anyhow." Oh, how true that was as far as healing was concerned – it didn't help, it only gave relief from the pain. So when she decidedly refused to take it, mother said that we will not force it upon her, but, oh, the pain and suffering she had to endure that day until the doctor came and changed her medicine.

She cried and screamed from pain. She could not sit. We could not hold her. The pain would drive her off our laps. She walked on the floor crying and screaming from pain until she was all tired out, and we could do nothing. We were at our wits end so that we were almost compelled to say, "My God, my God, why hast thou forsaken us?"

When she was too tired to walk anymore, she came to me and said "Papa, carry me." Oh, I was just too glad to do anything I could for her, so I lifted her up in my arms and carried her around the room, although she was really heavy. I

83

talked to her about the pictures on the wall so that she forgot her pain for a while, but it soon came back with force so that she said, "Walk faster, faster." I walked back and forth carrying her until I became too tired, then I set her on her feet and took her hand walking with her from one room to another, back and forth. She was crying all the while when she again brokenly said, "I just wonder why Jesus doesn't heal me?"

"I don't know," I said almost brokenhearted. "Shall we pray? Can you keep quiet long enough to pray?"

"I don't know. I don't know," she cried.

So I kneeled beside her and prayed this short prayer, "Oh, Lord come quickly so she does not have to suffer so much, for she calleth for thee."

Then I lifted her up in my arms again and walked around the room showing her the pictures on the wall, talking about them to get her mind off her pain. When I came to the picture of the Baby Jesus in the manager I asked her, "Shall I tell you a story of how Jesus had to suffer when He was here?"

She said yes, so I told her the whole story (although she heard it often before) about how many people didn't believe what He said and they tried to stone Him and kill Him, and how He was arrested by the soldiers, mocked and scourged and nailed to the cross.

These words came to me with force as I said, "Jesus also prayed but God didn't keep Him from the cross. He had to hang there all by Himself until He died. Then God took Him to heaven, and He had no more pain."

When I made an end to speaking, the tears were running down my cheeks. I always tried to hide them from her but there was no hiding them now. So with her in my arms, I with difficulty got my handkerchief and told her to wipe my tears, and with great tenderness, she dried my eyes. We sat on a rocking chair with tears still running freely. I said to her, "They just run, I can't help it."

Then she said in ever so small and gentle a voice, "If you pray to Jesus, He will help you."

I could say nothing. We sat very quietly. Her pain was all gone. After a while, she said very gently, "You don't have to cry for me. The doctor will soon come."

I was made to think of the words of Jesus when He said, "Weep not for me." She sat very quietly and soon fell asleep and slept for a long time, as if she had her medicine. But when she awoke, her pains came with renewed force. The doctor soon came and gave a different kind of medicine that was easier for her to take.

From then on, her pains were less severe, although, she suffered exceedingly for another week. Her feet were swollen, and sometimes she would get stinging pains. "Oh, oh my feet, rub them," she would say. Often have we rubbed her feet for long periods at a time.

Her abdomen was full, and the skin stretched so hard that it was quite blue. Sometimes she cried saying, "I am too fat," while her face, neck and arms became thin.

Although she ate very little, she was very hungry. She often asked for things to eat, and we gave her whatever she desired, but as soon as she tried to eat, she would turn away crying. "My head hurts," so she ate very little, and to make matters worse, she got vomiting spells so that she threw everything up. So with all her pain and suffering, it seemed that we would have to see her starve for lack of nourishment, for she now gave up trying to eat. "It just gives me pain," she said. Her hunger seemed to have left her so for the last seven days of her life she was without food. She had very little pain the last week. She rested peacefully most of the time.

The last few days of her life she was able to lie down to sleep for a few hours at a time. She became weaker and weaker although she was still able to walk a little. Her mind was very clear up to the very last. The last morning of her life she was very restless, and she had some pain. She called for Mamma to hold her and not being able to rest, she called for me to hold her, and so from one to the other.

It was Sunday, January 25, 1942. We were all in the house at the time. It so happened that I was holding her, and she asked Mamma to sing, when she said, "I'm afraid I must vomit," and got on her feet like she always did when she had to vomit. And while she was thus standing, her head dropped to one side, and she was gone. When the doctor said she would possibly last about six weeks, it was hard to believe, but after a few weeks we did not think it could last that long. The six weeks were up Saturday when she passed away Sunday morning about 9:30 a.m.

Glad was she to answer the summons to "come up hither," for without a sigh and without a struggle, she passed away to be with her Maker, where there is no more sorrow, no more tears, no more pain.

No one heard the footsteps,
Of the angel drawing near,
Who took from earth to heaven,
The one we loved so dear.

Her willing hands are folded,
Her dear warm heart is stilled.
A place is vacant in our hearts,
Which never can be filled.
(But)
We humbly bow in submission,
Though our hearts are bleeding and sore,
For Lucile is sweetly resting,
With Jesus forever more.

No one knows the silent heartache,
Only one who has lost can tell,
Of the grief that is borne in silence,
For the one we loved so well.

Friends may think we have forgotten,
When at times they see us smile,

But little do they know the heartache,
That is hidden all the while.

The funeral text was Revelation 21:4: "And God shall wipe away all tears from their eyes; and there shall be no more death, neither sorrow, nor crying, neither shall there be any more pain, for the former things are passed away."

Every time I read this touching story I am reminded of how uncaring I was as a child and adolescent, growing up in the company of Grandpa Gehman. He carried a great burden, hidden beneath a courageous skin. The pain of losing a child – and one so young – is almost beyond fathoming. How I wish, now as an older man with so much more experience and knowledge, and my own painful stories, I could tell him that I am sorry for his loss, how I admire his kindness to us while he carried the pain of it, and how I wish I could have comforted him and honored him more while he lived.

We really don't know what other people carry, this weight of experience, a burden mixed with trouble and of joy, of failure and success, of life and sometimes of untimely death. Pain lives hidden beneath the skin, behind the face, out of reach to other human beings, even one standing right beside. How indifferent I've been to so many! To my own grandfather! How I wish, I could be more like Jesus, who knows these deep things about us and is touched with the feeling of our infirmities, that I could be like Him, to offer more empathy and more understanding, or an outstretched hand of friendship, of affirmation, and with oceans more patience and grace.

7 Newport Road

My Mother, a few years younger than Dad, grew up on a dairy farm thirty miles south of Denver, near the town of Quarryville in southern Lancaster County. The two met as late teenagers, introduced by a friend – either Dad's cousin Phares Martin or Mother's friend Pearl – that led to a promenade of dating, romance and marriage, and the eventual arrival of yours truly as Child Number Two. After the wedding, in July 1952, Mother and Dad rented a small mobile home – "it was the size of a camper," Mother remembers – in Norristown, Pennsylvania. Dad got a job as an electrician. They started saving money. Three months later, Mother was pregnant. Judy arrived in September 1953; when I was born twenty-one months later, in June 1955, the little trailer had become intolerably cramped. That year Dad bought a half-acre plot of farmland on Newport Road outside of Rothsville and purchased a larger mobile home. He parked it on the lot, and the family moved in. This would be temporary housing while they built a proper home. I have no memory of our lives in either trailer, nor of our move into the fresh, new two-bedroom frame house. Only my parents' stories and a few faded Kodak pictures remain to tell the story. The pictures of my happy newlywed parents – Dad in a white shirt and bow tie standing beside his Fannie Arlene, in a flowery house dress holding baby Dougie, with three-year-old Judy, blonde hair and pony tails, standing beside them, the proud, happy family in front of a dirty hole in the ground, or beside the rough wood frame skeleton of a house-in-the-making, with a little trailer in background and building supplies scattered everywhere – are the only remaining evidence to a young family's stressed excitement over first home ownership. What a time in their lives! During our childhood, Dad and Mother often talked about those early years of marriage and about how they built that house.

With apologies to my contractor friends for the over-simplification, there are basically two kinds of houses in the world: those with basements and those without. Houses without basements are typically built on "concrete slabs" or are "off grade," meaning the house stands on short stilts above the ground. Off-grade homes are common in coastal areas – this I learned after moving to Florida – because of low elevation and high water tables. Beach-front houses sometimes lengthen the stilts to sit high above tidal force waves. Basements are the norm in northern states where freezing temperatures require house foundations to dig down below the frost line. Our Newport Road needed a basement. On the first days of construction, the builder's arrived with a backhoe and dug a big hole in the ground. When they finished, the front yard, just beyond the trailer steps, had disappeared into a sprawling, ten-feet-deep rectangular chasm! A week later a block laying crew finished building the foundation, a ten feet high walled rectangle inside the dirt hole. After dinner one evening, before the workers back-filled dirt around the block foundation, Dad and Mother decided to take a walk in their cratered yard to survey Building Project Stage One. Mother carried Infant Me while three-year-old Judy pushed a doll stroller by her side. For a brief moment, Dad, distracted by the emerging dream house, left Judy unattended. He didn't notice when she pushed the doll stroller too close to the hole. Before their horrified eyes, and before they could stop her, Judy and the stroller rolled into the abyss! Mother screamed, and Dad cried out to God. By Providence the stroller wedged abruptly between the dirt chasm wall and the new block foundation. Judy's leg caught on the stroller and stopped her from plunging to the bottom. There she hung, upside down, snagged by the foot, suspended between heaven and earth. Dad got down on his belly, reached into the hole, and hauled her and the carriage out of the chasm. Three months later the little family of four settled safely and thankfully into their new home. Another year passed, and in February 1957, child Number Three, Dale Curtis Gehman arrived, completing the Gehman family tree.

My earliest memory at Newport Road was my first birthday party, organized by Mother, to celebrate the beginning of my fifth year. I remember the party only as bland distractions and faceless children consuming party food and running noisily in our backyard in yellow and green birthday hats because I was pre-occupied with presents, and cake and candles, but especially presents, one hoped-for present in particular. It wasn't customary for guests to bring large presents in those days – not like today when our grandkids are lavished with mountains of gifts every birthday – but I did receive one gift from Mother and Dad, and perhaps a few other simple surprises wrapped in colorful paper. I opened them all in front of my kid guests, eagerly tearing open paper and packages looking for ONE THING. I was terribly disappointed when I didn't get the longed for western-style revolver. I so wanted to be Roy Rogers and fight Indians! But Mother didn't like guns, so thanks to her, who had warned me beforehand that we weren't having any guns, I was unarmed. Mother loathed my adolescent propensity for killing, even pretend killing. Years later, she boycotted Bill Cosby records because of his constant reference to killing this and killing that, or being killed by his dad. We thought Cosby was hilarious.

Father Cosby, after repeated visits to the boy's bedroom, declares, "If I have to come back up here one more time tonight, I... AM... GOING... TO... KILL... YOU! Do you understand me?!!"

"Yes, Dad."

"NOW, GO TO SLEEP!!" The bedroom door slams and Mr. Cosby's feet clump, clump, clump down the stairs. Cosby was a magician with a microphone! But Mother didn't like Bill Cosby, especially his murderous subject matter. Mennonite parents can't reconcile their pacifist ideology even with pretend killing, so little Mennonite boys grow up deprived of this most primal form of male self-expression. A decade later, a high school friend once bragged, "My Dad said if anyone ever hits me, I should hit him back even harder so he won't do it again." Sound advice, if you are okay with the possibility that within a year the entire planet will be dead. Eventually, someone has to back down. Pacifism simply maintains that it should come early in the conflict. Pacifism isn't the best answer in every scenario, but it works well most of the time. "A soft answer turns away wrath."

While I focused on being Roy Rogers, Judy was falling in love with horses. The equine love affair started early and continues today. Lancaster County farm country offers the perfect environment for horse husbandry. Dad and Mother weren't initially enthusiastic about allowing a large beast to live on our new property, so Judy satisfied her interests by drawing horses, reading horse stories, and collecting horse paraphernalia. Their lack of enthusiasm about beasts was the result of childhoods raised on the farm. Mother grew up on a diary farm where the smell of cow manure lingered eternally in the air, indoors and out. Dad was raised among sheep and chickens, probably the two stupidest life forms on earth. So, for the first few years of married life, and though the love of country living kept them out of the city, they were done with farm animals.

Enough of cows, bulls, goats, sheep, chickens, and all of their shit. Okay. I know, the "S-word!" The English-speaking world – especially the suburban Christian sub-set – has disconnected the word from its origins and reassigned it to a short list of taboo vulgarities. Not so farmers. Where I grew up the word was an essential farm item referring to a disgusting but useful, nutrient-rich by-product of animals. Farmers don't go around saying, "Tomorrow we'll clean out the cow manure from the barn," or "Don't step in those chicken droppings!" No, apologies again for further insulting my readers, but farmers, including my pious grandmother, call the stuff what it is: "Take off those shitty shoes before you come into my kitchen!"

Anyway, after a lifetime of farm life my mother wasn't having any… well, you know… in her new house on Newport Road. Judy needed time to formulate a persuasive argument (whining was definitely a part of it) on the issue of horse ownership. So Judy saved her allowance, drew, painted, and sculpted horses, and read every horse story in America. When she was eleven, Dad capitulated and let her buy a horse. Calling the animal that arrived on our property a "horse" stretches things to the extreme, because the little beast was stubby, short, and as round as an apple. But it had four hoofs, a long white mane, and it ate horse food in the front and pooped horse manure out the rear. And, to get to the real point, a saddle fit on "Molly's" back. Judy was in horse heaven. Dad built a wooden stall in our garage next to the car for Molly. A year later he bought an old shed from our neighbor, Mr. Henley. Mr. Henley loaded the shed onto his huge flatbed trailer – he owned an excavation business – and delivered it to the back corner of our property. Dad and Mr. Henley dragged the shed off the trailer and set it up on concrete blocks. Then Dad removed the flooring from one section so Molly could be on firm ground.

I didn't at first care about Judy's interest in horses. A horse was a lot of work: feeding, brushing, cleaning, etc. The benefit of riding the animal didn't offset the maintenance. But those empty burlap bags were interesting. We quickly accumulated a pile of them in the garage. "Horses sure eat a lot!," I observed. Dale and I had fun with the empty, and very scratchy, brown sacks. We stood in one, pulled it up to our waist, and then pulled another over our head. Thus adorned we began hobbling across our yard in the general direction of the Milford's next door. Gregory and Karla, the Milford's blond-haired youngsters were playing in their front yard. They looked up and saw two burlap "things" hobbling toward them, and Dale and I began shouting: "WE ARE THE BAG MONSTERS! WE ARE THE BAG MONSTERS!" Gregory and Marla's mouths flopped open and their eyes almost popped out of their heads. They dropped their toys, jumped to their feet, and sprinted hysterically to the house. "MAAAHHHMMMMM, THE BAG MONSTERS ARE COMING!! THE BAG MONSTERS ARE COMING!" Screaming and stumbling over each other, they clamored up their trailer's porch steps and dove through the front door.

Good grief! We didn't want to scare them! Well, maybe we did. I still didn't have a toy gun, so burlap was an adequate alternative. But we *didn't* plan for Big Momma Milford to be involved in this scenario, and quickly realized, after Gregory and Marla disappeared through the front door, that SHE would be coming out loaded for bear. Mrs. Milford was a nice lady, but nobody better mess with little Gregory and Karla.

The terrifying story got stammered to Mom: "Alien monsters have invaded earth and landed in our front yard!" Mrs. Milford exploded onto the porch while we tore at those stupid burlap bags, trying to get them off. Earlier we could not hold them up, but now the bags clung to us like glue. "Its just us, Mrs. Milford. Sorry, Gregory. It's OK Karla, it's Dougie and Dale." Mrs. Milford, wearing a flowery pastel housedress and apron, glared down at us from the front porch, legs apart, hands on hips, the militant matron. What an irony!

"Sorry, Mrs. Milford. We were just playing and the kids got scared." I put on my most innocent face and smiled lamely at her. Mrs. Milford leaned forward on her slightly heavy frame. "Okay boys. Go home." She was still glaring at us. "Don't you have anything better to do than scare my children? Don't ever do that again." We plodded back to the house, dragging our monster costume, hoping she wouldn't tell Mom.

My aversion to Judy's pony, especially the maintenance, did not eliminate a curiosity about riding. I was learning a lot about horses and their temperaments from this little beast. Like all Shetland ponies, Molly was short and pot bellied, physical features that seemed to exist in direct contrast to her strength and bull-headedness. Her disposition vacillated between the poles of reluctant indifference and passionate determination, depending largely on the direction in which she was headed from home. On the way out she was predictably apathetic, slow, uninterested, reluctant to trot, refusing to gallop, and continually trying to turn back. At the end of the outward journey, after the turn toward home, she miraculously transformed. Her head lifted and her gait quickened. There was almost a sparkle in her eyes and she wanted to run. Only with difficulty could the rider hold her to a manageable trot. As our property neared, she was determined to gallop and resisted every attempt to hold her back. Judy could control Molly. No one else, including me, ever mastered the technique of reining her in.

One summer day I took Molly out for a ride by myself. Judy helped me get her bridle fastened around her head and made sure the saddle was snug on her back. After a brief trip down the road past the Milford and Hustin mobile homes to Skyline Park (a mobile home community about a half mile from our house), I turned around and headed home. Molly followed her normal routine, which was part of the reason I decided to cut the trip short. She just WANTED to go home the entire time. When we turned to her preferred direction, I pulled back on the reins to keep Molly at a slow trot. But no amount of restraint or vocal commands made any difference at all. Molly went from walking to trotting to all-out gallop. At the Gehman – Milford property line, marked by a waist-high line of bushes, the stubborn little beast bounded over the hedge, and abruptly stopped on the other side, dropped her head and started nibbling grass. I catapulted over her lowered head and landed in the grass with a thud still clinging to the leather reins. Injured, angry, and fighting off unconsciousness, I leaped to my feet, jerked the reins, and shouted. "Molly! What are you doing!?" Molly reared up on her back legs, and pummeled me directly on the head with her hooves, knocking me back down onto the ground. Reeling, I let go of the reins. Molly finished a few more bites of grass and then trotted off to the horse shed.

I was still nursing a lump on my head when I recounted the story to Judy. "You just have to take charge and let her know who's boss," she said dismissively. Right. I think we already discovered who is the boss. Not long after the hedge incident Judy sold Molly and bought a bay-colored quarter horse named Ginger. Compared to Molly, she was twice Molly's size and incredibly even-tempered. Most of the time. I once made the mistake of going into her pen without pre-warning her and almost got my head kicked in. I never saw the hoof that flew past my head. THWACK! against the shed wall behind me at head level. Whew! Cardinal rule: never walk behind a horse without warning her first.

The term "quarter" horse is a curious designation. To the layman, it seems to refer to the horse's size, like a smaller version of a larger breed. In truth, the term is derived from the fact that these horses are lightening fast in a quarter-mile race. Quarter horses are sprinters, and can outrun most thoroughbreds in short distances. Their relative low center of gravity also gives them incredible agility and maneuverability, attributes that have endeared them to cowmen for herd work. Quarter horses were brought to the Americas by Spanish conquistadors and were later domesticated by the Comanche and other native tribes in the western Great Plains, while their "Mustang" cousins proliferated in the wild. In time, quarter horses were put to work by our nation's emerging cattle industry (aka the cowboys). The breed continues to be prized by horse lovers for their recreational, competitive and showmanship qualities.

When Judy bought Ginger she unwittingly purchased *two* quarter horses. Right after we acquired Ginger, we left for a weekend family camping trip, an annual tradition with the Mennonite "Camp Lighters" group. On Friday evening, after Dad arrived from work – he was now working for RCA as a technician in television tube Research and Development – we packed up our camping gear and left for the weekend. When we returned Sunday afternoon Judy jumped out of the car and ran to check on Ginger. To her surprise, Ginger had "foaled" over the weekend. All by herself, during the solitude of the weekend, Ginger gave birth to a healthy colt. We called the previous owner; he didn't know she was pregnant either! Judy named the new colt Tanner for his dark tan coat and darker mane and tail that included a distinct black pin stripe on his backbone. He wasn't a prize horse, but he was ours, born on our little "farm." Judy later sold Ginger, but she kept Tanner for many years. She broke him, and training him for riding. She had Tanner gelded (i.e. castration) which helps temper the wild stallion characteristics of adult male horses.

8
Rothsville Elementary School

Most people of my generation remember the place where they were when President John F. Kennedy was assassinated. That moment for me was on the front lawn, under the tall oak tree of the Rothsville Elementary School. Nearly fifty years later, the schoolhouse still stands, now refurbished and serving, not for the education of young minds, but as an apartment complex for low-income families. Even from the perspective of half a century and the tempering of middle age, the two-story red brick building, a huge rectangle monolith, looms larger than life. It still appears in reality exactly as it does in my memory when I, on my first day in Kindergarten three years before President Kennedy was shot, walked up its expansive gray concrete front steps holding (more like squeezing) my mother's hand. Through the huge green double doors we walked into a cavernous worn-wood plank hallway that to my childish eyes seemed as ominous as the nation's capitol building. At the door of my new classroom, I tentatively released my mother's hand – or perhaps she pried herself free from mine – as she introduced me to Mrs. Gardener, my Kindergarten teacher, whose kindly eyes and motherly voice only partly assuaged growing panic in my chest.

With a hug, a wave, and an off-hand remark, "Well, Dougie, you'll do just fine..." Mother left me to Mrs. Gardener and a buzzing horde of child strangers in the room. The door slammed shut behind me, and I was a captive. From that moment forward, there was no going back on the academic education and social conditioning of James Douglas Gehman. The academic track, I confess, I didn't fully embrace until many years later – a very late bloomer – when I entered graduate school. I did, however, immediately take to the social offerings – both male and female – of school life. Within an hour, I was immersed in the joys of new friendships. I spent five years at Rothsville Elementary School until the system, overwhelmed with children, so many children, who would in time become known as the baby boomer generation, moved our fifth grade class to a rented facility – the Lutheran Church – five miles away and across the street from Warwick High School, while they completed the new Kissel Hill Elementary School, built to handle the expanding horde.

On the afternoon of November 22, 1963, three years into my education experience, while I dawdled in the shade of an old oak tree in front of Rothsville Elementary School, President John F. Kennedy died in Dallas, killed by a bullet shot from the rifle of Lee Harvey Oswald. I was eight years old, near mid-point in my third grade education, too far distant in history to remember details. One moment, however, is frozen in time. Mr. Myers, the school Janitor, a person I rarely noticed before this day. He lingers in my memory after five decades for only one reason. On that day, when we encountered each other beside that oak tree, he was crying. The school day was over, and the children were exiting the building, walking, riding, chattering, and climbing onto big, yellow buses parked in a neat row. Kennedy was shot at 12:30 p.m. Central Time in Dallas, 1:30 p.m. in the east. Add extra time for the event to unfold and for news to travel across the country via 1963 communication systems, and the news reached Rothsville at the end of the school day.

As I exited the school down those big concrete steps I saw Mr. Myers standing by that big oak tree in the schoolyard. He was dressed in custodial grays, with a wide brim hat on his head. Tears were rolling down his face. I walked up to him as he wiped the tears from his cheeks. I asked him what was wrong. The inquiry, now that I think about it, was rare for most children. We would not be inclined to venture into an incomprehensible adult world, even when one of them was crying. But, it seemed the right thing to do.

"President Kennedy was just shot," Mr. Myers replied. I don't remember what happened next – Mr. Myers fades from memory – but the news jarred me. I knew who President Kennedy was – most eight year olds know such things – so I knew this was important news. It seems strange to me now, but I don't remember the ride home on the bus, or talking with my Dad and Mother about his death over dinner. I don't remember discussing the subject at school the next day. Certainly in every one of those scenarios the death of the President was on people's minds, in their conversations, and in my hearing, but the only memory that remains for me are the tears and the words of Mr. Myers on the front lawn of the Rothsville Elementary School.

There are other memories at Rothsville Elementary School, less traumatic but equally vivid. Several involve experiences with gym class and competitive sports. Others include the disgusting subject of vomiting. Funny thing, I don't remember any of my own experiences with nausea, but I do vividly remember what happened to other kids. Frankly, I don't understand the childish obsession with this particularly disagreeable experience. For some kids it is a thing to be avoided at all costs, dreaded and loathed, only death itself surpassing its awfulness. To others the ability to vomit is a tool, used when necessary to gain the upper hand over parents, teachers and other authority figures.

I knew a few boys (and yes, they were all boys) who applied the latter regularly. If they wanted to stay home from school, up came breakfast, usually in front of Mom, and the decision was quickly made and back to bed they went. If they wanted to go home from church early, it was, "Mom, I feel sick," and Mom, conditioned by previous episodes, dropped her socializing and commitment to library duty and hastened the little liar to the car. One kid I knew got so brazen about vomiting that he began to use threats: "Buy me that toy or I'll blow chunks right here in the department store!" I'm guessing he's in the state penitentiary now.

My brother's aversion to vomiting was probably closer to the norm. He hated and feared it! Of all of life's possible nasty experiences, vomiting rated worst in Dale's estimation. Tooth extraction, OK. Injections, no problem. In-grown toe nail, give 'em to me, two at a time. But, please God, don't let me vomit before I die. So, what does one do when nausea is growling in one's stomach, and an explosion is inevitable? Dale denied it until the chunks blew. Many years later when I became a parent, our third child, not knowing what to CALL the disgusting experience, used the best comparison he could muster. Trevor came running to my wife yelling, "Mom, the poop came out of my mouth!"

My brother's incident happened in the family car on the way home from a camping weekend with "Camp Lighters." Dale was feeling bad all morning, a tactic I assumed he was using to avoid helping us strike the campsite. He sat around at the picnic table looking gray while Judy and I grumbled our way through tearing down and packing the tent, stowing the kitchen into boxes, and stuffing everything into the trunk of the car. In hindsight, I realize Dale was indeed sick. Denial was working, because he held the churning bile down all morning.

But nature is going to take its course one way or the other. The nausea would not be denied forever. The moment arrived about fifteen minutes after we were in the car heading toward home. Dale was sandwiched in the back seat between Judy and me. As the car swayed and hummed along, Dale turned grayer and grayer. Mom kept looking back at him with a worried expression. I honestly missed most of this - he was my punk younger brother and I was not interested. I was just mad at him for sleazing his way out of packing the car, so I ignored the gray and green version of him. Sitting to Dale's right, behind my Mom in the front passenger seat, I gazed out the window at the farmland and cows.

Turning back one final time, Mom said, "How do you feel, Dale?"

"Okay."

"Do you feel like you're going to vomit?"

There it was, the dreaded word. My Mom should have never used the "V" word. You know, the power of suggestion and all.

Dale attempted a feeble, "No," but Mother's inquiry was an invitation. Dale burped, and the chunks blew. He could have done the decent thing, you know, and spewed straight forward onto himself and the back of the front seat. But no, he didn't want to get any nuclear waste on his own clothing, so he turned toward me - probably some kind of subliminal brotherly revenge reflex - and emptied himself on my pant legs. I got morning breakfast and who knows what the rest of that stuff was, all over me, from thigh to toe. Talk about scrambled eggs... Dad slammed on the brakes and pulled over while I screamed the best benign obscenities I could get away with. When we stopped, I jumped out onto the grassy shoulder. Dale stayed seated where he was, and sort of stared into noxious oblivion while his color changed back to normal! Mom leaped out of the car and got to work. Thankfully we were in the middle of farmer's fields in the heart of rural Lancaster County. Mother told me to pull my pants off and stand between the open car doors in my underwear while Dad opened the trunk. Then Mom dug through all the dirty laundry to find something clean for me to change into. She handed me a pair of Dale's pants.

"I'm not wearing those! Those are Dales!"

"It's just till we get home. Put them on."

"They're too tight."

"Put them on and be quiet."

Dale sat stiffly in the car, looking obviously better, trying not to look at the floor where his insides were splattered all over. Mom cleaned up the car as best she could so I could get back in. Dale didn't need any cleaning up. He was fine.

"Make Dale sit there. It's his mess," I demanded.

"I'm not sitting there," Dale said.

"Just get in and be quiet." I climbed in. Mother stared wearily at the three of us, scrunched into the back of the family car. It took months to get rid of the smell. Months more passed while we regularly found little nasties in hard-to-reach cracks and crevices in the car.

A few years ago my wife and I returned to Lancaster to celebrate my twenty-fifth high school reunion. About one fifth – fifty out of two hundred and fifty – of my classmates showed up for the event. They all looked pretty good. I had to wonder, "Does this group reflect the condition of the whole class, or did only the success stories come back?" I should talk. This was my first reunion, having missed all the others. Jane Mayer was there. It's amazing what you remember about people. I had forgotten her. But there she was, sitting on the bleachers of the high school football field where we had gathered to watch the Warwick Warriors challenge (and get defeated by) Hempfield High – a nostalgic walk through personal history. The moment I saw her I remembered her. But, dear reader, the nostalgia did not go to high school romance, a first kiss, or other such adolescent pleasantries. Some musings go in other directions, and this was one.

I first met Jane in kindergarten in 1960, at Rothsville Elementary School and from there we continued in the same class all the way through to high school graduation. There were many other moments with Jane in classes and extra-curricular activities through all those years, none memorable, but on this night, when I encountered her sitting casually on the bleachers, now an attractive middle-aged woman, a single memory leaped into my consciousness. The picture returned in vivid, living color: A seven-year-old Jane Mayer sitting across the table from me in the Rothsville Elementary School cafeteria at lunchtime. When I saw her on those bleachers, I almost made the mistake of blurting, "Jane Mayer! I remember you from the Rothsville Elementary School cafeteria in second grade..." Thank God, wisdom, learned after a decades of adult life, prevailed, and I kept my dumb mouth shut.

Here's the scene: A table full of second-grade kids are eating lunch, those government issued rations for which we paid something like twenty cents in those days. Jane sat across the big lunch table from me and had just finished eating. Other kids on both sides were busily digging in or jabbering away. The scene is basically a packed table in a packed cafeteria. Our plastic trays, plastic plates, plastic cups are mostly empty and we are talking and wiggling and being, well, elementary school kids. Suddenly, Jane grabs her tray with both hands, puts her face down, and blows her entire lunch right back onto her plate! I watched it happen, in stunned living color slow motion. It of course happened fast and was over fast. My stomach reacted first, before my brain could process the shock, and I almost wretched up my own lunch. I quickly turned away and put my hand to my mouth, trying to hold it down. Someone yelled, "Jane is sick!" When I looked back, she heaved again, and again I turned away to keep from losing control. Mercifully, a teacher ran to the rescue and helped the poor girl who by now was sobbing. Teacher and Jane quickly vanished from the embarrassing scene. I guess somebody else carried the ghastly tray to a nuclear waste disposal facility because it too quickly disappeared. I got out of there and ran for fresh air.

So, with this memory lingering in the cool Friday night air at a high school football game, I stared at the unmistakable resemblance of an older Jane sitting quietly on the bleachers.

"Jane Mayer, right?"

"Yes. Doug Gehman!" She remembered me.

"Hi. Good to see you."

Jane's memory of me was hopefully not rooted in the same awful episode. We chatted for a few moments. As I said, she looked pretty good. Maybe the vomit incident is why we never dated in high school.

9 Lancaster County Covered Bridges

Lancaster County has the most covered bridges in Pennsylvania. Only one other county in the nation has more. Park County, Indiana has thirty-one. The twenty-nine covered bridges of Lancaster County are protected by the National Register of Historic Places.

Zook's Mill Covered Bridge spans a quaint and shaded section of Cocalico Creek only three miles from my childhood home on Newport Road. Its eighty-nine-foot "Burr Arch Truss" single lane span over the creek was built in 1849. The bridge is quintessential Lancaster County. The two rugged wood inner arches, the red-painted wood plank outer skin, and the cedar shingles on the bridge's roof comprise for me one of Pennsylvania's most nostalgic symbols of quaint country living. A unique feature of Zook's Mill Bridge is the windows. There are two of them, one on either side in the middle of the span at a comfortable adult height. They beckon all comers to park the car and walk through the bridge, where for a moment one can pause and gaze through the opening at the surrounding farmland hills and shaded creek below.

The Covered Bridge survived Hurricane Agnes in June 1972. I was seventeen, and despite the fact that the Cocalico Creek rose seven feet above the bridge's wooden floor and blew out most of her wooden siding, the bridge didn't budge an inch. Caring Lancaster County people got together after Hurricane Agnes and raised money to restore the bridge. Decades later, a sign still hangs at the south entrance marking the apex of the floodwaters. For me the bridge is ageless: strong, red, an immortal symbol of my childhood. A century and a half and it still handles normal automotive traffic.

The "Covered Bridge" – the only name I ever knew for this landmark – is etched in my memory as an icon of my childhood. I had to look up the proper name – Zook's Mill Covered Bridge – to offer it here. I cannot make a trip to Lancaster County without diverting from larger roads that pass it by and hide it from everyone except the locals, to visit this nostalgic haunt. I make the journey every time I am in Lancaster County, just to drive through its arches and remember. It was too this bridge my parents drove our young family of five on summer Sunday afternoon picnics. Under the shade trees we filled our tummies with sweet bologna sandwiches, apple slices, and whoopee pies or chocolate chip cookies. Then we three young children pulled off our shoes and waded into the clear, cool water beneath the bridge, up to our knees and sometimes more while Mother and Dad lingered on a red and white patchwork blanket in the grass by the creek bank. Such afternoon outings go all the way back to Dale in diapers, when two-year-old Dougie, hand in hand with four-year-old Judy, ignored Mother's warnings to explore the rippling water and rough rocky creek.

A few years later, when I was eight and got my first bike, Judy and I – a few years later Dale joined us – rode from 125 Newport Road to the Covered Bridge to play on its rafters and frolic in the water for an hour or two on weekend afternoons. We climbed the bridge foundations, swam in the water underneath, and skipped flat stones on the creek's rippling surface. After an hour or two we rode our bikes to Sheffield's Grocery Store a mile away to buy Sugar Daddy's, that chewy golden-colored caramel candy on a stick. It cost a nickel and was all we could afford.

The Covered Bridge and the quiet country roads that surround her haven't changed much in fifty years. The same dairy farms, now owned and operated by Mennonite and Amish sons and grandsons, still stand, like memorials to another era, not yet gone, not yet forgotten. The same pasturelands feed a new generation of cows, steers and sheep, and the same rippling Cocalico Creek runs through them, nourishing the rich, green Lancaster County grass the animals crave. The trees are bigger, older, and offer more shade, but they are still there, or have been replaced by a new generation of healthy foliage. The narrow road still winds around the same curves, over the same hills, and past the same white farmhouses, red or white barns, and rail fences.

A lot has changed in Lancaster County, but quiet country life still abounds. Urban professionals from Philadelphia, Baltimore, and Washington DC have moved here, craving the quaintness and affordability of the area. They buy primary homes or weekend escapes for their families in a sincere quest for a more wholesome and safer existence. And, for the most part, they find it in this county, my childhood home, along quiet country roads, near red covered bridges.

10 Mr. Graybill

Old Mr. Graybill lived with his wife and daughter on a farm almost directly across Newport Road from our house. He was a constant presence in my childhood world, an old farmer neighbor, and was, from the impressionable perspective of a ten-year-old, a benign yet dreaded creature. His long protruding nose – the nose endures most profoundly in my memory – his wrinkled face and glaring eyes, peering out from the shadows of a wide-brimmed farm hat, atop a hulking bent-over figure, sketched a terrifying image on my young psyche. In adulthood, rationale now balancing childhood impressions, I know Mr. Graybill was nothing more than a tired old farmer. From his weary point of view, the neighbor kids were the terrorists! Adults have their limits when dealing with the unbounded intrusions of children. If adulthood and maturity has taught me anything, now, fifty years later, I defer to Mr. Graybill.

But to a six year old he was a horror. Whenever we ventured into his fields across the road from our house, or over the tree line to the north, we first scouted the Graybill house and barn. We scanned the landscape too, to see if the dreaded old man was anywhere around. When the coast was clear, or we could no longer resist the allure of imagined adventures in his forbidden fields, we ventured forth.

Unfortunately, his adult cunning usually outdid our childish sneakiness, and he'd catch us. Mr. Graybill never protested when we played in his cow pastures, or plodded through the rippling stream in the valley behind his farm, or rode our sleds down his snow-covered slopes in the winter. Perhaps he never saw us, since those tempting destinations were out of easy view of his house and barn. His cornfields were a different matter. In full view from his kitchen window he could see us, and he did not want us messing with his crops. Woe unto any reckless young soul who sought amusement in his cornfields.

Mr. Graybill did everything the old fashioned way, even in the 1960s. Mr. Graybill was definitely a 1940s man. My Dad observed some of his antiquated farm methods and once suggested to Mr. Graybill that he take a course in agriculture at a local community college to learn new agriculture technologies. Mr. Graybill replied, "Humph! I don't even do everything I already know!" End of conversation. So old barefoot Mr. Graybill planted his corn with a team of horses. He had an ancient tractor too, and used it occasionally. Both tractor and horses pulled the plow or disc through the fields to prep the soil. For planting, Mr. Graybill used his horses. With them, he could plant solo. He'd sit on the planter behind the horses, hold the reins in his toes, and drop seeds or seedlings into the furrows while the horses did their familiar work walking straight rows. There are some benefits to animals. No tractor has yet learned that skill. At harvest time Mr. Graybill picked his corn by hand, standing in a horse-drawn wagon with the reins wrapped around his waist. After the harvest, Mr. Graybill walked through the field again, in weathered hat and bare feet, cutting down the barren stalks and gathering them into neat Indian Teepee-shaped bundles, where, they would dry in the open air. To a curious child, the rows of corn stalk bundles looked like an Indian village, waiting to be explored. Each pale yellow bundle was spread out at the bottom creating a dark little opening like a doorway into its bowels. It was an irresistible temptation. To this day, whenever I pass that field – it was sold years ago to developers and transformed into a sub-division where new generations of children romp without the cornfields – I see only pale yellow teepees, calling me to come and play.

To explore the corn bundles, we had to get past Mr. Graybill's eagle eye. One day the Gehman three, the Milford two, and the Hustin gang, another neighbor family whom you will meet shortly – were gathered in our backyard. We spied the stalks of corn and scurried into Mr. Graybill's harvest field, momentarily forgetting the threat. Within minutes Mr. Graybill emerged from his barn and heard the adolescent glee across the road. He grabbed his pitchfork and marched into the field. When we saw him coming, the entire gang minus one sprinted to the safety of our yard and took refuge behind the garage, where eight pairs of little eyes peeked cautiously around the corner to see what would happen next.

I was the minus one. I sprinted with the gang to our yard, but at the property line I stopped and waited for Mr. Graybill. I wanted to run too, believe me. I was not brave, I was not a hero, nor I was a glutton for punishment, and I had no interest in getting Mr. Graybill's lecturing nose in my face. I did however, analyze the alternatives, a process that passed through my child-brain within seconds. Children get little credit for their analytical abilities, skills they in fact develop early in life. With simple reinforcement, even a two-year-old grandchild can suddenly adjust behavior from tantrum to quiet stoicism.

Me, to a screaming grandchild: "Do you want a surprise?"

"Yes, Papa." Loud protesting suddenly evaporates into diminished whimpers.

"No more crying. Ok?"

"Ok, Papa. Can I have a surprise?"

"We *are* going to the car. It is time to go home. But first let's go get you a surprise."

"Ok, Papa."

"No more crying, Ok?"

"Ok, Papa."

So, off we go to my office where from a desk drawer I pull out the magical box of chocolate surprises. Problem solved. My two-year-old grandchild did a quick analysis: Choice Number One: continue crying and get no chocolate. Choice Number Two: Stop crying, listen to Papa, and get chocolate. Chocolate wins every time.

In situations, such as the one I now faced on our property line, with Mr. Graybill steadily approaching, I compared negative consequences, weighing the rebuke of Mr. Graybill against the wrath of my Mother. If I didn't stop to let Mr. Graybill vent on me, I correctly calculated, he'd walk to the kitchen door and vent on my Mother. She'd get a tongue lashing about "this wild gang of neighborhood brats who have no discipline and no respect for other people's property, and doesn't she know by now that I won't tolerate these kids fooling around in my crops because one of them will sure enough get hurt and then you'll sue me and say it's my all fault because your kid was trespassing in my field!" Then old Mr. Graybill would stomp off to his house and Mother would send the neighbor kids home and give us a spanking, or a work assignment. She might even take away television privileges for the evening.

While the child horde ran for cover, these scenarios flashed through my child-brain. So, I stopped on the property line, standing erect, hands clenched into fists by my side, waiting to face Mr. Graybill's nose. He plodded towards me. He was wearing the familiar wide-brimmed hat, and his long sleeve dark shirt was tucked into worn britches that were cut off below the knee at mid-calf. He was bare foot, and carried a pitchfork that he used like a walking stick. The bare feet and pitchfork handle made a sort of step – clump sound as he approached.

I nervously waited, standing on our side of the property line. I felt safer on OUR side. By calculation, I was also staying out of range of Mother's ears and eyes. Precise work, this confrontation was. Maybe he'd think twice about hitting me on OUR property. Mr. Graybill was a tall skinny man, and even though age had begun its irresistible bending process, giving him a slight stooped appearance, he was still tall and strong. His stern eyes, shaded but visible under the large hat, stayed fixed on me as he drew near. Step – clump, step – clump, step – clump. He stopped two feet in front of me. I was too ashamed to look into his face, so I stared at his big old hairy feet and bony ankles… and the pitchfork handle. I could smell his farmer B.O. and his warm farmer breath. The breath was coming out in a heaving rhythm. After an eternal pause, I lifted my head and looked at him. Here it comes…

"What are you kids doing in my fields?" One long Mr. Graybill arm pointed at his fields. The other arm held the pitchfork, spikes in the air. The pitchfork handle rose off the ground a little. I kept the corner of my eye on it and said nothing, knowing he really wasn't looking for an answer.

"I want you to stay out of my corn!" Gesture, gesture at the corn stalks. The pitchfork gestured too.

"Don't you know you could knock one of those stalk piles down and get hurt and then go off and blame me for your fooling around?" I was more worried his pitchfork might go off and poke me somewhere.

"We're sorry, Mr. Graybill. We forgot. We were just playing and forgot. We won't do it again, Mr. Graybill." What was all this WE stuff? WE forgot. WE were just playing. WE won't do it again. I'm here all alone, getting the treatment from Mr. Graybill's nose and pitchfork, and apologizing for the cowards hiding behind the garage. The bunch of chickens!

Mr. Graybill softened a little. "Well, I have half a mind to talk to your Mother and Father about this." (Oh, no! Please don't!) "You kids need a good spanking to teach you some respect. Just make sure you remember to stay out of my fields!"

"Okay, Mr. Graybill. I'm sorry, Mr. Graybill."

Mr. Graybill sighed and I could see his face soften just a little. He gave me a final long look, then turned and trudged back through his field and across the road. He disappeared into his house. I know, because I watched him walk the whole way. Step – clump. Step – clump. Step – clump. I guess he gave us a break. No pitchfork treatment, and he didn't tell Mother. He really wasn't a mean old man after all. He probably was a kindly old gentleman. Maybe he was sick too, after all those years of working in his fields, and taking care of cows, and harvesting corn and tobacco. He had been pretty out of breath from that walk.

I walked back into our yard and met the cowards near the garage. They were glad to be off the hook, but I got no hero welcome back. Kids never really thank other kids who save their necks from the chopping block. They're just glad someone else got it instead of them. Kids don't hold grudges either. Some qualities of childhood might be better retained in adulthood. Within five minutes we were running wild again.... far from Mr. Graybill's fields. No discipline. No respect.

Every winter in my childhood life on Newport Road, after the first freeze secures its icy grip on the countryside and snow lays a white blanket on the entire countryside, Judy, Dale and I dug out rusty sleds, stored for the summer above Molly's pen in the garage, and cleaned them up for downhill sledding in Mr. Graybill's fields. We piled on cumbrous layers of winter clothing, including hats, boots and mittens. Mother usually insisted on wrapping a colorful scarf around each neck and over each nose. "Keep your scarf on!" she insisted, "Or you'll catch cold." After a quick inspection, to be sure every nose and finger was adequately protected, she squeaked open the kitchen screen door and out we marched to trek through white mounds. We plodded across Newport Road and onto Mr. Graybill's pastureland, and then, for an hour, until achy toes and fingers turned red with cold, we dashed our sleds down icy hills, made snow forts and then barraged each other with snowballs.

The hill at the back of Mr. Graybill's cow pasture descended gently into a valley where a stream trickled. Near the water's edge the valley dropped sharply, ten feet and more. Testing our daring, we sprinted our sleds down the hill as fast as we could, and then rolled off at the last second while the sled careened over the cliff into the frozen stream. During the dead of winter, thick ice covered the flowing water. The only real hazard was the sharp drop. The unfortunate soul who failed to eject experienced a brief airborne descent that ended in a teeth-grinding, heart-stopping impact. After a few rides down the hill with arduous treks back up we just played around the stream, poking holes in the ice to see what we could find.

On one such day, when the night before temperatures had dropped to twenty degrees and fresh snow had fallen, Mother took extra care to properly protect each kid with layers of outerwear. She gave special attention to Dale, and when finished, he looked like the Michelin Man! Mother stuffed him into an oversized coat, and forced something on every protrusion and appendage: thick hat and ear muffs, scarf over nose and mouth, and two pairs of jeans jammed into snow boots. Dale could barely move, and if he fell he wasn't getting back up without help. Finally, we got out the door, and plodded to the stream through a foot of snow. The trek made a path, a desecration in the pristine snow, a track that began at our kitchen door and meandered around the house, through the front yard, over Newport Road, and across Mr. Graybill's expansive pasture. It disappeared over the hill towards Mr. Graybill's stream. We stopped at the valley bottom, and peered over the cliff at the frozen stream.

The cliff was barren, too steep to catch the falling snow. Only a dust of white clung to the brown dirt. Dale stepped too close to the edge and fell. Down he went, a quick, steep slide on his butt to the ice-covered stream ten feet below. The force of the plummet and the abrupt stop at the bottom drove his feet through the snow and through the underlying ice, into the stream's freezing water. Dale jumped up immediately, but he was anchored in place, up to his hips, held by snow, ice and water. He squirmed, trying to step out of the stratums but it was simply too much for his short legs and all the clothing. He grabbed at the snow, but of course there was no nothing to grab hold of. Thrashing didn't help, but he thrashed anyway, and the motion only mixed snow, ice and freezing water into slushy pool around him. All of this happened while Judy and I watched from above. At first the scene was comical. We both just stared at him in shock, like entertainment at a circus. But then, we realized he might actually be in trouble. The slushy hole around him got bigger, Dale got wetter, and he was making zero progress getting out of the stream. Judy shouted at me to go down there and help him. Hearing her, Dale started panicking, shouting for someone to help pull him out. Judy began screaming, making adulations that her beloved brother (whom she ignored at home) was about to die. I started getting that panicked racing feeling in my chest. I wasn't sure if this was serious trouble or not, but figured I better get down there and help my pesky brother. I inspected the cliff. There was no way to get down there without ending up wet too. I plunged down on my butt and landed in the water next to Dale.

Now, I must emphasize, Dale was never in any danger. The water under the ice was hardly six inches deep. It was only because of the thick layer of snow and the angle at which he had slid into the water, that most of his legs had gotten wet. If Dale had gathered his senses and looked at his feet he would have noticed the water was flowing just over his ankles. But these were eight, ten, and twelve-year-old minds conditioned by adult-written scripts, horror stories about the dangers of falling through thin ice. The story goes something like this: While skating and playing on thin ice, little Susie fell through the ice and was lost, trapped in a watery grave. Her pathetic frozen body was never found, at least not until the spring thaw, when her despairing family members and rescue workers finally dredged her ghastly corpse from the bottom of the lake. Kid's interpretation: broken ice and cold water kills.

Such drowning stories filled our terrified imaginations as we watched Dale get his leg wet. At any moment, in our view, the flowing water under the ice was going to pull Dale under and drag him downstream for a half-mile. He'd be lost forever. Other pertinent facts, like the four-inch depth of the water, were of little rational importance. Dale had fallen through the ice!

Judy screamed from above, "Dale fell through the ice! Dale fell through the ice! Help him! Help him!"

Dale was screaming beside me, "Help me! My leg is caught. It's all wet! I can't get my leg out!"

I wanted to be the rational one, but with all the excitement I started screaming too. I can't remember why, the intensity of the moment formed its own stimuli. I looked around to see if anyone might be in the area. Perhaps Mr. Graybill had come outside to survey his land. But, there was no one. We were all alone and far from home. It was only a couple hundred yards to our house, but it felt like miles. I wasn't sure, even if I could get Dale out of this mess and save him, Judy and I would be able to drag him all the way back home. Judy slid down the dirt bank and together we grabbed Dale by the arms and pulled him free from the stream's death grip. We rested for a moment, leaning on the dirty cliff, but then the cold wetness of our clothes, especially Dale's legs which were soaked up to his waistline, introduced another threat: Without immediate attention, the freezing temperatures and soaked conditions meant frostbite and pneumonia, maybe even gangrene. We had no idea what gangrene was, but we knew it was awful, and Dale was on the verge of contracting all three terminal maladies.

So, with frostbite, pneumonia and gangrene setting in, we dragged Dale, who was now whimpering, up the bank and through the meadow toward home. Judy on one side, me on another, we draped his arms over our shoulders and half carried, half dragged him all the way home. Once inside the warmth of the house and the comfort of Mother, Dale made a miraculous recovery. Mother pulled off his coat, boots, socks and jeans. She examined his pink legs. No frostbite! No gangrene! Amazing! Absolutely providential! We sat on the floor and warmed our bodies in front of the warm air vent on the den wall while Mother calmed our anxiety with cups of steaming hot chocolate. Over the simmering brown brew, we recovered, reminiscing about our amazing survival.

Mother was the likely originator of all the thin ice horror stories. My Dad would never venture into such melodramatic territory. His stoicism simply didn't allow the behavior. The stories – however they were told and exaggerated – worked! In my lifetime, I have never fallen through the ice anywhere and have never gotten frostbite from exposure to the elements. If she indeed was the originator of the warnings, Mother succeeded in getting the point across. I am still alive and gangrene free.

Measured by the ethics of parenting, sometimes the ends do justify the means.

11 The Hustins

Black-Bumper Mennonite's operated a chicken farm north of our Newport Road home. We walked there to buy fresh eggs. The opposite direction from our house, a Mennonite-run dairy farm was about two miles to the south. Judy and I walked THAT distance, carrying a two-gallon stainless-steel milk jug to buy fresh milk. "Black Bumper" Mennonites got their nickname because their conservatism allowed for automobile ownership but not for gaudy amenities like chrome bumpers and bright paint. So, after they purchased a black automobile (the only color that was permitted) they had the chrome bumpers repainted black to match the car. There didn't seem to be a prohibition against chrome hubcaps.

Besides these few local Mennonite farmers, the rest of our neighbors appeared to be unregenerate heathen, the Mennonite leaven not being sufficient for the community loaf. The Hustin family, for example, lived on the other side of the Milford trailer, two hundred feet from our property line. They provided steady exposure to the ways of the Outside. The Hustin clan was a combination of two families, Hustins and Bakers. Mother Hustin had three boys by Mr. Hustin. After his departure for unknown reasons, Mr. Baker moved in with his girl and boy. They all lived together in a doublewide trailer.

As soon as they could afford it, Mrs. Hustin and Mr. Baker dug into the hill on the property and set their double wide on top of a new basement. Because of the incline of the hill, the raw cinder block basement opened at ground level on one end. A door on that wall allowed for human entry, and two windows provided the only natural light into the basement's cavernous bowels. The basement was unfinished, except for an inside stairway to the house above. Gray block walls and gray concrete floor accentuated the damp gloom of the place. As soon as the cavern was completed, the three Hustin boys were promptly relocated there.

Robby, the oldest, who was my age, told me they never went upstairs, by parental decree, except to use the bathroom. All their meals were delivered to the top of the stairs. They ate in the basement and returned the empty plates. Generally speaking, they lived like three little pigs. Maybe King Pigs. From an eight-year-old point of view, it looked almost like a perfect setup, except for the glaring lack of affection in the house. We rarely saw Mr. Baker. He mostly ate, slept, and drank beer in front of the TV. And we mostly only *heard* Mrs. Hustin: "Get the hell out of this house!" That scourge echoed all the way to our yard, indicating to me that the boys did have occasional access to life upstairs.

Mrs. Hustin was a hard woman, a Marlboro-smoking, motorcycle riding, stereotype. I don't think she rode motorcycles – the generalization is unfair to my riding friends – and I don't know what brand of cigarettes she smoked, but you get the idea. At the time Mrs. Hustin was probably not yet thirty years old, but to my child eyes, she was ancient, wrinkled, and worn out. My mother, by comparison, was young and beautiful.

My most enduring memory of Robby was the time he came to our house to play and decided to demonstrate the sex act, using a tree trunk as his partner, and the English language's most vulgar expletive to explain the process. I'll spare the reader too many details. "Hey look! I'm (expletive deleted) this tree! Look, this is how you (again, the word)!" On and on he went, repeating the vulgarity, very proud of his knowledge about such things. We were ten years old, so there is no way on God's green earth he had any actual experience, but again I shudder at what Robby and his siblings were being exposed to in that double-wide trailer. I was not ready for Robby's demonstrations or explanations. I ran inside and told my Mother, "Robby is doing sex with a tree!" She stormed outside and sent him home. In other circumstances, with other children, my parents would have called the parents. But, this was the Hustin/Baker house, and my Mother knew better. They probably would have laughed in her face and thought it was cute. So no phone call.

Amazing to me now, with their Mennonite emphasis on forgiveness and tolerance, my parents never forbade the Hustin boys from coming over. They must have thought we would be a positive influence on those boys, a sort of Mennonite or Christian osmosis. Fat chance. At this very impressionable age, it was the other way around.

On another such day of cross-pollenating osmosis, the Robby and Rick Hustin, plus Dale and I were in the basement of our house. My brother and I also shared a bedroom in the basement of our home. Yes, there is an irony here. Like the Hustin boys, Dale and I lived in the basement... but with several important differences. First, we ate our meals upstairs with the rest of the family. Also, we were allowed upstairs any time we wanted. And finally, at least once per week, my Mom came down to clean our properly finished, fully furnished, and heated and ventilated bedroom. Do I really have to explain the differences further? The four of us were lying on our *properly finished* basement floor happily drawing pictures of animals and people on old blocks of wood. The blocks of wood were the creation of my two Grandpas, both accomplished carpenters. What with houses, barns, sheds and chicken coups, carpentry is an essential skill for every Mennonite farmer. Thrift was another such skill. My two Grandpas would NEVER throw unneeded wood away! They saved everything for a future project. Even small pieces of wood were cut down into wooden blocks for the grandkids, an inexpensive and inspiring gift. Small wooden blocks, the precursor of Legos and other such building toys, are one of the most creativity-inducing playthings I have ever seen, for us a source of unending entertainment.

At some point during the fun – I want to blame Robby Hustin for the idea, but I must concede that these things are the mischief of every boy – I decided to draw a picture of a naked stick man on one of my blocks, with a complete but childishly simple anatomy. We had a good laugh. Then, the bounds of culture and conscience began tugging on my psyche. I looked over my shoulder. Were Mother or Dad coming down the stairs? I knew at any moment one of them might arrive and see what I had done. In my imagination, the little stick man, not two inches tall, began displaying his nakedness in life-size dimensions on the basement wall. I tried to erase the drawing, but the black ink clung like a tattoo, and the pen had etched the drawing permanently into the wood.

Dad's eyes began glaring through the ceiling rafters. With panic rising in my chest – I had to get rid of the evidence – I jumped to my feet and crept up the basement stairs. After checking that neither parent was watching from kitchen or den, I sprinted out the back door. When my toes were straddling the edge of the yard at the garden, tilled soil and rows of vegetables in front of me – I could not get my shoes dirty and make it back into the house without being caught by my sanitation guard Mother who would also ask me what I was doing in the garden at this hour – I heaved that dirty picture as far as I could. The block disappeared into the darkness and landed with a small thud far out in the garden. There. Like God, who threw my sins into the sea of forgetfulness, the naked man was gone and I was free.

Not so. One's sins will always find one out. God will not be mocked. Whatever a man sows he will also reap. The Bible doesn't directly refer here to a cardinal rule about the stupidity of sinners. Sinners tend to be ignorant and shortsighted about the difficulties of hiding criminal activity and incriminating evidence. I had thrown my sins, not into God's sea of forgetfulness, but into Dad's beloved vegetable garden. A few days later, when Dad was cultivating the garden with his rototiller, he uncovered a block of wood... with a now embarrassing drawing still vividly engraved on it.

He brought it to me. I saw him coming and remembered... Uh oh.

"Doug, did you draw this?"

"No."

"Then, who did?"

"Robby Hustin."

Good ole Robby, a perfect, flawless alibi. If God wouldn't forget my sins, then I still had a scapegoat to take the blame. My parents would never call Mrs. Hustin to verify the story because she would only laugh. And if they talked to Mr. Baker he would probably get mad because Robby drew a naked man and not a naked woman. I blamed Robby anyway: we were Adam and Eve and he was the devil in our garden, beguiling us. I would have never drawn that insidious picture on my own.

The other two Hustin boys, Rick and Mark, were more trouble than Robby. Rick was two years younger and a big loaf of a guy. He had to go to special education classes at school. Intelligence is definitely hereditary: negligent parents. In this case, I'm not sure Rick's academic challenges were the result of genetics. If those poor kids were given some love and affection, role modeling, and a little encouragement, they might have been the valedictorians of their classes. Sadly, however, Mark, the youngest of the three, was a criminal in the making. We played together and shared toys; our family had more to share than the Hustins – bikes, balls, and whatever – and when we were finished, we would indiscriminately abandon toys everywhere, in our yard and the Milford's. Fifty years later, now with grandchildren, I have learned that the practice, utterly frustrating to adults, is common to all children.

Mark once announced to me that if we left any of our things in the Milford's yard, or anywhere else off our property, he would claim them, and we couldn't get them back. It had never seemed improper or even out of the ordinary to abandon unmarked toys all over the neighborhood. I assumed they belonged to us and we could retrieve them at any time. I never considered the practice might raise a question of ownership.

"Can he do that?" I asked my mother.

"I should think not!" This was a common Mennonite rebuttal, putting the negative after the verb. Think not. Afraid not. Better not. Thou shalt not. I don't think Mark ever actually stole anything – at least not from us, but from that day forward I brought my toys home.

Jody, the younger Baker girl, had blond hair and wore weird-looking cat's-eye glasses. I remember very little about her, and nothing about her younger brother, the fifth Baker kid, whom my sister Judy insists existed in the house. He was probably too young and insignificant to take up any space in a ten-year-old boy's brain. One vivid memory is that the three Hustin boys were pure and total redheads with all the complexion characteristics: hair, skin, freckles, and temper.

The three Gehman kids and the four school-aged Hustin/Baker children walked to a bus stop every school day. The stop was a mile away, along a busy country road. We walked past the Milford and Hustin mobile homes, past farm fields, a mobile home park, and finally down a long winding hill to an intersection. The location of the stop was convenient for the school and bus driver, not the children who convened there. Times have changed!

One gray, drizzly fall day, while the seven of us waited for the bus, my sister Judy got into an argument and then a shoving match with Robby and Mark. The two boys shoved Judy and she stumbled backward into a roadside ditch. I ran to her defense and shoved them both back. Mark fell down. We exchanged more insults and shoves, but before the tension escalated into a fight, the bus arrived. Under the watchful "hairy eyeball" of the driver, we returned to civility, brushed off the dirt and snow and climbed aboard. The suspicious bus driver glared at us but said nothing. During the ride to Rothsville Elementary School Robby hissed get-even threats from the back of the bus.

True to his word, Robby got his revenge. Heathen people never forgive. Only Mennonites. So Robby told his version of the story to our fourth grade teacher, Mrs. Strickland. His version went something like this: With no provocation I had attacked poor defenseless Mark and shoved him into the ditch. (Heathen people are also liars). Mrs. Strickland marched to my desk and pointed her long outstretched arm and bony finger toward the closet in the back of the room. Fire was coming out of her eyes. Her lips were pinched tight. "MOVE!" she said.

Every classroom at Rothsville Elementary School had a huge walk-in closet in the back of the room. On arrival, students headed to the closet to hang up coats and hats and take off boots. Mrs. Strickland followed me to the closet. We passed thirty pairs of inquisitive eyes, wondering what crime had I committed. This was kinder-court and Mrs. Strickland was judge, jury and executioner. Into the cloak closet door we walked, and the door slammed shut. Outside, thirty children waited in frozen silence for the axe to fall. Mrs. Strickland glared down at me. "What do you have to say for yourself!"

I couldn't conjure a single word to make my defense. The simple fact is I was scared out of my mind. My lower lip quivered so badly I couldn't speak. Tears welled up in my frightened, humiliated eyes. A little chutzpah would have helped, but I didn't have any. I really don't think Mrs. Strickland wanted an explanation. She stared at me for a moment, and then her countenance relaxed. I rather think she understood what happened, but with the need to maintain discipline, she had to do something. Mrs. Strickland sighed and her neck muscles relaxed around the collar of her lacey, white blouse. She opened the door and waved her hand for me to return to my desk. No punishment. The inquisition, and the humiliating walk back past sixty third-grade eyes that followed me in wonderment, was thrashing enough. I probably deserved it anyway, for lying to my Dad about a drawing on a block of wood.

Robby Hustin had revenge coming back to him, but like a good Mennonite boy, I forgave him and never retaliated. I didn't even want to get him back. Holding grudges and seeking revenge simply weren't the Mennonite way. In fact, until this day, I never told on Robby. That was not the Mennonite way either. Mennonites sort of have a "just take it" attitude. If the world hates you, just take it. If one slaps you on the right cheek, just turn the other cheek and take it. If you are persecuted for righteousness sake, just take it, and be thankful you are counted worthy to suffer shame for the Kingdom of God. At eight years old, I hadn't yet sorted through the theological implications of suffering and humiliation. I had, however, learned how to behave.

It wasn't long before we were playing together again with Robby tempting me to smoke one of the cigarettes he stole from his stepfather. I just took it. Our family's move to Kissel Hill a few years later probably saved my life. Robby and I saw each other occasionally after that, but the friendship was finished, the victim of geographical separation. Robby completed high school with me in the Class of 1973. He became a long distance truck driver and died two years later in a fiery crash in Florida. "Burned to a crisp," was the way my Mother related the story in a long distance phone conversation. I never heard what happened to the rest of the Hustin/Baker clan.

12 Farm Animals

Del Miller lived on a farm across the valley behind our home. Del had a murderer for an older brother. Tom was a sandy haired teenager with wide shoulders and bulging chest muscles that rose above a rotund waistline, strength and appetite developed over a lifetime of work on his father's diary farm. Tom liked to wear tight shirts to show off his biceps. Perhaps he just out-grew the family clothing budget. The shirts were disheveled, half tucked in and half hanging out at the waist. Tom murdered pigeons. I learned about this unique inclination one afternoon when I was visiting the Miller farm. He emerged from the barn and offered to demonstrate. "Look what I found," he boasted. In his hand he held a nest with four recently hatched pigeon babies and explained why they needed to be eliminated. Farmers understand. Pigeons are pests, a source of dirt and disease. Their droppings can defile a barn's storage of hay and feed. But, that pigeons should be eliminated for reasons of sanitation was wholly secondary to Tom's motivation. He *liked* to kill the birds. With me watching in starry-eyed shock, he plucked a baby bird by its head, and then whirled it like a helicopter until the helpless body launched into oblivion, leaving a bloody head in his hand. He dropped the head back into the nest, plucked another one, and repeated the grisly procedure. When he finished sanctioning all the hatchlings, he threw the nest into the meadow and walked casually back into the barn. Adult pigeons, who could fly away, were eliminated with a 22-caliber rifle.

Tom's behavior is a stretch even for farmers who regularly kill animals. It's a touchy business, this issue of animal rights and animal cruelty. Who decides, for example, which animals are protected, and for the rest, how they should die? Do we protect pests, or is our patronage extended only to cuddly domesticated mammals, canine and feline varieties enjoying most favored status? Not because dogs and cats are indispensible to society, but simply because we are fond of them? Historically, particularly in agrarian cultures, animals have been valued for their utility – horses for transportation, cows for milk and meat, oxen for heavy labor, dogs for hunting, etc. In early American tradition, the only purpose a cat served was to eliminate barn mice. Grandpa and Grandma Stoltzfus' had scores of cats on their farm. They came running, twice a day, when Grandma, bowls of milk in hand, called to them from the front porch: "Here kitty, kitty, kitty, kitty kittyyyyy!" Today, industrialized nations use machines for heavy labor. Hunting with dogs is mostly about sport, and traps or poison do the job with mice and rats.

Country people remain pragmatic on the issue of animal rights. Most make a distinction between the rights of humans (unqualified favor) and the rights of every other living thing (negotiable). Debate about animal rights for a farmer, is as idiotic as gourmet cat food. Let a few urbanites speculate about the morals; the rest of us schmucks must deal with pigeons and rats. Argue all you want, my dear reader, about balance, Mother Earth, and the equality of all living things. Carnivores are still eating herbivores; they have been eating each other since Adam and Even left the Garden of Eden, and will continue attacking, killing and ripping into the flesh of their hapless prey until the end of time. And farmers, well, they still eliminate pests and raise livestock for our supermarkets. All due respect to vegetarians. Your dietary choices haven't engendered gratitude in the animal kingdom or saved a single beast. Only humans are discussing the issue. Most farmers do actually care for their animals. But they treat them like, well, what they are. Will Andersen, John Wayne's character in the movie "The Cowboys" groused: "A cow is just a bunch of trouble wrapped up in a leather bag. And a horse isn't much better." Mr. Farmer doesn't abuse his chickens, sheep, pigs and cows. He might be a nasty old brute, and his neighbors might not like him, but he doesn't have time for such nonsense.

People complain about modern milk and egg production facilities, where controlled environments reduce a day from twenty-four to eighteen hours to speed up natural cycles, and feed is infused with hormones, all to increase production of milk and eggs. Some of these practices go too far, but, we the American consumer shouldn't fuss too much! Until we adjust our proclivity to over-eat – we are the most obese nation on earth – and until we stop ordering omelets and cheese, hamburger, steak, racks of ribs, and chicken nuggets, the breadbasket of America will do what needs to be done to supply the voracious demand.

No one disputes the fact that killing animals is gruesome business. I grew up killing chickens, so I know how it goes. Memories of my grandmother chopping off a chicken's head and releasing the decapitated animal to flop around in the front yard are permanently etched on my brain. For a gruesome minute the terminal fowl scrambles, flails and jerks around the green grass until the bloody mess of feathers finally expires! One would expect the headless beast to make awful gagging and croaking noises, but the scene unfolds in complete silence. No head, no vocal chords. It is barbaric, but how else will we have roast chicken? After the headless fowl stops moving, Grandma retrieves its bloody carcass and places it in a bucket of scalding water for a few minutes. The hot water leaches out the blood and softens the skin for plucking feathers. Finally, Grandma cuts the cleaned torso from anus to breastbone and then scoops out all the entrails from the chest and stomach cavity. The organs – liver, heart and kidneys – are kept for later consumption.

The modern beef industry is perhaps the most sophisticated animal killing machine on the planet. It provides America's supermarkets, restaurants and delicatessens with a steady supply of fresh steaks and ground beef. To meet demand, cows are killed by the thousands in assembly lines, their lives ending by a pressurized ramrod to the forehead. The shot-gun-type device kills quickly and painlessly, and the warm carcass is immediately scooped up and hauled to huge machines, where hooks, razors and saw blades skin, disembowel, and quarter the animal before it cools. Fresh sides of beef are sent to cold storage and later shipped to wholesalers, retailers and finally dinner tables and outdoor grills.

Efficiency aside, let's not kid ourselves about the ghastliness. Putting down a large beast is disgusting. Killing thousands in an assembly line is a job for professionals only. Eric Schlosser, author of "Fast Food Nation," wrote a gruesome account about this uncaring and alleged unethical industry. Good reading, but I'm not buying it. It is grisly, but it is also necessary, and for the most part is hygienic and humane. How else do we dispatch large numbers of large beasts? As long as modern man wants meat – and that, if you will forgive the pun, will continue until the cows come home – there will be people and industries doing the deed. Rant all you want, opt for a vegan diet if it makes you feel better, but you will not convince this Mennonite country boy about the ethics. The vast majority of homo-sapiens are unrepentant carnivores, so get over it.

For a few years we had chickens at our house. Mother and Dad purchased them – they were little baby chicks when they arrived at the house – perhaps thinking the experience of feeding and nurturing chickens would enrich our young souls. There was no plan to murder the chickens for an evening meal, at least I remember no such discussion. These were pet chickens. After they matured, which for chickens happens in a couple months, the hens began laying eggs. When we could find them we collected the eggs and ate them for breakfast. We hadn't planned to raise egg layers either, but the fresh eggs were a nice plus for Mother. Most of the time, however, the hens laid their eggs under the horse shed. The off-grade floor of the shed was less than a foot above the dirt. We had to crawl ten feet on our bellies through cobwebs, chicken shit and other unrecognizable filth to get those stupid eggs.

"Hey kids, do you want bacon and eggs for breakfast?"

"No thanks. We want cereal."

The six chicks were sexless when we bought them. Weeks later they began emerging into chicken manhood and womanhood. Thankfully, only one was a male. When he was old enough, as males are inclined to do, Mr. Rooster began crowing every morning. He also took over the entire property, dominating the hens and everything else. Mr. Rooster was no ordinary, run-of-the-mill chicken. He was King Chick, and woe unto any living, breathing creature that imprudently wandered into his domain. Roosters can be very territorial and aggressive.

Most people think chickens are cowards, the ultimate incarnation of fear and timidity, and every waking moment of their anxious lives is obsessed with flight from everything. Hence the insult "You chicken!" In "Rebel Without a Cause" Jim Stark (played by James Dean) immortalized the stereotype during the famous car-race-to-the-cliff with the challenge, "Are you chicken?" The younger generation remembers the same insult thrown at Marty McFly in "Back to the Future." To be a chicken in American culture is to be weak, timid, and without valor. Our rooster was no chicken. He was an attack bird, and he reigned over the backyard, threatening anyone who ventured into view, including Dad's wheelbarrow when he was working in the yard. Karla Milford, the little neighbor girl, came over to play with us one day. Before she got to the kitchen door, King Chick charged and knocked her to the ground. He then stood on her chest and flapped his wings in conquistador pride. We found her after a few seconds, pinned to the ground on her back, screaming bloody murder and flailing her arms and legs. We ran over and shooed the bird away.

King Chick stood head and shoulders above the hens, a big, menacing bird. His eyes glared, perpetually irritated. Long, razor talons grew from the sides of his tough chicken-skinned legs. King Chick stomped around the yard, flapping his wings, standing up on this toes, and crowing as loud as he could. Generally he was a big nuisance. He didn't scare us because we had raised him from infancy. All this posturing was a big joke. When he attacked us, we would play along, challenging him, acting scared and sprinting away. He'd chase us but we could easily outrun him. Chickens are not fast, but they can dodge, and for that reason they are almost impossible to catch. I don't know why we put up with him as long as we did. His sudden demise came as no surprise.

Mrs. Milford didn't know about King Chick, an oddity after what happened to her daughter Karla. Perhaps she figured a chicken would never come after her. She came over to visit my mother one day. When she walked into his view, ten feet from the kitchen door, King Chick attacked from behind, leaping on her with a fusillade of wings, pecks and squawks. What he lacked in size, King Chick made up for in aggression. Before Mrs. Milford could gather her senses and realize she was being attacked by a measly bird a tenth of her size, she was overcome. With the bird pecking at her heels, Mrs. Milford turned around and sprinted for her mobile home screaming, "Get this chicken away from me!" King Chick gave up at the property line. When she got home, Mrs. Milford called Mother and declared she would never visit us again until we got rid of that chicken. That afternoon Mother cut the head off of King Chick and we ate him for dinner. The meat was pure unadulterated shoe leather.

One of our Newport Road dogs met his untimely end due to the juvenile idiocy of one, well, juvenile idiot. Because of another untimely dog death on Newport Road – that happened because I was chasing "Trixie" through the yard and he ran onto the road in front of a car – this new dog was leashed to a tree in the back yard. The black and brown mongrel terrier (the dog's name is forgotten) was snoozing in the shade while I mowed, back and forth, each pass bringing me and the mower closer and closer. When the mower reached the radius of the leash, I made a big mistake. Rather than move the animal to another location, I decided (logically, of course) that I could just mow over it. VERY BAD IDEA. Startled by the roar of the mower, the dog jumped to his feet and ran. Another VERY BAD IDEA. The rope lifted off the ground, snared on the whirling blade, and reeled the poor victim in. In one graphic, bloody instant the dog was dragged under the mower (only partially, thank God!), and "WHUMP!" lost a front leg. Mercifully the blade cut the rope and set him free.

You can imagine what happened next: A massive pandemonium of canine yelping, crying, flopping around and other assorted berserk behavior as the ghastly leg injury spouted blood all over the place. Hearing the pitiful yelping, Judy and Dale came running, with Mother not far behind. All three kids began yelping, crying and basically going berserk too. The poor dog simply could not be quieted down, no matter what we tried, and who could blame him. The grisly scene unfolded on the brick patio just outside the kitchen. Frantic to get the yelping hound to SHUT UP, Mother took a brick from the patio and whacked him over the head with it! The blow didn't knock him out but he quieted down immediately. Witnessing this unfold I honestly thought for a moment my Mother was going to beat my dog to death with that brick! But she hit him only once. I also have this fleeting wisp in my memory of the incident about a child's shame-filled reasoning: "Killing the dog with a brick was an act of mercy after what I did to him with a lawnmower."

To this day, if I come upon a rope, a hose, twig, or any linear object in the grass while I am mowing the lawn, I get this pit-of-the-stomach feeling that I'm about to do something stupid. One thing prevails: I cannot mow over the object. I must see if a dog is attached, and then, to prove I am a rational adult and to avoid another catastrophe, I remove the linear obstacle.

We wrapped the poor animal's dripping stump in a towel and Mother ran into the house to call the vet. The line was in use – in those days party lines were common. We shared a line with a few other houses in the neighborhood. Mother hung up and returned to check on a now whimpering dog and three whimpering children. After a few minutes I followed Mother back inside for a second try at the phone. The line was still in use, and I could hear two ladies airily talking about hair and makeup or who knows what. Exasperated, Mother butted into the conversation and declared, "Excuse me, but we have an emergency and must call a doctor immediately."

The women relinquished the line and Mother called the doctor. She hadn't really lied, under the circumstances. A vet is an *animal* doctor. Mother got the vet on the line and explained what had just happened. "Bring him in immediately!" he said. Three kids, one whimpering dog, and the responsible adult in charge, piled into Mother's little Volkswagen bug and scurried to the veterinarian. He examined the now relatively quiet animal and explained that yes, he could save the dog, and yes he would heal eventually, but he would be a three-legged animal for the rest of his life, and did we really want to go through the arduous and difficult recovery period with the expected handicap at the other end? We said, "Yes, we do!" Mother said, "No, we don't!" So, that was that. We left the dog with the vet and drove home. I don't remember crying too much over the dog's imminent demise by lethal injection. At least, I don't remember being too overtaken by it. I think by this time I was hardened to the death of pets. Trixie's tragic murder by a speeding car, witnessed by yours truly in graphic, crunching detail, King Chick's deserved decapitation, and now canine terminal amputation by lawnmower pretty much cured me of sentimental attachment to animals.

Judy or Dale might remember things differently. And we do have a pet Pug now whom we love.

13 The Paper Route

Two people, Del Miller and Robby Hustin, hold for me the honor of "Persons Who Made the Most Enduring Childhood Impressions." The Millers were Mennonites. At least that is how I classified them. The Millers could have been outright pagans. But, from the perspective of an eight-year-old country Mennonite kid, all farmers were Mennonites. What other possibilities existed? The Miller family did not attend our church, but even I knew there were other Mennonite churches in the community. Del and I never talked about church stuff, and I paid no attention to his parents.

Del was the youngest of three boys. Tom, the oldest, remains in my memory for only one previously mentioned skill. Del and I played together in the Miller fields or in the valley between our properties. We climbed birch trees as high as we could go, and built dams in the valley stream, using rocks, dirt, sticks and whatever else we could find, forcing the water to back up. Then we waded in and splashed around in our own homemade mud hole. I'd go home at dark covered in dirt, and Mother would make me undress outside on the patio, all the way down to my underwear. "Look at you!" she gasped from the kitchen door. "How did you get so dirty?! You're not coming inside covered in that filth! Take your clothes off and then go straight to the tub. Hurry up! It's time for dinner."

Del and I had lots of outdoor fun in that valley, so I never understood what fueled his changing moods, but sometimes Del Miller got angry and when he did, he directed his rage at me. Abuse, mostly taunts, would follow. But sometimes Del got violent. One time he trekked into the valley and broke down our dam. When I discovered the demolition and asked him about it at school. He retorted, "Because you're a jerk, and I didn't like your stupid dam!" No reason, no further explanation. The emotional shifts were an oddity, but like most children I spent no time analyzing them. Sometimes Del was my friend and sometimes he wasn't. On the off days I steered clear of him. It wasn't always possible. One day after school, when Del was acting particularly hateful, he stalked me onto the bus and from a seat several benches back taunted me with spitballs and verbal abuse.

"Hey Gehman, you runt! Why don't you come back here and let me give you what you got coming. Or do you like sitting up there with all the other girls?" Judy was sitting next to me. She turned around and told him to shut up. Judy never fully bought into Mennonite pacifism, and unlike me was not intimidated by Del Miller. I sat in my seat, facing forward, third grade eyes brimming, trying to hold back tears, angry, humiliated, and clueless about what was bugging this so-called friend. I hated to admit it, but I was scared of him, I didn't understand this aggression, and had no idea how to rebuff the taunts. "Hey Gehman, can't you talk? Or are you so yellow you have to get your ugly sister to fight for you too?" That did it, for Judy that is. She jumped up and walked back to old Del Miller and gave him what he had coming. Wham! Right on the ear.

"Hey Miller, why is your ugly ear so red?" Judy taunted back. She returned calmly to her seat next to me. She said nothing, and didn't look at me, which was a kindness. I knew she wanted to spare me further embarrassment. My sister had her moments. Judy wasn't a fighter, but unlike me, she was afraid of nothing. She could beat me up way into our teens. Judy and I usually got along. Any squabble that turned physical was more about playing than fighting. I was never afraid of my sister. We'd "fight," wrestling around on the ground, more playing than actual fighting, and Judy could always beat me. The "tussle" always ended with her sitting on my stomach and pinning my hands to the ground.

Dougie: "Get off me!"

Judy: "Say, 'Uncle!'"

Dougie: "Just let me go!"

Judy: "Say 'Uncle' first."

Dougie: (sigh) "Uncle."

The experience was humiliating, but she would never tell anyone else. Judy was a beautiful out-doors-kind-of girl: tossed blonde hair and flashing blue eyes, a sweet feminine mixture of perfume, horses, barns, and leather. I learned not to mess with her. The guys at school never took her toughness seriously either, because she was too pretty to be a threat. The femininity simply came with allowances. Even when she whacked Del Miller and made his ugly ear turn red, Judy was safe from retribution. In those days a girl had nothing to fear. No macho man in his right mind would actually hit a female.

Before we moved to Kissel Hill, I got my first job, delivering the Lancaster New Era newspaper to a hundred Rothsville homes scattered on the south and eastern side of town. Remembered now, from the perspective of middle age and current realities, I shudder at the thought of a ten-year-old boy riding his bicycle two lonely miles along winding, narrow country roads to the Rothsville Fire Station each morning. In today's environment – with child endangerment issues at the front of public consciousness – that bicycle ride must contain at least three violations of parental oversight.

The Lancaster paper was an evening edition, but my job started in the morning. I rode to Rothsville, parked my bike behind the Fire Station, no lock needed, and joined a bustling group of eleven, twelve and thirteen year olds who were waiting, without adult supervision, for a school bus to take us to Lititz about five miles away. In the afternoon I rode the bus back to Rothsville, fetched my bike, still safely leaning on the wall of the fire station, and rode to Marty's Garage where a neat bundle of string-bound fresh newspapers waited for me. On Marty's Service Station floor, I folded each newspaper with a rubber band and then packed them into my bike side-baskets. On weekends the newspapers were like firewood logs. I stuffed the logs into the side and front baskets and then loaded remaining newspapers into a Lancaster New Era issued shoulder bag. Lugging that load of Sunday papers to the first twenty or thirty houses until the load got lighter was a dangerous affair. Every day I whizzed along, throwing newspapers onto porches and driveways. At first, this whole new experience of riding my bike to Rothsville, waiting for the bus with the gang of new kids, and hanging out at Marty's Garage with the greasy adult mechanics and assorted customers who frequented the place, was exhilarating fun. The Hustins were history; I was in the big time with the "hip" Rothsville gang.

Exciting as this outside world of Rothsville was, I was not prepared for Marty's nefarious crowd of mechanics and customers, or for the Rothsville gang of juveniles. Marty and his friends were not inclined to protect a young Mennonite boy from worldly vices. Let him get an ear and eye full was his philosophy. I'm sure Marty tempered the rhetoric in my presence, but nobody turned it off completely. Crude language among automobile mechanics was lightweight, however, compared to the morning mob-fest at the fire station bus stop. Every morning about twenty-five kids waited – and I use this term to describe a very disorganized cacophony of activity – in front of the fire station for the school bus. Everyone participated, Rothsville's finest Future Felons of America, throwing insults at each other, and generally working up for a rumble. Male and female, with no hesitations because of gender, fomented a stream of raw jokes, blasphemy, and tough horseplay, all bad and worse. And this

142

was only a prologue for the real action that erupted when the bus arrived.

On the first day, I tried, uncomfortably, to fit in. I didn't actually join the rowdiness, but hid my shock and *pretended* I was familiar with it all. I assumed that, as soon as the bus pulled up, when an adult bus driver entered the picture, the wild behavior would stop. Not so. Writing this account now, I am still incredulous, but I swear I am relating it accurately. Every day when the bus rolled up, turned on its lights and cracked open the side door, before the wheels stopped turning, twenty-five kids condensed into a ball and frantically pressed toward the entrance. The pulsating human ball jammed against the side of the bus while every individual in the ball frantically tried to be the first person on board. Seriously. It was total, unmitigated mayhem, every morning, one pulsating pile of pubescent adolescents pushing, shoving, shouting, and scratching at each other trying to get on the bus at the same time. Girls and boys, with no respect for gender, lunged for the doors, their bodies squeezing together into a tight ball of frothing frustration. It was like trying to jam a beach ball into a coke bottle. One at a time a teenager popped out of the fracas and onto the bus steps. Every day, the fat old bus driver turned on his seat toward the door, and shouted above the din: "Get back! Stop pushing! One at a time! Get back for God's sakes! WHAT THE HECK IS THE MATTER WITH YOU!"

If he could have gotten away with it, and kept his job, I am sure that bus driver would have climbed down and knocked a few heads. But, every day, all year long, it was the same ritual at 7:35 a.m. Nothing ever cured that Rothsville mob of their moxie to get on that bus, ride into Lititz, and flunk out of school as quickly and violently as possible. Somehow I survived, and then we moved to Kissel Hill.

It was into this Rothsville scene that Del Miller strode for his revenge. My sister Judy had drawn first blood on the school bus, and Del was biding time to get me back, a day that for me will live in infamy. One afternoon while I was delivering newspapers I spotted Del walking toward me on Skyline Drive bouncing a basketball. Del saw me lumbering towards him on my newspaper-loaded bicycle. I knew I was in trouble, but couldn't turn around because I had newspapers to deliver.

As I write this, I am astounded by my sense of responsibility at this age. Where did that come from? Again, Mennonite culture is to blame, those incomprehensible Anabaptist roots. Most children would have cut and run from danger. Forget the stupid newspapers, I'm saving my hide. Not me, the good Mennonite boy. An innate Mennonite sense of responsibility kept me on the path. No turning around to save myself. Newspapers must be delivered, down the street, on the other side of Del Miller. Sheep to the slaughter.

Del quickened his pace and the gap closed between us. I scanned the area, searching for a way of escape or an adult who might deter him. Even with the newspapers, I had speed advantage on my bike. On foot, Del had maneuverability ... and a basketball. Twenty feet away, Del ran towards me and threw his basketball at my head. It hit my chest. Top-heavy with newspapers and careening to get away, I skidded off the road and landed in soggy, black, Pennsylvania farm dirt. Newspapers flew everywhere. The mud covered my shirt and trousers and a bunch of the undelivered papers. Del came over to finish the job. As I was getting up, he jumped on my back. I jabbed at him with my elbows, but that made him even madder. He grabbed my neck, put me in a half nelson, shoved me back into the dirt, then punched me a couple of times in the ribs, and rubbed my face in the mud.

"There. That'll teach you, you sissy. You better watch out when you come into my neighborhood." Del gave me one last kick with his dirty sneaker and strutted off, bouncing his basketball down the road. I got up, brushed myself off, and tried to rub the mud off of my clothes and the undelivered newspapers. At that moment I hated Del Miller. I hated him for beating up on a fellow Mennonite and for making me feel so weak and powerless. What had I done to deserve his abuse?! I hated myself for not being able to stand up to him. The dirt would wash off. And he really hadn't hurt me. But my wounded pride, splattered in the mud with so many newspapers, was a more difficult recovery. Some of it just stayed there for a long time, in the mud down the road from Del Miller's house. I gathered the papers, stuffed them back into the side baskets, and climbed on my bike to finish my route. Limping and humiliated, I hoped my subscribers wouldn't notice the grungy delivery boy and the dirt in today's headlines.

No such luck. As if to accentuate Del Miller's victory and my humiliation, at 5:30 p.m. – I was at home and the family had just sat down to supper – Mrs. Craymore and her daughter Beth, one of my school classmates, drove into our driveway, walked to the front porch, and knocked on the door.

"Who is that at this hour?" Mother asked.

Jumping up, I made some excuse about a school project, and went outside. I closed the door behind me. Mrs. Craymore presented me with a mud-covered newspaper. "What is the meaning of this?" she demanded. Beth stood beside her Mother, head down like she was inspecting the porch floor. Feeling stupid and self-conscious – I was still wearing those mud-covered pants – I stared dumb-founded at Mrs. Craymore. She glared at me, waiting for an explanation. What could I say? Mrs. Craymore looked at my trousers, and I could almost read her mind: "Don't these people bathe?" I finally managed a rambling monologue about what happened: I fell off my bike and dumped the load of newspapers into the mud, and I didn't have any extra newspapers, and it was getting dark, and I had to get home, and I was terribly sorry, and if they'd like I can give them a clean newspaper now because I had a few extras here at the house that I brought home from Marty's service station... I left out the part about getting beat up by Del Miller.

When I stopped to catch my breath, Mrs. Craymore was scrutinizing me with an incredulous "you poor kid" look.

During the entire confrontation, Beth just stood sheepishly beside her Mom. She shifted her weight from one foot to the other, and kept her eyes fixed on the porch floor. After an eternal pause, Mrs. Craymore handed me the dirty paper with a sigh, "Never mind. Just don't let it happen again." Then, shaking her head, she turned and walked to the car. Beth gave me a final parting glance and shrugged, a sort of "Sorry about my Mom, but you're an idiot" look. They got in the car and left, without a fresh a clean newspaper. I watched them go. Right, Mrs. Craymore. Don't let it happen again. I stood on the porch with Del Miller's dirty newspaper in my hands as they disappeared up Newport Road toward Rothsville. Sigh. Pacifism is a great idea as long as no one comes after you. And you don't have to newspapers to deliver.

14 Kissel Hill

In 1966, our family moved from Newport Road outside of Rothsville to Kissel Hill on the southern side of Lititz, Pennsylvania. The move, from country living to a four-acre "farm" on the edge of the suburbs, covered only seven miles, but the distance was almost global in contrasts. In those days, Kissel Hill was home for a few hundred middle class families seeking, as it appeared, family values and sub-division lifestyles. Much of Kissel Hill was built on farmland, sold over the years to development planners, split into lots, and covered over by rows of houses and cul-de-sacs. When we moved, the latest addition to the community was the Kissel Hill Elementary School. It opened that year and I was in the first sixth grade class.

The "farm" we purchased was a wispy residue of the original. The once fully functioning dairy farm was reduced to four acres of land, a two-story brick house, four-car (or tractor) garage, a couple of dilapidated chicken houses, and one gem: a classic Pennsylvania red brick barn. The brick treasure was concealed inside an ad hoc arrangement of wood add-on buildings that doubled the footprint of the original and completely hid the brick treasure inside. The property was beautifully nestled in a green valley with – I'm not making this up – a gentle brook running through it. Again, the farm was quintessential Lancaster County. Dad found the property on a fatherly real estate hunt to satisfy his daughter's equestrian dreams, his two son's aspirations for the game of baseball, and his own yearnings to plant more fruit trees and cultivate more vegetables. While visiting the real estate he peeked inside the wooden monolith and discovered the hidden brick barn! Dad promptly made an offer and bought the place, for the 1966 price of $27,000!

So, we sold my childhood Rothsville home and moved to Landis Valley Road in Kissel Hill where James Douglas Gehman would now enter a wondrous new existence in the suburbs. I had no way of knowing how monumental the move would be, having only one point of reference. But besides the fact that I was twelve and entering adolescence with all the complications of pubescence, the move from one spot on the globe to another an insignificant distance away, had immeasurable cultural implications. It was transition from hick-town-in-the sticks to suburbia.

What a contrast was Kissel Hill! On the first day of a new school year, Dale and I joined a gang of neighborhood kids at a new bus stop fifty feet from the end of our drive way. We didn't know anyone, and had no clue what to expect. You must remember I alone experienced the mayhem of the Rothsville Fire Station. Neither Judy nor Dale, and certainly not my parents, ever followed me there, and I never told them about the daily goings on. Dale and I stood around watching the other kids, wondering how to behave, and feeling the apprehension: a new neighborhood, a new group of teenagers, and a BIG new school. I would only attend Kissel Hill Elementary School for one year – sixth grade – and then, in 1967, head to the real challenges at Warwick Junior and Senior High School. But a year is an eternity for a thirteen-year-old.

I surveyed the crowd of nicely dressed teenagers for clues about who might throw the first insult and to whom it would be directed. But nothing happened! The boys in one group and girls in another, separated by a comfortable distance, stood around talking quietly. The boys weren't telling dirty jokes and saying insulting things about the girls. And the girls weren't laughing and cursing in their faces.

I thought perhaps they were waiting to get on the bus, out of sight of their parents. When the bus approached I prepared myself to fight. I may be a Mennonite, I may be a pacifist, but I'm not going to be last! When the bus stopped at the corner and turned on its lights, the door cracked open and two gracious lines of young people formed automatically, boys in one line, girls in another. The girls climbed onto the bus first, one at a time, while the boys waited. In Rothsville, even the girls tore at each other to be first - scratching, screaming, and cursing female curses. I observed this orderliness with incredulity. When the girls finished boarding and the last one was safely up the stairs, the boys began entering, one at a time! To my pre-conditioned brain, this was miraculous! I scarcely believed a place like this existed!

Off to a new school to quickly discover that Kissel Hill wasn't everything I had hoped for, especially after the initial introduction at the bus stop. A few introductory days passed, then the student body started warming up to each other, and the real topics on everyone's mind bubbled to the surface. The top subject in sixth grade? Not history, algebra, or English. Sex was the favored theme, Sex Class met on the playground, and the "teachers" were my classmates! At this stage in life, I am sure none of my new friends had ever done anything. This was still 1967, and these kids were only thirteen years old. Consenting adults were certainly doing "it" in New York, and the sexual revolution had gathered a good head of steam in California, but beyond the voyeuristic braggadocio of pubescent boys and a few renegade high school juniors and seniors, promiscuity hadn't gotten too ensconced in the heartland, especially not in Lancaster County, Pennsylvania. But talk is cheap on the Outside. This too was an otherworldly idea for a Mennonite boy, raised as I was to believe words have power and produce consequences. These sixth graders knew how to talk cheap! At recess the boys gathered in one corner of the playground and exchanged glances with the girls, making muffled commentary about the sex terms they were learning. The girls huddled at the opposite corner, giggling and looking our way.

That year one of the neighborhood girls, who rode the bus and always sat near me, wrote an erotic story about her first sex experience. She passed it around in the bus. It got a lot of giggles, jeers and comments, and ended up in my hands. I curiously scanned the handwritten lines for a page or two. Whew! I did not believe this thirteen-year-old girl author had actually done these things – I figured she was just daydreaming – but what an imagination! And, her knowledge of the terms, mostly vulgarities, and the boldness to write it all down on paper! Aroused and intrigued, I squirmed in my seat, and handed the paper back. This was all the way Outside! Sex talk was way more radical than A.M. radios playing Simon and Garfunkel. At home, when the subject of sex came up, my parents stammered uncomfortably over explanations and Dad's voice modulated to a slightly higher pitch. When I was twelve Mother gave me a book called "A Doctor Talks About Sex." It contained simple drawings and explanations, so I understood the physical distinctions and terminology. But no one had prepared me for these human development discussions at recess and on the bus.

I was a normal adolescent, and got the familiar pounding heart and warm feelings when I read the doctor's book and gazed at the pencil drawings of naked females. But talking and writing shamelessly about sex in casual peer-to-peer conversation was more than I was ready for. I was taught that sex belonged exclusively to the marriage bed, no exceptions. I stood hesitantly at the edge of the playground crowd with an invisible Leash pulling me away. The sixth grade guys sensed my caution and squinted at me, figuring I was just dumb.

I tried to explain my reticence to Kent Cannon. Kent and I had a little history – I had visited him in the hospital and in his home after a bike accident a year before. Our entire family saw the bike accident happen. Our family car was loaded and we were all on our way for a weekend camping trip. As we drove through Rothsville we came upon Kent and a friend riding double on a bicycle. The front wheel of the bike was wobbling crazily as the pair coasted down a hill. Dad slowed down behind them. "That bike is in trouble!" he said, hardly getting the words out before the bike hit the curb and threw the boys onto the pavement. Kent hit his head hard and was knocked unconscious. The other boy jumped up, bruised but uninjured. Dad stopped the car and we jumped out. Dad and Mom started helping Kent who was flailing around and banging his head on the ground, a sort of unconscious reflex action I figured. Someone ran for help. The ambulance arrived and carted Kent off to the hospital.

When we got home from the weekend, Mother insisted I visit Kent in the hospital and then go over to his house a few times. So a bond developed and we became friends, which gave me a little extra credit on the playground at Kissel Hill Elementary School. Kent listened as I explained to him that I knew what "bleed" meant, a vulgar reference to female menstruation. I didn't join in the mockery, I continued, because it wasn't respectful to the girls. Kent nodded as I made my case. I don't think he really bought it, or cared, but he didn't join the group scorn. He didn't defend me either, which would have been social suicide.

The Eberlys were a part of our Inside group, family Mennonite friends of my parents, part owners of a supermarket chain. My folks figured Dan was a safe companion for their youngster. Dan, the oldest son in the Eberly family, became my friend when we were both eight, while I still lived on Newport Road. After we moved to Kissel Hill, our homes were only half a mile apart, so bicycles helped ramp up the friendship. Later, when we got our driver's licenses, we added automobiles and girls and trouble to the relationship. What had started well in childhood, shifted radically sideways when we both reached adolescence.

"Look, this thing flushes so well you can drink the water right out of the toilet." Thirteen-year-old Dan threw a

Styrofoam cup into their new shimmering bathroom toilet bowl. He turned, obviously expecting me to dip out a cupful and take a drink. I said thanks but I'm not thirsty. Dan sometimes surprised me. He was related through his mother to a successful business family, the Kauffmans, who owned a large produce market and garden center in Lancaster County. The business was doing well, and the wealth provided Dan some of life's extras that we couldn't afford. Dan wore more expensive clothes, played with more expensive toys, and took more expensive vacations with his parents.

He also had extra refinement, on most days at least. Today didn't seem to be one of them. But in my mind Dan's family was sophisticated, so an occasional off day didn't damage the trademark. Dan's parents joined an exclusive stamp collector's club at Lancaster's downtown Public Library. Stamps were definitely not part of my interests. Stamp Club would have sounded incredibly boring if my Dad suggested we go. But when Dan told me he was going to the Lancaster Stamp Club, I figured it must be cool. Until I was seventeen, Dan set the standard for coolness in my life.

One Saturday afternoon, I went to Stamp Club with Dan and his family. A very formal affair I found out too late. Dan wore a white short-sleeve shirt and tie, with nice slacks and dress shoes. Not being forewarned, I wore casual clothes with old sneakers. The experience, already unfamiliar and prickly, was not starting out well. As soon as we arrived at the looming gray, granite library in downtown Lancaster my anxiety peaked. We gathered in a dimly lit, stately library room with high ceilings, dark hardwood floors, and large, book-filled walnut shelves on every wall. We found seats in a circle of old oak chairs. An elegant crystal chandelier hung above our heads. I settled into a chair and tried to act inconspicuous. I was sure everyone was staring at my dirty sneakers and wondering who brought the hick.

The group's first item of business, so said a distinguished older gentleman in shirt, tie and blazer, was to elect a new chairman. I had no idea what a chairman was, but figured it had something to do with chairs. Why was that so important? Who would arrange the chairs before the meetings and put them away afterwards? I couldn't understand why this grown man - apparently Lancaster's king stamp collector - was so concerned about chairs before we even talked about stamps. I suspected that a chairman's job involved more than taking care of chairs, but I had no idea what that might be. I couldn't understand why they called this person a chairman. I mean, if the job wasn't chairs, why the title? I didn't want to be the chairman, because I didn't even know where they wanted me to put the chairs and if I had to ask then everyone would know how stupid I was. I started getting a panicky feeling in my gut that they were going to pick me to be the chairman. Trying to act invisible, I pushed my dirty sneakers as far as I could under my chair and slumped into the chair back trying to blend into the stained oak, hoping the old man wouldn't look at me. I didn't even want to be sitting in this stupid chair because it made me a candidate for chairman. If he picked me, then I'd have to ask, "Uh, chairman? Yes, sir. Sure. I can be chairman. When do you want me to move the chairs? Now or later? And, where do you want me to put them?" To my great relief they picked someone else. I remember nothing else about that dreadful day at Stamp Club, and never went back.

So, on this day, Dan, the classy stamp collector in his elegant home, was asking me to drink out of the toilet. The Eagles were right. "Every form of refuge has its price." Either Dan was living a jaded existence in his ivy-covered tower, or he was deliberately testing me, trying to find out how gullible I was. Maybe this was a science class experiment: Test the intelligence quotient of a friend. But I wasn't buying it. I may not know my way around the Lancaster Stamp Club, I may not know where the chairs are stored, but I know where to get a stupid drink of water! "No thanks, I'm not thirsty." I didn't have the guts to tell him he was full of it if he thought I was going to drink out of his commode.

But being friends with Dan had its benefits. After-hours adventures inside the Kauffman supermarket were definitely among them. The business was spread out over several acres of hodge-podge buildings and property including a supermarket, an outdoor garden center, and huge refrigerated produce storage rooms. Discreetly hidden behind wooden fences and outdoor wholesale areas, Kauffman's stored empty crates, old wooden skids, forklifts, two-wheel carts, customer shopping carts, lumber, and mountains of unidentifiable junk. Once when we were foraging through the supermarket late at night – during one of many campouts on the Kauffman's property – I asked Dan about the free food we were eating. He said, "Oh, we keep an account at the house and write down what we take, and then settle it at the end of the month." He must have had a good memory: five peaches, four bananas, two small fruit pies, six plums, and a bucket of cherries.... I sort of lost count by the end of the night, but I figured Dan would take care of it.

On this night we – Dan, his cousin Gerald Kauffman, and I – were camping out in a storage building at the Kauffman Garden Center. Bored at 2:00 a.m. – sleeping was definitely not a part of the plan – Gerald suggested we climb the big tree in front of Dan's house. It hung out over the highway. He'd done it before, Gerald bragged, adding that he dropped cherries on the cars as they passed underneath. We fetched a small bucket of soft, deep-red sweet cherries from the Kauffman store, shimmied up the tree quietly to not wake Dan's parents, and waited. Soon we were splatting cherries onto the windshields of Friday night college preppies on their way home from their girlfriends' houses.

The sequence went something like this: (1) a car came north up the road in the lane that passed directly under our tree perch; (2) we timed the cherry drop to hit the windshield; (3) SPLAT!; (4) the car's brake lights illuminated briefly; (5) the red-stained car continued down the road. We experimented with timing and thrust. Sometimes we aimed for the car's grill or hood. Or we threw the cherry down with a good whip of the arm, hanging onto a limb, to see what extra velocity might do. Once or twice a massive semi trailer went by, passing very close beneath us and shaking the branches. Cherries made spectacular splats on the truck's vertical windshields. With all of the laughing and carrying on, it's a miracle we didn't wake Dan's parents or fall out of the tree onto the road.

The fun lasted for about thirty minutes, about half of bucket of cherries. I climbed down to the front yard. Gerald whispered loudly from the tree, "Wait, I've got all these cherries left! I'm gonna unload the whole schmeer on the next car." I wondered about the wisdom of this plan. Nothing we were doing on this night was wise, but I knew whoever caught Gerald's final load of bottom-of-the-bucket blood-red, squashed cherries was not going to like it. Dan climbed down out of the tree and the two of us hid behind a bush, nervous. Crazy Gerald. He was always ready to push the edge of good, sane, fun. He descended to a lower branch for a quick escape, and waited. The road wasn't buzzing with traffic at three in the morning. Finally, a lonely vehicle came into view, a little white British sports car. Its convertible top was up, thank God! With perfect timing Gerald unleashed the glutinous mass of red yuck. It poured out of the bucket in slow motion, fell through the night sky and with a loud PHLAAAT it hit the car's windshield. The driver slammed on the brakes and careened into the Wash 'N Wax Car Wash down the street. The car squealed into a U-turn, gunned the engine, and roared back onto the road toward us. We took off running, around the house toward the back lot of Kauffman's store. We hadn't planned an escape route or hiding place! Running out of time – we could hear the car screaming toward us out of sight – we ran for the trucks.

Dan reached the truck first and tried the door. It was unlocked. He dove in. Gerald and I followed and we slammed the door shut just as the car screamed into the parking lot. We ducked onto the seat and floorboards. I lifted my head, peaked out the window and saw that the rabid driver had stopped near us, only twenty feet away. A big red stain smeared the car's hood and windshield, and streamed over the convertible top. The driver looked around for a moment, then gunned the engine, whirled in a tight circle, and squealed out of the parking. We waited for a few minutes, frozen in fear, breath panting and hearts racing. Whew. That was close. After we were sure the car was gone, we emerged from the truck, and crept through the parking lot quietly, eyes fearfully looking around. Back at the storage building we climbed into our sleeping bags. Enough adventure for the night. Nothing like a near-death experience to top off an evening.

The experience was typical Gerald Kauffman. Dan's cousin was two years older than me and was the Kauffman family clown, always suggesting dangerous adventures and pushing us lemming participants to the edge of sanity, moral decency, and legal safety. During another campout, at two in the morning, Gerald led the lemmings down the road to the Northridge Club's private outdoor swimming pool for an illegal entry and free swim. It was easy getting into the pool grounds. We simply walked to the fence line at the outer edge of the property and climbed over. Then we waited for fifteen minutes until the Lititz Police made a patrol drive by. Knowing he wouldn't be back for another hour we made a headlong rush to the pool and leaped in. Splashing around made a lot of noise in the middle of the night. We tried to splash silently, and kept reminding each other, especially Gerald, to "Shut up!" and keep the noise down. For the most part we were unsuccessful.

As usual, Gerald led the way. He suggested we drop our drawers and go skinny-dipping. He dropped his pants, exposing his nearly hairless thirteen-year-old body, and climbed the high dive. From this pinnacle he danced around suggestively for a moment and then dove in. No thanks. No complete nudity for me. I wasn't proud enough of my anatomy, nor morally liberated enough from the family framework, to exhibit my carnal side from the high dive. And if the police came again it would be much harder to run and climb over the fence while you were pulling your pants back on. Dan declined the invitation too. We waited in the water near the side of the pool for Gerald to get done expressing himself on the diving board. After about ten minutes, cold night air and cool water overcoming enthusiasm, we climbed out, got dressed, and headed back to Kauffman's grocery for a free mid-night snack.

A few days later my Mom got a phone call from Mrs. Eberly. We got busted... and grounded. No more campouts with the Kauffmans for the rest of the summer. It turned out that when Gerald got home after the nude dancing, he felt guilty. So he confessed our sins to his parents. Then his parents confessed our sins to Dan's parents and they called to confess our sins to my parents. Thanks Gerald. You lead us naked down the paths of unrighteousness and then confess that WE sinned. I guess we were all guilty, but I wanted to kick him in his cowardly behind. I'm sure it was that naked dance on the high dive that did us in. In later teenage years Gerald's conscience was his redeeming grace – it protected him from a lot of really bad behavior.

One benefit of getting into trouble with friends like Gerald and Dan was that I didn't have to hide or explain my Mennonite heritage. The three families were Mennonites to the core. All attended different Mennonite churches in Lancaster County – the Kauffman's home church was very conservative, which might explain Gerald's propensity for edgy behavior, a quest for Dan's and my approval – but we understood each other. To the rest of the world I minimized my Mennonite heritage. The paranoia was mostly unfounded. How many teenagers really care about church membership? Teenagers are more concerned about clothing and athletic performance or academic achievement than religious affiliation. Peer pressure is harder for girls, especially the blessed ones from conservative branches of the Mennonite faith that eschew female fashion and require women to wear their beliefs on their heads and bodies. It's a heavy burden, those head coverings and long skirts.

The deep religious and cultural paradigms evoked in me a form of pastoral protection of my people, mostly for the girls. The empathy did not drive me to their defense in public. I was not ready to make that big a sacrifice, tempted as I was toward the Outside and looking for acceptance. A real hero here.

Mrs. Kurtz once asked our English class to write a television ad treatment. We were to create a product idea, and then write copy for the marketing campaign. A friend of mine, Jerry, decided to sell a product called Miracle Toilet Bowl Cleaner. He stood in front of the class and read his advertisement:

"Miracle Toilet Bowl Cleaner! This amazing product is the best on the market today! Pour a cap full into your toilet bowl, and Miracle foams up into crud-scrubbing bubbles. Like a million little men, Miracle bubbles scrub and scrub your toilet bowl to a sparkling yellow! And when the foam disappears, the little men are dead. Buy Miracle Toilet Bowl Cleaner today!"

We all had a good laugh. Another friend, Bill, raised his hand and volunteered. "I have a product, Mrs. Kurtz!"

"Okay, Bill. Come on up and show us your ad." Bill sauntered to the front.

"Tillie Caps!" he started, holding up a crude drawing of a Mennonite head covering. *"Everyone needs a Tillie Cap! They are great around the house and kitchen, they can be used as soup strainers and...."*

"Alright!" Mrs. Kurtz jumped from her seat and shut him down. "That's enough, Bill. Please sit down."

Bill sauntered back to his seat, grinning. Muted giggles wafted through the room. Two girls in the class were wearing head coverings. They sat staring at their desktops in shocked silence. No one looked at them. I wasn't wearing a Tillie Cap, but my throat went dry and I couldn't breath even after we moved on to the next ad.

I REBEL

A bunch of years have passed since I first sat down to write this tome. Much has changed in the interim. In short, after only a year, we left Lancaster County and moved south. Except for the rather abrupt departure from Pennsylvania – my hoped-for white picket fence not yet built – it wasn't a bad relocation. We resettled one thousand miles away in Florida, and now after fifteen years in another home, and thirty more nations that I have been privileged (or ill-fated) to visit in my professional capacity since *that* move, those earlier yearnings for tranquility have been adequately fulfilled. My wife, distraught at first to be uprooted yet again, has settled nicely into the new assignment.

I'm sitting here in my chair from the comfort of a white picket fence existence, now in the sunny coastal Florida panhandle. What began in Lancaster County Pennsylvania as an ethereal hope has matured into real existence in the nation's Southeast. Three of our grandkids (we now have eight – my how time has passed!) just left with our daughter and her husband. He is an orthopedic surgeon specializing in ankles and knees, a career-track – tested and proven over the last six years – that landed him work at a prestigious medical group in the area. Beth is at the office, urgent business of some kind, so I'm left alone in our living room in front of a cozy fire with my thoughts and memories.

My earlier quest for a white picket fence, as it was briefly experienced inside the quaint farmlands of Pennsylvania, lasted a few weeks short of one year. What with the need for a job and the inevitable angst that possesses a man without professional livelihood, plus a twelve-month study sabbatical that wore itself out, and finally a thirty-year record breaking frigid and snowy winter that befell the Northeast and practically drove the entire family to cabin fever insanity, conditioned as we were to tropical warmth for fifteen years, Pennsylvania never had a chance. Come spring, and a job offer in Florida, we sold the house, moved south, planted ourselves in Pensacola, and now another fifteen years have passed. My wife has settled contentedly into house, home and family. On planet earth there is no better barometer for happiness than a wife's state of mind.

Now again, with some time on my hands – my profession demands my attention in clumps of time rather than as an analog flow of activity – and until the next crisis makes the phone ring, I can write. Perhaps I'll finish this project before time takes both memory and skill. Frankly, most of my adding to these pages happens on the weekends, especially Sunday afternoons. There isn't any magic to the formula. At my age, energy and inspiration are increasingly limited commodities. I must make the best of them.

I'll get into "my work" shortly. My readers are certainly curious, especially since the glaring fifteen-year gap after Chapter One: *What on earth has he been doing all those years?!* It's a subject of some importance to the theme of this book. But even if it were not, my male readers would feel cheated if I failed to deliver on the career subject at some point. There is a reason questions about profession arise early in man-on-man conversations. No mystery here. We males define ourselves by what we do, and genuinely want to know what the other guy does. Female readers will have to trust me on this point. The "What do you do?" question comes up early in male conversations. It helps men size each other up, gets us to common ground if there is any, and keeps conversations going. And conversation, as most wives discover about their husbands, is not a man's best work. We need all the help we can get.

I just returned from two weeks in South East Asia. That region of the world, our home for fifteen years, is changing more rapidly than any other place on the planet. American businessmen long ago discovered that hard working Asians will produce goods for a pittance of what their fellow Americans demand. Factories are popping up all over. Even in Sri Lanka, where this tome began, one of the most remote corners of the planet, the international textile industry has invaded and hired the local population to manufacture name brand clothing for the fashion-obsessed west. On my arrival, Pastor Yoganathan met me at Katunayake International Airport and drove our team to his home in Nuwara Eliya. On the way into the mountains we passed several new factory buildings nestled in the green background, unmarked on the outside. I had to ask him what they were. He and I have been making this five-hour road trip since 1988, so I know the route, but the buildings were new. Factories: a hopeful sign of change for a nation that has been in the throes of civil war for twenty-four years.

I didn't go to Sri Lanka for the textile industry. "Yoga" (as everyone affectionately calls him) and I have been planting churches together for many years. He is a church-planting machine. When we met over twenty years ago this Tamil pastor had planted three churches – the "Mother" church in Hatton, and two others in the towns of Maskeliya and Bogawantalawa. Today there are over ninety churches scattered throughout the hill country, touching nearly thirty-five thousand people. Our original ten-year goal was fifty churches. This trip we opened another church. Our typical methodology: a three-day outreach ends on Saturday night with an announcement about a similar meeting the next morning. A fledgling group of interested souls comes together for their first Sunday service.

Jesus talked frequently about "the harvest." Few places on the planet show more evidence of harvest than the hill country of Sri Lanka. If war produces anything good (I hesitate to suggest the possibility), it is that people awaken from indifference and get serious about more important things in life. Crisis has a way of re-ordering our priorities. Sri Lanka is learning a brutal lesson through racial war. Tamils fight for independence, determined to throw off the discriminatory policies of their Singhalese-controlled government, and the Singhalese resist them, unwilling to compromise or divide a tiny island into tinier pieces. Enough blood has been shed, and lives lost, that one wonders how much more suffering the nation must endure before the citizenry and their politicians make concessions. I'm hopeful, but have learned to expect very little from human nature.

In the meantime Tamil people turn to God. From their oppressed perspective, Christianity offers a hopeful alternative to state-sponsored discrimination. "For God so loved" on the lips of Jesus is gold for suffering people. I've spent my adult life working in Asia and have seen a lot of suffering, most from human origins, the stronger oppressing the weaker. Oppressed people are desperate for good news, and the message of Jesus is the best the world has ever heard. If human aspirations could be measured, love and hope are the weightiest of all, and no one offers more of these commodities than Jesus.

But, we have more adolescent ground to cover before we immerse ourselves into the Asia part of this story. So, off we go, back in time to the 1960s and a little community called Kissel Hill.

15 The Slippery Slope

I don't remember the moment or the specific issue that led to my departure from faith and decline toward the outside. Adolescent flights from the safety and familiarity of home usually need no more explanation than the allure of raw curiosity and the accompanying propensity to break rules. Like a hatchling that peers over the edge of the nest for the first time, young people are fascinated with the great, big world out there. Still, in most cases there is impetus, which in my case was the influence of friends, the pull of pubescence, and a mixture of hypocrisy and meaningless tradition at church. I can't blame my parents, like so many are inclined to do, some with justification. My parents were not perfect, but there was no glaring dysfunction or abuse in our house. I only remember one time in my entire life that my Dad lost his temper.

Except for the temper episode, which I'll get to shortly (I'm sure my readers are now curious to know the sordid details) – in this singular confrontation Dad's anger was directed at Mother, not me. Neither he nor my mother ever did anything that scared or hurt the children. Okay, I remember one *other* time when my Mother chased me around the Rothsville house threatening to take my trousers down and whip me with a wooden spoon, which I certainly deserved, inclined as I was toward mischief. I outran her, first to the basement and then back up the stairs and out into the garden. She gave up the chase at the kitchen door, promising retribution when I returned to the house. Predictably, I grew bored standing alone in the garden. When I re-entered the house, I submitted to a mild form of discipline, Mom's anger subsided. The older I get and hear about other people's formative experiences, the more grateful I am for the rarity of such drama in our home. The blessed legacy of love, nurture, and boundaries was a gift.

So, the incident. My Dad is off to heaven now, and my Mother is too old to care about her reputation, so here it is. The entire family was in the kitchen/dining room area of the house. Our Rothsville home had an open floor plan where kitchen and dining room were divided only by a breakfast bar. Dad was cutting my hair with an electric clippers. I sat submissively on one of the kitchen bar stools, while he trimmed and snipped away. He and Mother were not having a good day, and I think the hair cutting routine was just an excuse for them to snip at each other. He was complaining about having to take the time to cut my hair after work when he had a million other things to do outside, and why hadn't she cut Dougie's hair during the day, she isn't working full time and has lots of time, etc.... Mother retorted with comments about the way he was cutting my hair, adding that she was just as busy as he was, taking care of three kids at home all summer, and besides I have my AVON deliveries to do so I'm not just sitting around the house, and if you don't have the time, why don't you just take him to the barber and quit your griping about it, and anyway look at what you are doing to his hair! Dad normally didn't argue with Mother, but this time he shot back, waving the clippers in the air, with comments about trying to save money, which you know by now was Mother's trump card, now used against her. The comment served Dad's real intention to enflame Mother. She retorted with comments about going to a barber who wasn't that expensive, and anyway, it was *your* idea to buy that stupid hair clippers and look at Dougie's hair! You're making clipper lines all over his head! That will take a month to grow out!

All this while I perched quietly on the stool, covered from neck to toes in a white bed sheet – I looked like a snow-capped mountain with a bad hair cut on the top – and growing anxiety, not about the parental conflagration, but what my hair was going to look like at the end of it. As they argued, my gaze shifted stiffly back and forth, at Dad then Mother. Judy and Dale sat nearby averting their eyes and keeping their mouths shut. Judy, all of thirteen and old enough to snicker at such goings on, had an amused look on her face. Our presence usually tempered such arguing between the parents, but today was a low point.

Well, the remark about the barber and the clipper lines in Dougie's hair tipped the scales. "OK!" Dad shouted. "YOU take him to the barber!" and with that he threw the black electric clippers to the floor and crushed them with a stomp of his shoe. The clippers squashed into a thousand pieces. Dad stomped out of the room. For a moment, everyone sat in stunned silence. Dad never did anything like that before! The air sort of echoed with "YOU take him to the barber!" Eventually Mother got up and left the room. She was never one to back down, but this time Dad got the last word. I pulled the sheet off my body, climbed off the stool, and started picking up the smashed pieces of the clippers, a sort of cathartic attempt to fix what felt broken in our family. I couldn't reassemble the clippers – they were broken beyond repair – but by the end of the evening the family returned to normal rhythms and Dad and Mother sorted out the dispute.

Now that I'm thinking about it I recall another similar clash between Mother and Dad during a summer Camp Lighters camping trip. This one happened in the family car. We were late for a canoe outing. The whole family was packed into our station wagon, and while Dad drove frantically down forest roads to the rendezvous point, Mother hounded him:

"We're late! And, there is no way you are going to drive nine miles in two minutes!" Dad drove as fast as safety allowed, murmuring something about "let's just go and see..." but Mother kept at him, "We'll never make it. You can't drive nine miles in two minutes!" The words became her stubborn rebuttal to every attempt Dad made to appease her. He drove, white knuckles gripping the steering wheel, shortening the distance to the elusive meeting point, while Mother repeated the mantra, "You can't drive nine miles in two minutes!" After all the hounding, Dad finally gave up and turned the car around.

"We're not going!!!?" three kids protested in unison from the back seat.

"No," Mother retorted. "We're late, and Dad can't get there in time."

So, we missed the canoe trip. Technically, Mother was right. You can't drive nine miles in two minutes. But then when does any campout activity ever leave on time? We probably would have made it, but after all the tension and the constant reminders about the distance and shortness of time, we sort of lost interest.

I gave my heart to Jesus in the middle of this flawed godliness. Five years old, I walked out behind the garage to our shed, and knelt on a pile of wood and asked Jesus to be my Savior, knowing from parents and Sunday School that I was a sinner in need of a Savior. And while I didn't understand the deeper theological issues, and wasn't interested, I wanted to make my peace with God. The nearest I had gotten to a sense of God's call by this time was Mother's comment, a regular one, usually following a noisy boyish outburst: "Would you please quiet down, Dougie! You are going to grow up to be a preacher with that loud mouth of yours!" One wonders about the prophetic accuracy of maternal declarations.

On a forgotten day in 1960 a five-year-old seeker was simply trying to get to first base with God. So, down on my knees I went in the dirt by a woodpile. I finished the prayer with an "Amen." Nothing happened except that I marked the moment as having done what needed to be done. Saying "nothing happened" is an inaccuracy. Something did happen, and fifty years later I remember it: I made peace with God, He heard me and accepted my prayer. This was not an emotional experience in the way modern culture seems to think all religious experiences must be. What can I say? We were wired differently. I could not have explained the internal experience. Philosophers and theologians define moments like this an awakening of conscience. Jesus said, "Let the children come unto me, and forbid them not." He wasn't just patronizing kids. When given the chance, and when they are pointed in the right direction, children experience God, perhaps more profoundly than adults. Innocence can be an incredible asset. Jesus talked about child-like faith. The world could use more of it.

No major transformation happened at that woodpile. After only five years I had little to report on a repertoire of sins *committed*. My emerging conscience, nurtured as it was by godly parents and the larger Mennonite community, certainly knew that good and evil existed. By the time I was ten, thanks to Sunday School Teacher Katherine Hershey – who will forever linger in my memory as one of the most inspiring teachers in the universe – I could recite all the names of the Books of the Bible from memory, and could quote Bible verses like John 3:16 and John 14:1-6. Even at five, because of this teacher and my parents, I knew about sin in theory, and was aware of the common human propensity toward the dark side. But *that* shadowy place was mostly uncharted territory. On this day God just gently pushed me a little farther away from its edge. After the prayer I was back to chasing chickens, playing baseball, and, with "that loud mouth," making noise and bugging Mother for snacks.

But making one's peace with God on bended knee beside a pile of wood doesn't guarantee protection or insulation from insidious Outside influences, a fact taught me in shocking detail by Robbie Hustin, re-emphasized by a gang of youth at a Rothsville bus stop, and then re-introduced half a dozen years later when we moved to Kissel Hill. In this new venue, Scott Breeley, who lived only two blocks from our little farm, was my apt teacher. One afternoon after school he invited me to his house to hang out. When I entered his bedroom I encountered on the walls a shocking reminder of life on the Outside: poster-size photos of completely nude women, centerfold models from Playboy magazines! He had the magazines too, a whole stack of them. I asked him if his parents knew about the pictures – an unthinkable, cardinal sin in my house. I knew the answer but couldn't muster the real question: DO YOUR PARENTS LET YOU HANG THESE PICTURES ON YOUR WALLS!? He shrugged. "Sure." No big deal. This was *us meets them* on the grandest of scales. Our friendship lasted about a year, occupied more with outdoor activities than gazing at pornography (thank God!). We caught several abandoned baby raccoons in the woods behind his house and turned them into pets. We set muskrat traps in our local stream, and played baseball and football in our farm pasture. I never told Mother and Dad about Scott's bedroom art.

After we moved to Kissel Hill our Neffsville Mennonite youth group made a winter weekend trip to Greenwich Village, New York City. Our goal was an outreach effort to the beatniks, homeless and alcoholics. Unfortunately, in my declining state of mind, the only "reaching out" I did was in the form of conflicted comparisons, weighing the sheltered Pennsylvania existence against a very alluring urban world to which I was hungrily drawn. The beatniks (or hippies, as the culture was starting to call them) and their girlfriends, with their clothing, hair, cigarettes and devil-may-care attitude were definitely reaching out to me. One young lady – who still lives in my memory after four decades – was sitting casually at a table with friends in a smoky Greenwich Village coffee shop when we entered. A cigarette dangled from her left hand. Her gleaming black hair flowed over elegant shoulders to her waist, and black bangs hung low over dark brown eyes.

To complete the alluring picture, she was wearing only a white, over-sized T-shirt. It hung off her bare shoulders, and barely covered her thighs, exposing long, shapely legs, strategically crossed. High heels, totally out of place on this cold wintery New York day, completed the exotic picture. But there she sat, as real as life, nonchalantly chatting with friends, smoking a cigarette and brushing her hair out of her eyes!

I don't remember why we entered that coffee shop, perhaps for a warm drink or snack. The reason is lost to my memory, pushed out by a beautiful woman in a white T-shirt. The trip to New York City took me too far from home and didn't bring me all the way back. We returned to Lancaster County on Sunday afternoon with a budding teenager harshly aware of how different he was from the rest of the world, a frustrating disparity he resolved to change.

Opportunities have a way of presenting themselves to the determined soul. My first big step in the wrong direction came in the seventh grade through the good intentions of an English teacher named Miss Kurtheimer. This beautiful, just out of college, newcomer to Warwick taught English with a marvelous mixture of grace and toughness. What male teachers could not do to force a rowdy mob of pubescent adolescents to be quiet and focus on academic goals, Miss Kurtheimer achieved flawlessly. She was amazing and I loved her for it. Miss Kurtheimer got married that year and became Mrs. Nabor, but before the wedding a few football jock seniors in our school boldly asked her for a date. She declined of course – against school policy – but I doubt she ever explained it that way. More likely she just looked at them, raised a condescending eyebrow, and walked away. Lucky guy she married, whoever he was. I admired Mrs. Nabor – okay, I had a crush on her – but I was never stupid enough to make an advance toward a teacher! To my delight, Mrs. Nabor noticed me too, for all the right reasons. Her attention, and its result, was a huge boost to my neophyte identity. The high school Drama Department needed a junior high male for the fall high school play, Camelot. Mrs. Nabor submitted two names –

mine and one other – for the role of Tom of Warwick. I had absolutely zero acting experience, but was intrigued by the invitation and Mrs. Nabor's advocacy. I went to the audition and beat out the competition for the part. Maybe size was good for something after all! The skinny kid, now Tom of Warwick, met King Arthur behind the battle lines! Landing the role was my first foray into the performing arts.

Acting awakened an interest in making music too, not just singing but creating and playing songs, so I bought a guitar, and began scratching and picking until I mastered three or four chords and could roughly execute a few popular lead riffs. Led Zeppelin's acoustic opening to *Stairway to Heaven* was my favorite. Two songs, *Hotel California* by the Eagles and *Stairway to Heaven,* for many years ruled the top ten list of every teenager's most replayed songs in the universe. The two bands got insanely rich from royalties, and I'm sure Robert Plant and Don Henley got sick of singing the songs.

Through the rest of my junior and senior years I acted in as many plays as my parents' patience (dependent as I was on them for transportation) would allow – Camelot, The Mouse that Roared, J.B., The Music Man – to name a few. Except for all the fooling around between girls and boys in the dressing rooms and backstage, Drama Club at Warwick High School was a positive high school experience. Meanwhile music, especially the rock 'n roll varieties, steadily drew me away from the family heritage and into a new and darker world of experimentation. I eventually abandoned every other distraction and became absorbed with rock music and the life it encouraged. The fixation lasted through high school, including continuing mandatory attendance at church and the other existence I was forced to live in front of my parents. By the time I turned eighteen, the rebellious, deceptive duplicity had reached critical mass. Even my appearance had turned pathetic and neglected, and I no longer cared what other people thought.

I can't blame the downward slide on a single event or person, and I'm not going into the sordid details. Imagine a rebellious teenager and you get the idea. It wasn't Robby Hustin, or sex talk on the Kissel Hill playground or Scott Breeley's magazines that pushed me in the wrong direction. I can't blame a pretty girl in a Greenwich Village coffee shop, Led Zeppelin's *Stairway to Heaven,* or a cold church experience, although our church was biblically sound but spiritually lukewarm. The journey was an angst-driven adolescent exploration away from the fold and an unwitting immersion into an unknown abyss that closed in around me. I wanted to rebel, against what I am not really sure, I wanted to jump from the sheltered nest, into what I do not know. The world offers an infinite variety of titillations for the curious soul. Jesus' Prodigal Son parable is not an isolated experience of one Jewish boy. It is the story of all humanity.

16 The Vietnam Generation

At the fresh age of eighteen, with the Draft still in place, and my numerical designation worrisomely low, I braced myself for a call to war. I should not have been worried. I could not claim to be a conscientious objector. My position on military service was more a derivative of Mennonite tradition, not of personal conviction. I did not know how powerful that affiliation was until I innocently used it on a spring day in 1973 when the telephone rang in our kitchen. A male voice on the line asked, "Is James D. Gehman there?"

"Uh, well, I'm James, but everyone calls me Doug." *Who is this!*

"Okay, Doug. How are you today?"

"Fine. Thanks." *Okay, what does this guy want?*

"Great! You are about to graduate from Warwick High School, aren't you?"

"Uh, yes, in about a month."

"That's great, just great. Have you decided what you're going to do next?"

"Well, I'm going to college in the fall."

"Great. A college education is always a good choice. In fact, I can help you with that."

Okay, is this a college recruiter?

"Have you ever thought about military service?"

173

"Uh, not really." I really had *not* given that option any thought, other than what I would do if I were drafted. It wasn't a regular topic at the Gehman dinner table.

"Well, Doug. I'd like to get together with you to talk about it. The Army has some great programs and benefits, including help with a college education."

There was a brief pause while I tried to think of how I should answer this man. I wasn't afraid of military service. Dying in Vietnam, maybe, but not the service itself. The issue was better framed in terms of familiarity – like being asked if I wanted to, say next Thursday, take a rocket ship to Mars.

"Uh, I'm a Mennonite."

"Oh." An uncomfortable pause followed, during which I imagined the man looking at a clipboard and checking a box beside the words, *Not a Chance in Hell.* "Okay, thank you for your time." Click. The Armed Services hung up on me! Give a Mennonite a chance! A short time later the Draft was discontinued, so that was that.

That summer my parents bribed me. There was no other way I would attend Jesus '73. Military service didn't want me, and I wasn't interested in religion either.

We'll get to the Jesus '73 milestone in the next chapter, but first a little groundwork. The months leading up to this auspicious August weekend were marked by a growing internal war: desiring change but being powerless to do it. At one point that summer I even considered becoming a "Jesus Person." Jesus was becoming a hit on the west coast, and His new popularity was finding its way east. The idea was a whimsical social option, driven by a genuine spiritual hunger that hadn't reached critical mass. It didn't stick, I had too much partying left to do, but things were heating up.

That year, at some point, I decided I was an atheist, therefore any more attention to conscience and the divine was pointless. Initially, the decision was liberating. No more worrying about a disapproving deity. No more tedious moralizing about right and wrong. I got enough of that at church, what with the long hair, disheveled clothing, and obvious attitude. I was weary of hairy-eyeball hypocrites anyway. I found ways to avoid church as much as I could, outwitting my parents with excuses until they gave up. I did not declare my newly embraced atheism directly, because ironically I respected them too much. But I was finished trying to please an unreachable Entity whose standards I, and no one else I knew, could live up to. Such was my atheism: more an expression of spiritual frustration than an academic analysis of existentialist philosophy about life and meaning.

While I gave up on faith, I did not give up on the belief that the world should be a better place. Pursuit of such a goal was good in my new humanistic view. I was not alone in this skepticism or hope. During the sixties and seventies, the idea of a better world drove millions of American young people to search for something better. Weary of war, and distrustful of the status quo, of government, big corporations, and organized religion, aka "the establishment," and hungry for peace, love and meaning, young people of the 1960s birthed a movement – sometimes they were called "Flower Children" – that reached critical mass in the early 1970s. Like all movements, this one expressed itself, with a rebellious edge, in the wider culture: new genres of music, art, fashion, media and engagement in social issues, environmental concern, and a return to simplicity with spiritual experimentation. Millions of young people questioned the status quo, specifically a definition of life around the norms of education, family, and a career. The new ideas and their expressions impacted a generation, for both good and bad, and transformed America.

The War in Vietnam was the fuel that drove this cultural engine. Dear reader, do not underestimate the cultural impact of the Vietnam War. During a twenty-five year period the United States deployed over two and a half million people to this tiny tropical South East Asian nation. One out of every ninety Americans was directly involved in the war in some way. Everyone in America experienced Vietnam, one way or another. The war officially lasted from 1965 to 1975, but CIA advisors were present in Vietnam – including unofficial combat operations – starting in 1950. I was born in 1955. The influences of Vietnam shaped the entire generation of the Baby Boomers. Most people think of the Baby Boomers as the offspring of World War Two veterans. True enough. World War Two produced us. But Vietnam *defined* us. To understand this time in history, and the Vietnam War's influence on it, is to understand, at least in part, the worldview of millions of Americans who came of age in that time. The residue of Vietnam's influence continues to filter through Americana to this day, and will not stop until the last Baby Boomer dies, probably sometime in the decade of the 2050s.

Generalizations are never fully accurate nor do they ever represent every point of view. Prudence requires me to concede on this point: not everyone in the United States of America protested Vietnam or got caught up in the controversies whirling around Washington and the Pentagon. Indeed, many young men and women enthusiastically went off to fight in or serve the war effort. Many others avoided the hippie/flower child movements, completed their college degrees, got married and entered the professional world unscathed and unaffected. But, everyone knew about Vietnam, and millions were active on both sides of the controversies. The massive controversy shifted the American psyche permanently.

Nearly 60,000 Americans died in the Vietnam Conflict. Especially when measured against the outcome of the war, this one statistic triggered the anti-war movement. The question was simple: Why are so many of our young men dying in this little South East Asian country? We went to Vietnam, not to protect America – there was never a direct threat to our national security – but to assuage a lingering fear of the Cold War and the global advancement of communism. This fear was exacerbated in 1962 by the U.S. confrontation with Russia in what became known as the Cuban Missile Crisis during the Kennedy Presidency. Premier Khrushchev's placement of nuclear warheads in Cuba brought us to the brink of nuclear war. America was deeply shocked by the crisis. The fear of communism's advance, especially communism's influence on our allies, led to our build up in Vietnam. Our involvement in Vietnam was not about helping the South Vietnamese people. Let's not kid ourselves. Vietnam was meant to assuage an American fear and make a statement to Russia and China about the advancement of communism. Vietnam was a line in the sand, nothing more. The line didn't hold, and by the late 1960s, the mounting numbers of dead Americans pressed us to the breaking point. A frustrated and beleaguered citizenry began demanding an explanation about why our boys were dying in Vietnam. Unfortunately, nobody had an adequate answer to the question.

Country Joe MacDonald summed up the national exasperation in an appropriately named song:

I Feel Like I'm Fixin' To Die Rag

Come on all of you big strong men, Uncle Sam needs your help again
He's got himself in a terrible jam, way down yonder in Viet Nam
So put down your books and pick up a gun, we're gonna have a whole lotta fun

(CHORUS)
And it's one, two, three, what are we fighting for
Don't ask me I don't give a damn, next stop is Viet Nam
And it's five, six, seven, open up the pearly gates
Ain't no time to wonder why. Whoopee! We're all gonna die

Well come on generals, let's move fast, your big chance has come at last
Gotta go out and get those reds, the only good commie is the one that's dead

And you know that peace can only be won, when we've
   blown 'em all to kingdom come
(CHORUS)

Come on Wall Street don't be slow, why man this war
   is a go-go
There's plenty good money to be made, by supplying
   the army with the tools of its trade
Just hope and pray that if they drop the bomb, they
   drop it on the Viet Cong
(CHORUS)

Well come on mothers throughout the land, pack your
   boys off to Viet Nam
Come on fathers don't hesitate, send your sons off
   before it's too late
Be the first ones on your block, to have your boy come
   home in a box
(CHORUS)

That the body count among the South Vietnamese who
fought along side us was exponentially higher also became a
huge ethical issue when the American public started hearing
about it. Compared to our sixty thousand dead, nearly four
million Vietnamese died in the North and South Vietnamese
Armies, and among civilians caught in the middle. Late in the
war another half a million died in the neighboring countries of
Cambodia and Laos when the conflict spread. The carnage
didn't end when we withdrew. Kampuchea's (formerly called
Cambodia) heartache – the genocide that began when Khmer
Rouge leader Pol Pot came to power in 1975 and then
murdered two million Cambodians – had not even started yet.
   Viet Cong leader Ho Chi Minh's strategy was to
demoralize American troops, not to beat us. He engaged us in
petty skirmishes, killing and maiming Americans, not to gain
ground but to wear us down and weaken our resolve. This
strategy, patiently implemented at the cost of hugely

disproportionate numbers of Vietnamese lives, was in fact very successful. Especially disgusting was our military's policy of measuring battlefield victories, not in ground gained and held, but by comparing the number of American deaths with Viet Cong losses. According to this grisly policy, as long as their death count was exponentially larger than ours, we won. By the early 1970s the ongoing tedium of American deaths became untenable for an American public.

We lost the war, not because we lacked the machines and the manpower to beat the Viet Cong, but because we lacked the resolve. Regardless of your politics on the issue of Vietnam, we all agree on one thing: No one fights more passionately, more sacrificially, and with more resolve than those who fight to defend their own land. Ho Chi Minh knew this to be true and simply held out until American pain overwhelmed American pride. Simply put, Ho Chi Minh believed in the war effort more passionately than we did and he outlasted us.

The news media harnessed the emerging power of video, and daily reported the war – displaying graphic film clips and pictures of death and mayhem on national television and in newspapers – day after dreadful day, month after dreadful month, year after dreadful year. The price America was paying to "stabilize Vietnam" became intolerable. American troops were putting too many dead comrades into body bags and families at home were burying too many sons. The carnage finally reached a tipping point, and America ran out of resolve. Public support plummeted, soldiers lost faith, drug abuse and other pathologies escalated at home and on the battlefield. The Viet Cong, however, were willing to fight forever.

In 1969 a series of events happened that tipped America's scales on the issue of Vietnam. That year President Nixon announced plans to reduce the numbers of troops in the country through a plan called "Vietnamization." The reduction didn't begin immediately. Impatience over its delay and exasperation from events that followed became a tidal surge that tipped the country against the war.

- October 16, 1969. A nation-wide public protest entitled the *Moratorium to End the War in Vietnam* drew over 200,000 demonstrators.
- November 12, 1969. Journalist Seymour M. Hersh broke the story about atrocities committed by Lt. William Calley and his "Charlie" Company troops in the Vietnamese village of My Lai. Calley and his men brutally murdered between 300 and 500 unarmed citizens – men, women and children, even babies – during a daylong rampage. For eighteen months, the army hid the event from public scrutiny.
- November 15, 1969. Another anti-war protest, organized by the newly formed National Mobilization Committee to End the War in Vietnam drew over 600,000 demonstrators.
- May 4, 1970. National Guardsmen, deployed around the country as a result of increasingly large and violent anti-war demonstrations, opened fire on protesters at Kent State University in Kent, Ohio. Four people died from the gunfire. A photograph by John Filo – of Mary Ann Vecchio kneeling in anguish over the body of Jeffrey Miller just minutes after he was shot by the Ohio National Guard – became an icon of the anti-war movement, and earned Filo a Pulitzer Prize. The widely published photograph coalesced the nation's frustration with Vietnam. The rock group Crosby, Stills, Nash and Young wrote and published a song entitled *Four Dead in Ohio* that became a national anthem for the protest movement.
- June 13, 1971. Excerpts from "The Pentagon Papers" are published in the New York Times. The information hits the public conscience like an earthquake. The Times front-page article stated that the volumes, officially entitled *"United States – Vietnam Relations, 1945-1967: A Study Prepared for the Department of Defense,"* revealed that "the Johnson

Administration had systematically lied, not only to the public but also to Congress..." on the subject of Vietnam.

- 1972. Under public pressure, President Nixon withdraws another 70,000 troops from Vietnam. The conciliatory gesture was quickly overshadowed by revelations of Presidential involvement in a break-in at the Democratic National Convention offices at the Watergate Hotel. The "Watergate" scandal embarrassed the White House and led to Nixon's resignation, the first of a sitting President in U.S. history.

The United States withdrew fully from Vietnam in 1975, abandoning a South Vietnamese Army who were entirely dependent on us for supplies and support, leaving them to fight the Viet Cong on their on. When the last helicopter lifted off from a CIA compound roof in Saigon on April 29 carrying its cargo of Americans and Vietnamese refugees, these and seventy thousand other evacuees returned to a confused and angry country.

The anti-war movement, like the war effort itself, was led mostly by university students, who, catalyzed by the Vietnam Conflict and the cultural machine that created it, were desperate to create a new and better world. They wanted love and peace. The dream may have been naïve but it was a driving force. "Make love, not war" became the banner cry of the movement, and for a brief time it reflected the aspirations of millions of American youth. Hatred of war gave rise to dreams of a utopian society defined by peace, love and social harmony. A whole new genre of music emerged to express this existential angst and idealistic hope. Singer/song writers like Bob Dylan, Arlo Guthrie, Janice Joplin, Joan Baez, and Jimi Hendrix, and bands like the Beatles, Buffalo Springfield, Credence Clearwater Revival, Jefferson Airplane, The Guess Who, and many others wrote and performed the anthems of an era, protesting war, condemning violence, resisting government and the establishment, and searching for a new kind of life, marked by peace and love.

Hippies, the name given to young people at the center of the counterculture movement (because they were "hip"), were composed mostly of whites between the ages of fifteen and thirty. Adopting a lifestyle of cultural dissent from the bohemians and the beatniks of the 1950s, hippies rebelled against established institutions, criticized middle class values, opposed the Vietnam War, and promoted sexual liberation. Purist hippies were against every kind of political and social orthodoxy. A new enigmatic term, *antidisestablishmentarianism,* represented the dropout mentality of this group. No one really knew or cared what the word meant, but like the nonsense word *supercalifragilisticexpialidocious* from the Mary Poppins movie, it rolled off the tongue nicely and made the dissension seem official.

The era produced millions of casual followers and not a few hedonists and narcissists who advocated, not social reform, but self-discovery and pleasure through promiscuous sex, experimentation with drugs, and a devil-may-care attitude toward life, responsibility, and relationships. Timothy Leary, a Harvard Professor and leader in this new self-preoccupation, gave a hallucinogenic drug called LSD to his students at Harvard University in a misguided attempt to help them find answers to their existential questions. He coined the phrase "Tune in, turn on, drop out." For a brief time Leary was hero of the sixties, but ultimately lost his job at the University for not showing up for class enough. Opportunistic young men like Abbie Hoffman and Jerry Rubin, who both attended the University of California, Berkeley – a seedbed of activism and protest, during the late 1960s and early 1970s – became self-appointed prophets of this unsettled generation, leading demonstrations and stirring violent uprisings against the status quo. Jerry Rubin participated in the leadership of some of the largest anti-war demonstrations of the time. Abbie Hoffman wrote "Steal This Book," a handbook on ways to undermine the system, promote anarchy, and be a general nuisance. One such Hoffman idea: Go to a local bank, rent a safe deposit box under a fictitious name, deposit a frozen fish into the box and leave. The book also provided instructions with diagrams about how to make gasoline bottle bombs called "Molotov cocktails." For a short time many of our generation took inspiration from Hoffman's and Rubin's rants against the abuses and deception of government, and while the anger may have been justified, these men, and many like them, were little more than buccaneers looking for a stage, skilled at tearing things apart but unprepared to work for positive change.

The Jesus Movement was born inside this bubbling cauldron, and was in truth a direct result of it. Many young people, having begun their journey with high ideals – protesting war, violence and the system that produced them – eventually succumbed to disillusionment, and began numbing themselves with drugs and sex. In time, because of the efforts of a few courageous Christian leaders who reached into the malaise and engaged the culture, many of these young people began finding answers in the message of Jesus Christ. By the early 1970s tens of thousands were abandoning drugs and promiscuous sex to follow Jesus.

Andre' Crouch's song *Jesus is the Answer* came out in 1973, boldly declaring:

> Jesus is the Answer
> For the world today,
> Above Him there's no other,
> Jesus is the Way.

This and scores of similar songs and songwriters emerged singing and talking about the life-changing answers that could be found in Jesus Christ. The movement started almost wholly outside the walls of the organized church, and in the early years, was looked upon with skepticism and suspicion by the Christian status quo. But the Jesus Movement got traction, first in southern California in the late 1960s when Pastor Chuck Smith of Calvary Chapel, Costa Mesa decided to welcome hippies to Sunday church services, regardless of how they looked or what they were wearing. Pastor Chuck didn't focus on their politics, and he didn't care what they had been smoking or with whom they were sleeping. His first concern was their souls. Smith's watershed decision drew waves of hungry young people to Calvary Chapel. Burned out on drugs, sex and rock 'n roll, but still hoping for a better world, they began flocking to Calvary Chapel in search of the peace and love they had not found in either political activism or existential escape. Within a few years a growing network of church plants made Calvary Chapel a principal force in the newly forming "Jesus Movement."

It would be inaccurate to give one leader or one church the credit for starting something that was happening throughout the nation. Young people all over the United States, confused and outraged, were desperately looking for answers. What began in California at Calvary Chapel quickly spread across the country as the message of hope in Jesus Christ and new ways to discover Him resonated with young people everywhere.

As we will see, I too was drawn into this movement and in time became a part of an army of young people who were abandoning everything to follow Jesus.

17 Jesus '73

Jesus '73 was Lancaster County's official immersion into the Jesus Movement. This first of its kind Christian festival was patterned after the ground breaking Woodstock music festival of August 1969 that drew half a million young people to a farm in New York State for "three days of fun and music." Jesus '73 didn't draw half a million young people – the numbers were closer to ten thousand – but the event was ground breaking for Lancaster County. A friend of my parents, Harold Zimmerman, organized Jesus '73. This entrepreneurial businessman and ardent Christian was concerned about our generation's young people. Jesus '73 was his way of communicating the Gospel to them.

Jesus '73 was the pivotal event of my young wayward life. Like its rock 'n roll progenitor, Jesus '73 was hosted by a farmer, this one in a potato field near Morgantown, Pennsylvania. The three-day event in August drew thousands of young people from all over the northeastern United States. The concert lineup featured several top Christian bands and performers including Andre Crouch and the Disciples, Randy Stonehill, Danny Lee and the Children of Truth, Danny Taylor, and Randy Matthews. National Christian leaders such as black activist Tom Skinner, Bible teacher Bob Mumford and Entertainer Mike Warnke also participated.

My life was convulsing that summer. The confluence of bad choices and their utter non-compatibility with my parents' values and the Christian heritage in which I was raised was finally catching up to me. Living outside of the bounds of parental approval, something I publicly disparaged but inwardly craved, added to the pressure. I graduated from high school in May and by my eighteenth birthday on June third only three months of summer remained until I would leave for college in Indiana. I had visited Goshen College in February, and came home boasting about the party life I would lead when I got there. My Mother secretly knew this and prayed, "God, I don't care if it is three weeks or three days, but get a hold of him before he leaves!"

Most parents do not really know what their kids are doing. Teenagers are experts at hiding unapproved behavior. Generally parents ignore the danger signs, choosing rather to believe in little Johnny's angelic innocence. My parents were no different. Denial, even with suspicions and not-so-subtle warnings, sometimes masks the truth until some event wakes the parents up.

Dad and Mother's wake-up call happened in the parking lot of a shopping mall. They had gone to Park City Mall for the evening, and when they returned to the car, or at least to where they thought it was parked, the car was no where to be found. They walked down one aisle, up another, searching for the missing car. Losing a parked car was out of character for my methodical engineer-minded father, who always noted such details. Becoming more frustrated by the minute, Dad finally said, "God is trying to tell us something." Another feature of my father was his openness to divine intrusions. Dad and Mother held hands and prayed – right there in the parking lot – and asked God what was on His mind. Immediately, a mental light came on and they got the message. As they told me later, "Our eyes had been blind to the trouble our son was in, but this was the turning point."

When they looked up from prayer, the car was right in front of them, two parking spots away! They drove home, went straight to my 1969 Austin Healey Sprite, and found contraband under the driver's seat. That evening they confronted me, telling the parking lot story, and appealed to me to change my life. Dad even sobbed at one point. I belligerently resisted, crossing my arms and glaring at Dad for being so pathetic. I cringe now at how cold-hearted I was. But a Higher Power was stepping in and nobody messes with Higher Powers. Pride before a fall. It was only a matter of time until this errant soul plummeted off a cliff at the end of a dead-end road.

After the confrontation, Dad and Mother stopped nagging me. Desperate to rescue their wayward son, but not knowing how, they sought counsel. "Give him lots of rope," the counselor said, "and he'll hang himself." They did, and I did. Unrestrained living has its own consequences, a harsh truth some wayward young people only learn the hard way.

So, for the summer of 1973, my parents gave me lots of rope. No questions about my late night activities. No comments about coming home smelling funny and looking disoriented. No pestering me about music. No asking about the people with whom I was associating or the girls I was dating. Their behavior was a curiosity at first; then it became exhilarating, full of possibilities, when I realized they had released me! No more harassment! No more inquisitions. "I'm eighteen-years-old and can do what I want!" I naively thought. "They finally get it!"

Such liberation is usually short-lived. The euphoria only lasts until the money runs out or reckless behavior lands the liberated soul in jail or the hospital. Then desperados are glad to have sensible friends or parents on the other end of the phone line. As I said, Higher Powers are serious business. I knew this – and it gave me nagging apprehension – but I wasn't initially ready to pay attention or alter my lifestyle.

One Sunday afternoon in April 1973, I picked up Ann – my current girlfriend – in my Austin Healey Sprite convertible, with the top down, and the two of us headed toward Lancaster Central Park to hang out for the afternoon.

The Austin was running perfectly, which if you know anything about British sports cars, is a rarity. There is always something wrong with these temperamental cars: engines, starters, brakes, shock absorbers, you name it! Mine was only four years old but had endless idiosyncrasies. On this Sunday afternoon the Sprite was purring. Ann was wearing jeans – she always wore jeans – and a cute white halter-top. Her brown hair flowed over her shoulders, and her wispy bangs danced on the edges of her John Lennon wire-rimmed glasses. She jumped into the car next to me and we drove west along Route 23 through New Holland toward Lancaster. In Leola we stopped at a light. Glass pack mufflers, poking out of a shiny blue Mustang directly in front of us, rumbled throaty noise up over the Sprite's hood and into our open windows while we waited for the light to change. Before I knew what was happening, a loud screeeeeeech pierced the air. I looked in the rearview mirror just in time to see a late model Datsun 240Z smash into the trunk of my perfectly running Austin Healey Sprite. The impact slammed us into the Mustang, and instantly turned my little sports car into an accordion. On impact, the Sprite engine screamed to five thousand rpms. Keeping my head, I turned the key and shut the engine down. Incredibly, the Mustang in front of us came out mostly unscathed, except for a few scratches on the bumper. Not so the Datsun, which, like my car, was totaled. No one was seriously hurt. Only the driver of the Datsun, a teenage girl with a brand new driver's license, needed medical attention to close a wound on her chin.

After completing the police formalities, I telephoned Dad from a nearby service station. The first thing he asked me was, "You don't have any drugs in the car, do you?" (I didn't). I was offended by the question, but okay. Dad came and took Ann and me back to the house, and then I drove her home in Dad's car. The interruption to our day felt like a "gentle nudge" from God to a prodigal. I, however, wasn't ready to pay attention. Ann and I continued dating that spring, but the accident knocked something out of the relationship, and now with God pestering me, interest waned. Then another girl, Sherrie Brubaker, entered the picture and the relationship with Ann became terminal. Sherrie was a Christian girl. We met at community youth choir practice. Ironically, I was still involved in a few such religious activities, motivated only by opportunities to meet girls and have fun. I first saw Sherrie across the sanctuary in the girl's soprano section. Her long brown hair and swimming pool brown eyes reached out to me from a mile away! "Who is that girl?" I asked my guy friends.

After practice, partly dared by friends, I worked up the nerve to cross the room and talk to the pretty brunette. She had looked my way earlier in the evening, so I was hopeful. Over the teenage din, we talked for a few minutes. Sherrie was definitely a good girl. And after a long line of disappointing dating experiences with girls from area high schools, I was ready to try anything, even a religious girl. The beauty was a definite plus.

A week later I asked her out, she said yes, and we began dating. By the end of July, Ann was forgotten. I had fallen for the pleasant young lady with the swimming pool brown eyes and high moral character. We went to movies, took long walks in the country, and ate picnics by Cocalico Creek. On my meager high-school-graduate-with-a-summer-job budget we occasionally dined at real restaurants. Sherrie was delightful company compared to most other girls I had dated. They constantly complained about the bad day they had, the stupid clothes people were wearing, or the *last* guy they had gone out with. I shuddered to think what they might say about me on their next date. By contrast, Sherrie was unbelievably pleasant. I had never met anyone like her. No complaining about other guys. No complaining about her parents or her job. No complaining about anything. And, icing on the cake, she was gorgeous! Fun and pretty! I didn't want to lose this girl. She made me want to be a better person. She made we want to behave. She made me want to do *anything* to keep her interested in me! Privately, however, when I wasn't with her, which, let's face it, was most of the rest of the week, I

189

continued running after trouble with my wayward friends, listening to weird rock music, getting high, and dreaming about a better world. The irony of those contrasts hadn't gotten through yet.

One June weekend, still without wheels after the car accident, I borrowed my Dad's 1969 Ford Econoline family van, picked up my party friend Jim, and we headed to Ocean City, New Jersey for the weekend to enjoy three days of fun, music, and beach life. We were going on the cheap because that was the cool hippie way of life. But also, we had no other choice. We wanted to look like hippies, we wanted to BE hippies, you know, living off the land, taking it easy, living in harmony with all things, etc. We wore the hippie uniform: t-shirts, torn jeans and sandals, and left Lancaster County pretending we had not a care in the world. Peace, love, freedom, and all that. Forget all the uptight parents, the square teachers, and the pig authorities! Up with antidisestablishmentarianism! Up with rock 'n roll! The fact that we still lived with our parents and would in three days return home to family and jobs didn't deter our enthusiasm, at least not on Friday afternoon driving east toward the Jersey Shore with the setting sun on our backs. It never occurred to us that most hippies were probably living this same inconsistency.

I am mocking my hypocrisy of course, but the reader must realize that a part of me was genuinely looking for a down-to-earth carefree life – even if I could only do it on the weekends. I wanted an existence defined by contentment rather than ambition, simplicity over possessions, and relationships defined by love, peace and community, rather than cutthroat lust and greed. The ideals were sincere, even if the execution was flawed. In mid-life I've come to learn that none of us pursues our ideals with absolute purity. Our baser humanity always gets in the way, even for godly people. In my case, at the ripe age of eighteen, the inconsistencies were taking over, the hypocrisy was gnawing at my conscience, I had lost my way, and time was not in my favor. So, on this weekend we drove to the beach, slept in my Dad's van, ate inexpensive food (mostly supplied by Mom from her pantry), and "winged it" in all the other details. A short three-day weekend hippie life was better than no life at all. We would work out the long-term plan later.

By the summer of 1973 the Hippie Movement was showing signs of age. The themes of the 1960s – "All You Need is Love" (the Beatles), and "Get Together" (the Youngbloods), had begun to wear out like so many overplayed vinyl LPs.

Come on People now, Smile on your brother
Everybody get together, Try to love one another right now.

After a decade, these existentialist ideals had wearied under the strain of reality. Trying "to love one another right now" takes patience and work. The live-in girlfriend isn't as cute as she was in 1969, money is tight, the roof of the house needs to be fixed, and all the protest marches haven't made that big a difference. An inevitable deterioration was setting in, and the once vibrant call for "love and peace" began sounding more like "Forget it. Let's party!"

I noticed the erosion. The 1960s songwriters who had inspired us with revolutionary music and lifestyles, by the 1970s seemed distracted. Some were downright compromised. Their new pre-occupation seemed about IMAGE, the SHOW, the MONEY and hordes of groupie girlfriends. Protest singers became sell-out entertainers. Many got addicted to hard drugs and acted like they could care less about anything or anyone. Some, like Janis Joplin, James Morrison and Jimi Hendrix made early departures from earth, dead from drug overdoses, a big contradiction to the whole idea of hope and change.

So, here we were, Jim and me, on the way to Ocean City, New Jersey for the weekend in July 1973, while the national chaos buzzed in the news, tired voices sang hollow anthems on the radio, and ideals and pubescent urgings raged for supremacy in our souls. On arrival at the shore we went to see James Bond in "Live and Let Die" and then found a place to park the van for a night's rest. As I drifted to sleep, James

Bond's devil-may-care attitude and temptress girlfriends nagged at me. On Saturday, after breakfast and a stroll down the boardwalk, we parked the van near the boardwalk, opened the side and back doors, pulled out our guitars, and started jamming. We didn't draw a crowd, but then we weren't really trying. True hippies aren't interested in drawing attention to themselves. True hippies are only concerned with being in tune, you know, with the universe. So we jammed and enjoyed the vibe. Jim played rhythm on his guitar while I picked out a lead riff, and then when the muse changed, we reversed roles. I would have enjoyed the day more if a couple of girls had come by to listen to the music and share our quest for universal oneness, but none did. Sherrie was on my mind of course, but I knew her standards were too high to run off for the weekend with a couple of guys in a van.

One person did come by however. He was a very large young man, about our age, tall and overweight. He was wearing combat boots, rough jeans and a t-shirt. Over one shoulder he had slung a worn out green army parka. A backpack hung over the other shoulder. In those days lots of young people wore Army surplus clothing, an ironic anti-war statement and show of solidarity with veterans. He stopped by our van and smiled. "Hey man! What are you guys doing?"

"Oh nothing much. Just jamming."

"Do you mind if I hang out for a while?"

Internal pause and an eye exchange between Jim and me... *who is THIS guy?* But then I chastised myself for the hesitation. "Yeah, man, have a seat!" I said, trying to represent hippie values – peace and love and all that. Jim picked up my cue and went along. He wasn't really feeling it either, but it was the right thing to do. While we resumed jamming, the obese visitor threw off his parka and backpack and loosened his shoelaces. He then squeezed his fat butt through the side door, and as we continued playing he moved in, a few inches at a time, until he was completely inside the van. At a pause in the music he asked, "Hey, I'm hungry. Do you guys have anything to eat?"

Again, pause and glance. But peace, love and harmony won out again. I replied, "Yeah, sure. There's some chips and cookies and stuff in that bag. Help yourself." He probably already knew this, because the overflowing bag of goodies was right next to him behind the driver's seat, which explained his maneuvers through the side door. While we continued the jam session, glancing sideways at each other, he dug eagerly into the food, devouring our cookies and chips. During the next half hour he consumed everything in the bag and then fell asleep, sprawled out on his back, chip and cookie crumbs sprinkled on his t-shirt and in the carpet. We tried to keep jamming, to keep the peace and love flowing, but the inspiration pretty much expired with our food supply. While he snored through heavy breaths, we stopped playing and stared at him in disgust – an empty bag of groceries and the fat guy who ate them – spread-eagled in our van. What to do?

After a few minutes we whispered, "Let's get out of here." We began packing up our guitars, making noise to wake up the intruder without *looking like* that was what we were doing. Maybe he'd get the message and leave.

I am writing this from a distance of nearly forty years, but still remember the wrenching conundrum. This fat young man in an Army parka and combat boots represented a battle for my ideals – peace and love and all that. For all my good intentions, and all my dreaming about a better world, and all my complaining about the hypocrites at church who weren't loving and kind, I could not deliver peace and love to a single person, especially when he arrived in a fat, disgusting package. The good intentions evaporated. I was clinging to ideals but was unwilling and unable to act in concert with them. In truth I had no peace, love or time for this intruder. I would have time for a pretty girl if she came by, but I knew that didn't count. That was pure selfishness. This guy represented an opportunity to be selfless, to help a fellow human being, but I wasn't up to it. He might have had a genuine story, he might be in real need, but I wasn't interested. He was intruding into my space, taking up my time, and eating my food. I wanted him gone. With all my peace, love and harmony rhetoric, I realized I had no capacity to give him anything. I was no different than the church hypocrites I despised and used as an excuse for my behavior.

I was a phony.

The inconsistency stared me in the face.

All this happened in milliseconds in my head as Jim and I packed up our guitars and shuffled about trying to wake the intruder from a deep sleep. The battle was on for Doug Gehman's soul, but on this day selfishness again won. I really couldn't bear the fat guy in my van. I'll deal with my hypocrisy later, I decided angrily. The intruder finally stirred. He rubbed his eyes, sat up, and asked, "What's going on?"

"Uh, dude, we're heading out," I said. Not really true, but we were definitely heading out of this parking spot.

"Great man! Where ya' goin'? I'll just tag along,"

"No, man. Sorry, but we're headin' home and we really can't take an extra passenger, and uh, because we'll be sleeping in the van tonight and there just isn't room." That was true.

"Oh, man, I don't have any place to go. And I'm out of money. Can't I go with you?" This guy was piling it on. I think he was telling the truth. I'll spare you the rest. We ended the conversation by giving him twenty dollars to get rid of him and assuage our guilty consciences. Twenty dollars was a huge amount of money for two poor high school grads. When he was out of the van and on the street we backed out of the parking space and drove all the way to Atlantic City in a fog of gloom.

The weekend was only half over, but the experience ruined the remainder. I returned home on Sunday night, my ideals and integrity discarded like the crumbs at the bottom of a grocery bag. I couldn't love a single unlovely person, I had no time for a young man in need, and was uninterested in his story. He might have been a freeloader, but I had to face the fact that I didn't care enough to find out. My only solution was a twenty-dollar bribe given, not with compassion or to offer a hand of mercy, but to send the problem away. So much for peace and love, and being one with the universe.

You may wonder how I extracted so much altruistic meaning from a fat guy in an army parka. But understand, I was living on the raw edge of rebellion, exploring the boundaries of convention in search of meaning, and like many wandering souls, I went too far and foundered. I wanted to be different, but I couldn't make it happen. A fat intruder forced me to face my hypocrisy.

When I got home I called Sherrie. I didn't tell her about the weekend. I wasn't ready to be that transparent. We continued to date through the remainder of the summer. Sherrie was the most intriguing girl I had ever dated. I was drawn initially to her beauty, but her devastatingly pleasant personality kept me coming back. She wasn't empty headed. She wasn't morally ambiguous. There were strict boundaries to be respected with this girl. Sherrie possessed herself in a way that was inviolate. Unlike a long line of other girls I had dated in high school, Sherrie was both solidly grounded and wonderfully upbeat. She listened to me when I talked, and had something meaningful to offer in return! Granted, I was a hypocrite, hiding a portion of myself from her – those *other* activities – but that summer of 1973 her gentle influence slowly moved me in a new direction... I wanted to be more like her and less like my other friends.

In July, Sherrie invited me to a meeting. A bunch of teenagers and college students were getting together in the home of a friend, she said. Her older sister Faith was going to be there too. I had met Faith once – another beautiful girl. The meeting was a Bible study, weird in my mind, but with two gorgeous women as escorts, the invitation was irresistible. Besides, thanks to a fat intruder in an Army parka, my hostility to religion had been diffused. I figured these religious nuts couldn't be any more hypocritical than I was. I didn't have what it took to be a better person, but these women

195

obviously had something I lacked. Maybe other people, like Sherrie's Bible study group, had it too. If the missing element was religion, or Jesus, or whatever it's called, well, I was open to the possibilities. For an hour, we sat in a circle, singing songs and sharing from the Bible. It wasn't an uncomfortable experience. I sat beside Sherrie and Faith and kept my mouth shut. These folks were genuine, I thought, another quality I lacked. The fat Army parka guy would have been welcome in this meeting! They had even invited me, the two-faced hypocrite, for heaven's sakes! The inconsistencies of my life had started stinging! I sat silently the whole evening, mumbling through the unfamiliar songs, and trying to blend in without saying anything. Thankfully, no one pressured me. I left with "my heart strangely warmed."

Sherrie and Faith *never* pressured me about religion and their beliefs. They had to know I wasn't being honest with them. I started realizing that these women were smart – so they had to know I was living a double life. I liked the acceptance, and the no pressure stance; both made me want to change. They kept inviting me to events, church services, bible studies, and various youth events. I went sometimes. Sherrie and I continued dating. What could I do? Say no to two irresistible women?

Warm, sunny July rolled into warmer sunny August. On Thursday afternoon, August 9, I finished my job at Klotz Kleaners and drove Dad's van to Morgantown for the first night of Jesus '73. Showing my pass at the gate, I followed the dirt path through a field and parked with a thousand other cars. An adjacent field sloped gently downward to a huge modular stage, a converted flatbed semi-trailer lit up under massive lights. Music blasted from huge speaker arrays. I found an empty patch of grass near the back of the crowd and sat down.

A Christian rock band blared away. Pretty good music, I thought. Maybe this will actually be a cool weekend. The great outdoors, lots of young people around, solitude with a good vibe, this might be fun. When the band finished, a guy walked to center stage and introduced the evening's speaker, a preacher named Tom Skinner. Tom Skinner was a black Christian activist from the mean streets of Philadelphia. I had never heard of him, but from the moment he took the stage, he had my attention.

"There are people all over this nation who are praying for this meeting tonight, and for this weekend we will share together. We are living in troubling times, and young people like you are looking for answers to the world's problems."

I like this guy, I thought.

"We live in a time where almost everybody now agrees that Humpty Dumpty has fallen off the wall. But what most people cannot agree on is how, in all the world, do we put Humpty Dumpty back together again."

Shouts of agreement from the crowd.

"We live in a society where people thought there were things we could have faith in. But in recent times that faith has been shaken. I grew up in a place that, to survive, you had to be a profuse liar. You had to be good at it. But in recent months I have listened to hearings and watched proceedings on television and have never in my life heard such great lying!"

More shouts from the crowd.

"'Did you pick up a suitcase?'"
"'I think it was a suitcase, sir.'"
"'Was there money in that suitcase?'"
"'I don't know, sir.'"

He continued on this track, obviously referring to the Watergate hearings.

"The confidence of people has been shaken, and where people have been holding on to certain norms, we now realize those norms have collapsed beneath us, and people are now asking, 'How do we put it all back together again? And, where does hope lie?'

"When we look at the world's system today, it seems we have three alternatives. Some people have suggested that we just go into the system, bomb it out, destroy it, and start all over again. Now, the only problem with this solution is it presupposes the world's system

is made of facilities, and that by destroying the facilities you can change the system.

"'How about General Motors? Yeah, let's get General Motors!' So, some guy plants a bomb and blows up GM. 'Aha! We got GM!' he says. The problem is you haven't gotten rid of GM! All you have done is INCONVENIENCED GM. Tomorrow the leaders of GM will get together and make a new plan to build a bigger, better GM and in a short time GM will be back and you haven't changed anything! Why? Because the system is not made of facilities. You cannot change the system by dealing with its brick and mortar. Systems are not facilities. Systems are people! And to change systems you gotta deal with folks!"

Enthusiastic shouts from the crowd. I, on the other hand, had started quivering inside.

"Some people say, 'We'll go inside the system, and change it from within! Yeah, that's what we'll do.' So, you go to college and get a good education, and then you get a job in a big company or in the government. You plan and work for years to get inside the system so you can change the world from within. The problem with this plan is that by the time you have worked your way into the system and fought your way to the top where you can actually influence change, **you have so prostituted yourself to get there that you forgot what you came there for!**"

Now I couldn't pull my gaze from this black preacher as he bellowed at us from that semi-trailer stage. "... No! To change systems you gotta deal with folks!

"You can't change the world by blowing it up or burning it down! And you can't change the world by going inside and changing it from within! If you want to change the world, if you want to create a new society, you've got to start with new folks! You need new people, and you've got to start with yourself!"

Never had any words hit me with such force. Never had any declaration rung so true. Skinner's words, "You need new folks!" penetrated into my soul. For the first time in my life, religion made sense. Jesus and His message, and all that I knew in my head, including a five-year-old prayer at the woodpile behind the garage, began to resonate inside. To change the world, I had to change first.

Tom Skinner continued. *"Jesus said, 'Unless you are born again you cannot see the Kingdom of God.' Jesus was talking to Nicodemus, a religious leader who knew everything there was to know about the Bible, about God, and the traditions of the Jewish people. But Nicodemus didn't get it. He came to Jesus one night to ask Jesus about his teachings.*

"'You mean I must go back inside my Momma, and be born again?'"

"'No,' Jesus said, 'You must be born of the spirit…'"

While Tom Skinner explained Jesus' conversation with Nicodemus, my heart ran way ahead of him. The conversation between Jesus and Nicodemus is Sunday School 101. I had heard it all my life, but it had never unnerved me like this.

"If you want to create a new society, you've got to start with new folks!"

As Skinner continued his message, talking about Vietnam, politics, and the angst of millions of American young people, something started rising from deep inside of me. I have no words to describe it, even after forty years. It was a plea, an earnest reaching, a silent desperate prayer coming from the center of my being, boiling up through the drugs, and the lying, and the betrayal of my parents, and the failure to help a fat young man who needed a friend:

"That's what I want," I said.

Four words – okay five – if you count the contraction. My desperate plunge into faith, a sinner's prayer reaching out to a patient God, was only five words long. Skinner gave an altar call at the end of the service but I didn't go forward. There was no need. I drove home in a glow and went to bed. The next day while pressing trousers at Klotz Kleaners I mulled over what had happened. The glow was palpable, obvious to no one else but me. Later that day I told Mother about the experience. Her response was subdued; maybe it was calculated so as to not bruise a delicate reed, or maybe she just knew God would answer her prayers – "THREE

DAYS OR THREE WEEKS!" I returned to Jesus '73 Friday evening to meet Sherrie. I couldn't wait to tell her about what had happened to me. Sherrie met me at the rendezvous point but the reception was not what I planned.

Before I could get a word out, she told me she didn't want to be my girl anymore.

"What? Why?" I asked, in shock.

"I don't know. I just don't have feelings for you anymore." Sherrie was trying to be pleasant – she was always pleasant about everything – but the conversation ended in awkward silence. We stared at each other, me in shock. She said some bland "I'll see you later" goodbye, and turned her back and walked away.

There *is always* more to every breakup story. I found out later what happened. While I was pressing trousers for Mr. Klotz, and mulling over my encounter with God, Sherrie spent Friday afternoon sitting beside my good friend Dan Eberly on a grassy hill at Jesus '73. So my best friend stole my girl friend! Shocked and reeling, I wanted to get his version of the story. For most of our teenage years Dan had gone farther and fallen harder than me in every rebellious activity. His head-long descent into darkness became so alarming that our friendship faltered. Then, a year earlier, in the summer of 1972, he attended Expo '72 in Dallas, Texas. Like me, his concerned parents bribed him to go. Expo '72 was a huge youth rally sponsored by Campus Crusade for Christ and the Billy Graham Evangelistic Association.

Dan returned from Texas transformed. The change alienated us even further, because I didn't want to hear his "Jesus saved me" story. Dan's pitiful attempts to reach me that year, to appeal to me, now with big innocent eyes, drove me crazy. My "Get-away-from-me-man" posture really hurt him, but I didn't care and wasn't having any. The darker, meaner Dan Eberly had been hard to deal with, but who was THIS guy? "I don't know what happened to Dan Eberly," I told my guitar buddy Jim. "It's like another person moved into his body and took over."

Not far from the truth, if you take Jesus at His word.

Dan prayed for me for a year, right up to Jesus '73. He missed my big event on opening night but then came for the Friday daytime sessions, and by coincidence bumped into Sherrie. He knew we were dating, so they sat together. Neither of them knew what had happened to me the night before. Dan didn't mean to do it, but the nice guy Dan Eberly romanced my pleasant girl friend all day long. So, Sherrie got a crush on my best friend, and when I arrived that evening she dropped me. Oh, the irony of teenage love! My girl friend, the pleasant girl, who had drawn me toward Something and Someone, who warmed my heart to God, dumped me like a brick for my best friend! I finished the weekend terribly conflicted – euphoria over meeting Jesus but in agony over the loss of Sherrie. When Dan and I finally unpacked the story, he assured me he had NOT tried to steal Sherrie and wasn't interested in her. They had only sat together because of me. He had not encouraged her. I believed him and accepted his explanation. But I still lost the *pleasant* girl.

I told Mother about Sherrie Friday night. She said, "You aren't going to turn your back on God are you?"

"Of course not, Mother!" The idea never even crossed my mind. Whatever happened to me on Thursday night, August 9, 1973 was burned, seared, tattooed, grafted into my soul. I can't describe it. "I was lost, but now I'm found. I was dead, but now I'm alive." The metaphors of scripture, attempting to describe in words this connection with God, are punchy, and powerful, but even these descriptions don't tell the whole story. Sherrie's breakup hurt me deeply, but this, this was SOMETHING ELSE!

It took a few months to get over the pleasant girl, which is an eternity for an eighteen-year-old. My newfound faith however, stuck like super glue. And the move to Goshen College provided the distance I needed. Maybe Sherrie served a higher purpose after all: A pleasant girl leading a wayward soul down a dusty road towards destiny.

18 The Land of Goshen

Three weeks after Jesus '73 I left for Goshen College. This Mennonite liberal arts college is named after the quaint northern Indiana town that is its home. Goshen was founded in the early 1800s, probably by Anabaptist pioneers searching for safe haven and good farmland. The State of Indiana fondly describes itself as the "Gateway to the West," a flattering label until one considers that it perhaps refers to the proclivity of pioneers to travel *through* it's flat landscape to more enticing western destinations. The few who settled in northern Indiana affectionately named their new home for the region in Egypt where Joseph, great grandson of Abraham, and his Hebrew family, settled after fleeing famine in the ancient land of Canaan. For Joseph's father Jacob and his eleven brothers and their families, the land of Goshen wasn't heaven, but it had food and was safe.

I decided on Goshen College in February – eight months before Jesus '73 – not for food and safety, not even for a good education, and certainly not for the school's spiritual or Mennonite climate. The interest in Goshen College was purely carnal: parties and girls. I had encountered these two attractive commodities during a college-sponsored weekend recruitment trip that started one cold February Friday afternoon when I climbed onto a tour bus with fifty other

Pennsylvania high school seniors for a twelve-hour ride from eastern Pennsylvania, through Ohio, to Goshen, Indiana. We disembarked in front of the College Administration building at 1:30 a.m. and were met by two self-appointed greeters. The guys had shoulder length hair and were wearing ratty jeans, flannel shirts, and green army parkas, protection from the bitter Indiana cold. Not that they were feeling anything. Their eyes shined a little too much.

"Hey, what's happening?" they asked as we poured off the bus into the chilly Lake Michigan air. The greeters scanned the females in our group and their eyes landed on Brenda, standing beside me. Brenda was a cute – well she was a knock out – blonde girl from Lansdale, Pennsylvania. Brenda and I had become friends on the trip. A lot can happen when two teenagers spend twelve hours inside of a bus. I wowed Brenda with my charm and wit, plus good doses of enthusiastic playing of Led Zeppelin's "Stairway to Heaven" on my guitar. Yes, I had my guitar. I dragged it everywhere in those days, this time onto the bus, stuffed into an overhead bin. I planned to pass the time and maybe entertain the crowd, but then Brenda came into view so I narrowed the focus. I had discovered a few years before that limited talent and a little enthusiasm on a guitar had an uncanny ability to attract the opposite sex. By the time we arrived in Goshen, Brenda was practically my girl.

"Where you guys from?" one of the hip college greeters asked. He seemed a little tipsy, but then it *was* one-thirty in the morning.

"We just came from PA," I replied, impressed that a Mennonite school would have students who looked, talked and acted like this. It was Friday night, but still.

"Cool. Welcome to Goshen College." I liked Goshen College already! The unofficial greeters wandered off when our sponsors started herding us toward the dorms. I said goodbye to Brenda and followed the male herd to the men's dorm. My room for the weekend was with two guys on High Park Fourth Floor. They welcomed me, pointed me to my bunk, and offered me a beer from their fridge. Beer was contraband – this was a Christian college and they were underage – but they didn't seem concerned. Pictures of bikini-clad women hung on the walls, another taboo, but again, the posters were hanging ON THE WALLS for crying out loud! Goshen College *was definitely* going to be cool. By the end of the weekend I was convinced Goshen was my school: wild enough to satisfy my cravings, but not too far Outside to be scary. Ironically, carnal motivations included, God was paving a path, guiding me down His planned route, six months before August 9, 1973.

When I arrived in early September, a few weeks after my Jesus '73 encounter with God, my life had changed. The news was a huge disappointment to my new roommate. Ron was a sophomore at Goshen College, from my home church, Neffsville Mennonite. We had pre-planned to be roommates, more for partying opportunities than academic or spiritual pursuits. When I dragged my bags and gear into our room, he jumped up, gave me a big welcome "Hey man!" and started gushing about the party scene coming up for the weekend. He stopped short when I pulled out a Bible and put it on my nightstand. I offered a brief explanation, which he accepted with silent, disappointed nods. Ron came from a Christian home, so a Bible and my new story was familiar territory. He respected my decision, too much religious heritage to do otherwise, but he wasn't following me down the road of righteous living, not with college party opportunities. We went our separate ways through the first semester, shared the room for sleeping and study, and seldom interacted, a real bummer for him, this turncoat, religious zealot roommate. Making one last attempt to change my mind, Ron invited me to drive up to Michigan with him and a carload of other guys. Drinking age was eighteen in Michigan, only thirty minutes away. "It'll be fun," he promised. I declined.

On the second day at Goshen College, I followed a crowd of several hundred nervous freshmen from the dining hall to the gymnasium for "Orientation." Orientation was a student-led evening to welcome newcomers, especially freshmen, with information about the college thrown in. I found a seat near the back of the buzzing crowd. At seven o'clock two guys in jeans and t-shirts walked to center stage.

"Welcome everyone! How many freshmen are here tonight? Give us a shout!" Cheers and catcalls from the crowd followed. "All right, then! Welcome! Welcome to Goshen College!"

"To start off," Host Number Two began, "we're going to do a little presentation. We need a volunteer. Who would like to come up here and assist us?" A guy on the front row raised his hand. The hosts pointed to him and, encouraged by cheers from the crowd, the volunteer bounded up the platform steps.

Host Number One shoved the microphone into the volunteer's face. "What's your name?" he asked.

"Jim."

"Where' ya from, Jim?"

"Kansas."

"What city?"

"Topeka."

"Great!" shouted Host Number One. "Everybody, give it up for Jim from Topeka, Kansas!" Whoops, hollers and clapping from the crowd.

Host Number Two: "Jim, this presentation will require a test of your physical strength. Do you work out?"

"Oh, a little." Jim looked fit enough, but he was no body builder.

"OK, Jim. No problem. But, before we do this exercise, we need to see your muscles."

"Host Number One: "Yeah, Jim, we need you to take off your t-shirt and show us your muscles."

"Uh, what?" Jim looked back and forth at the two hosts.

"We need to see your muscles, Jim. This is a test of your physical strength. Come on, pull off that t-shirt and show us what you got."

Now Jim looked scared. He backed up a step. "I, uh…"
I was feeling a little nervous myself. *What are these guys doing,
asking a volunteer to undress on stage?*

"Come on, Jim! Whata' ya waiting for?"

"Uh, no thanks, I don't want to…"

Host One: "Oh come on, Jim. Why so shy?"

Host Two: "Yeah, Jim, let's see them muscles!"

Jim looked around sheepishly and tugged at his t-shirt.
He looked ready to bolt off the stage. Now *I* was *really*
nervous… I've always had a problem with empathy.

Host One turned to the crowd: "Hey everyone! Do you
all want to see Jim's muscles?"

The crowd cheered and clapped. Jim started backing
away, but the two hosts grabbed him.

"Oh, come on Jim! Don't be so shy." Jim started
squirming to get loose. "Just take off that shirt and show us
your muscles."

One host grabbed Jim from behind, and the other
pulled his t-shirt up. The crowd gasped. Jim was wearing a
woman's bra! Jim broke free, jerked the shirt down, and ran
off the stage. There was a moment of stunned silence, and
then the room exploded in cacophonous laughter and
clapping. A few freshmen, me among them, sat in shocked
silence, our mouths gaping open. What just happened?! I
understood beer and girl pictures in the privacy of a dorm
room, even with my new faith, but this was unfolding on
stage, in full view of faculty. The skit was obviously staged.
After the raucous crowd quieted down, Jim returned to the
stage to assist in other progressively more risqué
"presentations."

Eventually things leveled off and ended with a
monologue, a dispensing of information. Boring but less
scandalous, thank God!

So the school year started, and everyone settled into an
academic rhythm – class, study, meals, study, sleep, study,
and precious little time for recreation and socializing, more
study, except for my roommate Ron who frequently stumbled

into bed in the wee morning hours. I studied alone and with a few new friends, in my room, in the library, and when the weather permitted, on the grass under the campus maple trees. Fall in Indiana can be a beautiful time of the year, and Goshen, the Maple City of Indiana, is a pretty town. Maple and oak trees abound on the college campus, casting shaded patterns on exquisite green lawns. Autumn season accentuates the beauty with changing colors and falling leaves.

My first encounter with Goshen College's religious heritage happened during a post-Chapel discussion group. Our discussion leader, one of the school's professors of religion, was presenting the social implications of the Kingdom of God as understood by our Anabaptist Mennonite tradition. He expounded on Christian community and social action, concepts that in a few more years would be skillfully put down by Howard A. Snyder in his book "The Community of the King." I listened for a while and then raised my hand to offer an opinion. The professor nodded at me, giving me the floor.

Making my best effort to look and sound informed, I stood up and stated to the group of thirty people: "Well, I agree with the whole community conscious aspects of our faith, and of the need for social concern and involvement in the community, but none of this matters if each of us doesn't have a personal relationship with Jesus Christ." I sat down, feeling good about my contribution to the discussion. Good job, Doug, pointing out a foundational truth of the Christian faith!

The professor didn't share my opinion. "Well, I just think that's heresy!" He retorted. He continued the retort, shifting his gaze between the group and me, obviously offended. "That's just holding to a belief that says our faith is me and God alone, just me and God, with no responsibility to a larger community, to God's people, and the bigger social issues in a community of faith and the world around us!" On he went, tearing into my "me and God" heresy. When he finished, I could hardly lift my head up to look at anyone. Me and God sat speechless staring into misty space. Everyone else – our little community of faith – remained silent too. This was my first semester at Goshen College, I was an eighteen-year-old newcomer, obviously too inexperienced to navigate the expansive oceans of academia, even with God by my side. The professor wasn't looking for a response, especially from a dumb freshman. For him the moment passed as one more forgettable dictum from an uninformed ignoramus. He moved on to more important community topics. I stayed for the rest of the discussion, but mostly tuned it out from embarrassment. Me and God left at the end.

I had better luck with Professor Bauman. He led our Wednesday night Bible study. Professor Bauman's weekly Bible study became my "church" at Goshen College. It wasn't a big gathering – about twenty people – but I made a commitment to never miss, not for any activity, even studying for tests and finals. Don't ask me where I came up with this idea, but it was another "me and God" thing. I decided early in my college experience that I would have priorities in my faith. Showing up at weekly Bible Study was one way for me to live it.

Professor Bauman was a devout Mennonite man, a serious academic, and a caring Christian leader. He lived his faith as both a personal relationship with God and community responsibility to his fellow man. Although we never discussed it, I was sure he was a "me and God" heretic. Professor Bauman was also an activist, willing to take a stand in public for his Anabaptist and pacifist beliefs. The year before my arrival, he stood on the streets of Goshen with hundreds of other anti-war activists, silently but publicly protesting the United States' presence in Vietnam. Don't confuse Professor Bauman with people who ridiculed the government, mocked our fighting forces, and put people's lives at risk. Professor Bauman was a patriot. He loved our nation, respected our leaders, cared about veterans and stood up for what he believed during a time of great national uncertainty. He watched me with a curious mixture of friendship and fatherly patience, putting up with my tendency to talk too much and ask too many questions. I consulted him once about an open letter I wrote to the student body voicing my disapproval of some edgy college activities. I wanted to post it on the public bulletin board in the cafeteria entrance.

"I wouldn't do it," he cautioned. "It won't change anything, and will only provoke backlash against you." His counsel seemed like cowardice, but I didn't post the paper, and later realized he had spared me a lot of ridicule. One must choose his battles carefully, a lesson I learned from a wise mentor. The world is not transformed in one day. I know now Professor Bauman was no coward for protecting me from my own naiveté.

During that first semester I met another "me and God" heretic, Brent Gray, who approached me in the library one afternoon. Brent's clothes – the blue jeans, ragged t-shirt, and sandaled feet – the obligatory uniform of college life in the 70s, blended with the twelve hundred other students on campus. What set Brent apart was an eternally frowning horse face below a disheveled crown of wiry brown hair. Even his smile couldn't erase the depressed look. But Brent's persistence at becoming a friend with a fellow believer in Jesus was compelling. Brent first appeared at my library corner table one afternoon lugging a huge pile of textbooks. The books were balanced on his hip and a loaded backpack was slung over one shoulder. The backpack and books hunched him over and bent his body slightly to the right.

"Do you believe in Jesus?" the horse face asked, frowning. Even the voice was melancholy. Igor, the donkey friend of Winnie the Pooh, comes to mind.

"Yes, I do," I replied. I was not ashamed of my faith, but this was not a typical introduction. I squirmed a little in my chair and sized up this odd-looking guy with the pile of books. A memory of Ocean City, and a fat guy in a green army parka wisped through my mind. Maybe the Christian community has moochers too. What did *this* guy want?

"I saw the cross and Jesus on your jeans," he said pointing to the ink artwork on my jeans. I looked down. There it was, in ink just above my knee. Sherrie Brubaker had sketched the cross during the previous summer, a romantic moment between teenage lovebirds. Pangs of Sherrie wafted into the library – I didn't need a reminder about the *pleasant* girl!

"Oh, yeah. I sort of scribbled it there," I said, rubbing over Sherrie's artwork.

"I'm a Christian too," Brent said, sitting down at the desk next to me. "I love Jesus with all my heart."

You should tell your face, I thought. "Uh, me too." I offered. "What's your name?" I couldn't just snub the guy outright. I wanted to give him a chance. I didn't like the way I was feeling either. Guilt is the operative word. *Have I not changed at all?*

"Brent. Brent Gray."

We exchanged names and stories. Brent lingered way too long. I needed to study, but he was obviously looking for friendship. He wouldn't normally be my first choice in friends, but Brent loved Jesus, so what could I do? Before we parted, Brent invited me to go to church with him. I declined – some excuse about studies and other commitments. No problem he said, maybe another time.

Through the fall term he kept asking and by November I was out of excuses. His stories about this church were tugging at my curiosity. They were a cool group of young people, he said, full of life, and they met in an old farm building. I went one Thursday night… and had the second big spiritual encounter of my life.

So, dear reader, an odd horse-face friend is how I came to know Zion Chapel, another step toward destiny. Zion Chapel was not a typical church in the 1970s. It started as a student bible study in a basement. Victor Hildebrand, a Canadian Mennonite and Goshen College graduate, married a local Goshen girl named Ruth Ann Yoder in the 1960s. Vic and Ruth Ann met at Goshen College. After graduation and marriage, Vic stayed in the United States and got a job teaching at Goshen High School. Then, in 1969 the couple experienced something powerful from the Holy Spirit, and began ministering to young people in the basement of their home. By the time I arrived in November 1973 the home group had exploded to a couple hundred young people, had long outgrown the basement, and were now meeting on Sunday mornings and Wednesday nights in an old gladiola farm warehouse along Route 33. The "glad farm" was a rundown, dirty excuse for a building, and utterly lacking in religious flare or creature comfort. The only alluring aspect of the place was God, who seemed to show up regularly. Zion Chapel was definitely a bunch of "me and God" radicals. Young people, strung out on drugs and sex, or just tired of the hedonistic routine, came by the hundreds to experience something divine. Even bored Mennonite youth were checking out Zion Chapel.

Religious leaders in the area, including the Mennonite Church hierarchy, didn't know what to do with "that meeting" at the gladiola farm. There was ridicule... and suspicion... but Vic Hildebrand didn't care. His was a raw faith, born of a powerful experience, and grounded in old-fashioned Canadian Mennonite sensibilities. He was utterly committed to reaching a new generation and rescuing them from their hell-bent godlessness. Like flies to light, young people flocked to his intrepid leadership. The church grew quickly. Like a thousand others across this great nation, Zion Chapel was one more Jesus People fire that started in the "Vietnam Generation."

One young man, plucked from the fire and mentored by Pastor Hildebrand, was Ron Manning. I first met Ron when he was leading worship at a "Holy Spirit" weekend at Goshen College. Goshen's Mennonite community was not going to be left behind in this growing national interest in Jesus and the Holy Spirit. The College hosted the weekend and asked Ron Manning to help with the worship. When I first saw Ron, he was sitting on the platform in front of the group, guitar on his lap, radiating like a neon light. The service hadn't even started yet, and he hadn't said anything. He just sat on the stage in front of the crowd, holding his guitar and glowing like a light bulb. That happened a lot in those days – people glowing. Ron was the genuine article, flaws and all. He loved Jesus, and the passion just radiated out of his pores.

Ron's faith was genuine, born of a radical conversion out of a horrible family background, and a troubled adolescence. Zion Chapel became Ron's family, and Vic his "Dad." In time, he met a young Mennonite girl in the church, and a few years later they married. Carolyn was a close friend of my future wife, so we all became good friends, as good as Ron could muster anyway. His quirky, melancholic personality limited intimate relationships with people. Ron was a great teacher and worship leader but was uneasy in one-on-one interaction. He once commented, during a teaching session, that he was "socially constipated." Awkward. But Ron was comfortable with God. I understood that. Human relationships are inherently unpredictable and complicated. The *pleasant* girl! People can be a lot of work for a recovering soul.

Zion Chapel started in 1969, almost a decade after the Mennonite denomination got its first taste of the Holy Spirit. That moment happened in Pennsylvania to a country preacher named Gerald Derstine. His church youth group started seeking God, and before long they encountered the Holy Spirit, with all the odd phenomena, including speaking in tongues. After too many late-night prayer meetings, and long times of worship, and falling down under God's power, and too many other odd manifestations, the alarmed parents complained to the Bishops. Pastor Derstine was called before the powers-that-be to give an account. It didn't go well. Derstine lost his church, the "Left foot of fellowship" as it is sometimes painfully recalled. Not to be dissuaded, Derstine started traveling, telling his story and preaching revival as an itinerant minister. He eventually relocated to Bradenton, Florida where he founded Christian Retreat. National interest about Holy Spirit phenomena was running high in those days, and a lot of people were telling incredible stories. Derstine, and many like him became nationally recognized Charismatic leaders.

In 1974, at a Mennonite renewal meeting in Lancaster, Pennsylvania, Derstine was officially reconciled to the Mennonite Church. Zion Chapel started at this time in Indiana, six hundred miles away. The Jesus Movement and the Charismatic Renewal were giving rise to hundreds of new ministries. The Full Gospel Business Men, Women's Aglow, Christian publishing houses, and scores of healing evangelists, emerged in the fervor. Many evangelists started by conducting tent meetings and later sought larger audiences through national television programing. Large sections of America were being impacted by interest in the Holy Spirit. Charismatic teaching infiltrated almost every denomination in the country. Even the Catholic denomination, a bulwark of tradition and orthodoxy, had to contend with "Charismatic Catholics" in their midst who attended Mass on Sundays and "Spirit-filled" Bible Studies throughout the week. Church leaders who refused to embrace the new vibrancy began losing their members to emerging independent Bible study groups and churches. Zion Chapel was the first such congregation in Elkhart County, Indiana. The influence quickly overflowed the boundaries of the Anabaptist community and touched many non-Mennonites in the area, including Ron Manning.

Zion Chapel became a pivotal influence in my life. I met my wife at this church in 1975, we married in 1976, and two years later Zion Chapel sent our little family to Asia on what became a fifteen-year adventure. All of this began because a horse-face friend named Brent Gray reached out to me in friendship at the Goshen College Library. God has His emissaries. Sometimes they are angels, about whom we are at first unaware. Brent and I remained friends for many years, mostly around my new church family. He graduated from Goshen College, married his college sweetheart, and went to medical school. After graduation he moved to Wisconsin and started a medical practice. We lost touch. I found him on Facebook recently, divorced and in poor health, but happily surrounded by his children and grandchildren.

In the early days Zion Chapel preferred simple music, another tradition carried forward from Mennonite influences. A cappella worship was common in Mennonite churches. Zion Chapel augmented worship with an acoustic guitar. Later, a keyboard, sometimes a violin was added. Drums were out. So too were organized bands and multiple singers. Too much noise, too much sophistication, too much temptation to show off. No need for instrumental noise when you had a few hundred enthusiastic worshippers. In fact, the leaders were not wrong on this point. Man, did we worship! Sometimes worship lasted for an hour. People jumped to their feet, threw back their heads, closed their eyes, raised their hands high above their heads, and worshipped God, clapping, dancing, kneeling, and singing in tongues. It happened in every meeting. Who needed a band when rivers of worship were flowing out of two hundred souls?

"He is Lord! He is Lord!
He is risen from the dead and He is Lord.
Every knee shall bow, every tongue confess,
That Jesus Christ is Lord!"

We worshiped and worshiped and worshiped and then waited for spontaneous outbursts, prophecies, utterances in tongues and their interpretations. Sometimes it got really weird and the leaders had to step in and separate the wheat from the chaff. There was a lot of chaff. As is common to every revival, fervency eventually wanes, weirdness and routine settles into predictable rhythms, the leaders sift out most of the chaff, and the church relaxes into new norms and traditions. Waning fervency isn't simply an indication of lost focus or commitment; it is just a fact of life and the passing of time. Eighteen-year-olds become twenty-year-olds; they get married and have babies, and babies don't tolerate long meetings, no matter how good the worship is. Mothers need to take their babies home, and fathers must get up to work at 5:00 a.m.. So the revival adjusts, and normal church life emerges, with children's ministries, family picnics, youth services and coffee socials. In time, Zion Chapel organized their worship services with instruments, including drums, keyboards and support singers. Today, Zion Chapel, newly named Harvest Community Church, and upgraded for the times, enjoys a full ensemble of instruments and singers. Worship services last for a predictable ninety minutes, and the church offers state-of-the-art infant, children, and teenage ministries and facilities.

Two hundred years ago Charles Finney declared that "revivals of religion" are a necessary part of every generation's spiritual experience. Christians oscillate between appetite and apathy, Finney declared, between inspiration and indifference. So, when God's people slide too far into lethargy, when they fall asleep in tradition and meaningless religiosity, God sends revival to wake then up. The wake-up call is necessary, even if it gets a little weird.

So, the weirdness at Zion Chapel drew me in and catapulted me forward toward destiny... first to meet and marry my wife in 1976, then to an overseas mission trip in 1977, and a call to Asia that followed it.

ASIA I

19 The Little Redhead

The Little Redhead came into my life in the spring of 1975 at a church-sponsored singles canoe trip. Eight young women and eight young men, some coupled up and others just friends, none married, joined together for a Saturday canoe trip down a local river. The entire group conspired to put Beth and me into a canoe together. Not that we were resisting. Our paths had crossed several times, introductions had been made, and interest was high, at least on my part, to get to know the cute little redhead.

I was determined to make an impression on the girl. On this day that work would be accomplished by demonstrating my skills in piloting a canoe. I made the impression, but not how I planned. Every river man knows that a canoe is inherently unstable, a side effect of its maneuverable design. So, instead of showing off my prowess, I drenched us both, twice, complete into-the-river dump overs that produced a lot of laughing from her and not a little embarrassment for yours truly.

Beth forgave me – somehow the debacle had an endearing quality to it – and agreed to start dating me. We quickly discovered that, besides the mutual attraction, our goals and dreams were the same. Within a few months, casual friendship blossomed into a full-blown love affair. I proposed in December 1975. We married in April 1976 and after a long, relaxing honeymoon that meandered south through the Smokey Mountain National Park in Tennessee, to Disney World in Orlando, friends in Sarasota, and back north along the eastern seaboard to my family in Pennsylvania, we returned to Goshen and settled into a simple startup apartment on Seventh Street. I got a job working for Coachmen Industries in Middlebury and Beth busied herself with keeping our house and managing our social calendar.

Wes Smith returned from a trip to the Far East that year and came to Zion Chapel to report. We listened, spellbound, as this fiery evangelist shared stories from Hong Kong and the Philippines – exotic places and people as far from my experience as Mars and its Martians. I had been outside the United States only once, to Belize in Central America in 1974 while at Goshen College, so stories from the Orient were compelling drama. Smith's style in the telling of them glowed with anecdotal humor and divine inspiration: millions of Asian people, thousands of them hungry for God, attentively listening to the Gospel of Jesus Christ on streets and crusade fields, crowds rushing to the front, weeping and falling down, praying and receiving Him as Savior, with signs following.

"These people aren't like American Christians," Wes quipped. "They don't know anything about being religious fanatics, but when the Holy Spirit comes on them, they jerk and twitch just like everybody else!" Everyone laughed. He continued: "A couple of years ago, Robert Ewing told me, 'The best fishing in the world is in the Philippines!' Well, I'm here to tell you, Robert Ewing was right!"

A month later, I heard Ron Manning was going to the Philippines with Wes Smith. Catalytic news this was! I whined to Beth about it. "Why does he get to go?" She countered immediately: "If he can go, so can you!" Great idea! I talked to Pastor Vic.

"Write to him and ask." Vic suggested.

I did, and a few weeks later Wes called Pastor Vic: "Who is this guy?" Vic assured him I was safe. With my pastor's blessing, an invitation from Wes, and reluctant permission from my now pregnant wife, I withdrew a chunk of money from our meager savings account and bought an airline ticket.

Ron wasn't going to the Philippines, he later told me. Never considered it. Where did I hear that? A baseless rumor inspired a journey to the other side of the planet. The irony. A rumor that launched an excursion that inspired a career! On a freezing morning in February 1977, my wife drove me to O'Hare International Airport in Chicago. I kissed her goodbye and joined Wes and two other men who had flown in from Fort Lauderdale. Airport security in 1977 was not what it is today. No scans, no pat downs, just a ticket and passport check. The terminal was not a restricted area. Anyone could wander freely throughout the airport, and in typical entrepreneurial fashion, the place was crawling with people and their agendas: travelers on their way, family members saying goodbye, airport employees scurrying about on assignment, and weirdos. A lot of weirdos. Odd-looking people hovered or wandered everywhere: selling stuff, handing out flyers and preaching religion. Hari Krishna devotees – both male and female, easily identified by their shaved heads and white robes – carried plastic buckets marked with "Help the Children" labels; they were making a nuisance of themselves at every corner.

"Can you help the children?" Two young devotees, a guy and a girl, handed me a flyer and held out their buckets.

"Uh, well…" I looked around for my companions. One was shaking his head. "Uh, no thanks." Wes was more direct. "If you were serving the Living God you wouldn't have to beg for a living." The white robes backed off, we walked away, and an hour later boarded a Boeing 747 airliner. This was my first experience on Boeing's mother of all flying machines. The 747 is a massive hunk of metal. The burgeoning aircraft lumbers down the runway, groaning to pick up speed, four engines roaring, and then the wingtips bend upward and the hunk of metal just leaves the ground. We landed in Anchorage to refuel and then continued west to Hong Kong. On its descending approach the hunk of metal skimmed over the rooftops of Kowloon's business centers and tightly packed high-rise apartment buildings, close enough to see tenant women on the roofs hanging their laundry out to dry. Terrifying for me – "Aren't we a little low?" – but the women ignored the massive metal beast passing overhead.

Hong Kong is one of the most unique places on earth. Set in the heart of South East Asia on the South China Sea, the territory is located on the southern coast of communist China. Still a British Colony in 1977, Hong Kong is a bastion of international capitalism: finance, business, wealth, culture... and people. The people! So many people! Our taxi dropped us in the heart of Tsim Sha Tsui, Kowloon's business district. Hong Kong is divided into three main areas: Hong Kong Island, Kowloon City on the mainland with its famous business district, and the New Territories, a large tract of less developed rambling city and land that stretches to the China border. When we stepped out of the taxi onto the sidewalk in front of our hotel, we entered a river of human beings, an uninterrupted mass of people flowing in both directions. This was the Hong Kong I will never forget. At any time, day or night, the streets are continuously alive with people. I saw more people in my first fifteen minutes in Hong Kong than I had seen in my entire life before! Everywhere we went it was the same: People, people, people. I have seen human congestion in many Asian cities since then – it is common in Asia – but in 1977, coming fresh from rural America, Hong Kong was a paradigm shifter.

Our host Dennis Balcombe drove us out of Kowloon through the New Territories to the border. From a hillside vantage point, we gazed into the People's Republic of China. It was an eerie feeling, standing there at the border of strictly enforced Chinese communism, peering into a mysterious, forbidden land. Forty years had passed since Mao Tse-tung established his version of Communism as the governing policy of the Chinese. Forty years of silence behind a "Bamboo Curtain." Nobody really knew what was going on in China. Except for a few government dignitaries and heads of state – a short list that included President Richard Nixon, who visited in 1972 – few western outsiders had been inside China since the end of the Second World War.

Dennis Balcombe, this blond-haired and blue-eyed American, had come to Hong Kong in the 1960s as a single man from the San Francisco Bay Area. He married a young American gal named Kathy a few years later and they returned to Hong Kong. Hong Kong was his home but Dennis' heart was in China. His work in Hong Kong, the church he planted, the ministry he led, were merely dress rehearsals for the big show. When the Bamboo Curtain finally opened, he was going in.

The reasons for "The Curtain" are fairly simple. Prior to and during World War Two, the United States supported President Chiang Kai-shek and his Kuomintang Nationalist Party in their fight against Mao. After the war ended, with the U.S. nuclear bombings of two Japanese cities, Mao marched on Beijing and pushed Chiang Kai-shek's armies backward toward the Pacific Ocean. The United States stood by their friend and ally on principle, but not enough to defeat Mao; we were too war-weary for another engagement, so our support was mostly symbolic. On December 10, 1949, Chairman Mao declared victory, and President Chiang and his government officials and their families fled for their lives, floating or flying across the Formosa Strait to Taiwan, where they set up a government-in-exile in Taipei. The "Republic of China" has ruled Taiwan since, waiting for an elusive future time when they hope to return and re-establish their rightful rule of the mainland.

The massive conflict for control of China was complicated. During the Second World War, prime real estate and coveted natural resources were up for grabs all over the world. Hitler's Germany advanced in Europe, taking Poland,

Czech, Austria, France, North Africa, etc. Then finally, Germany went after the Soviet Union. On the opposite side of the world, the Japanese Empire embarked on a hegemonic quest for control of the Pacific Rim, including China. In 1931 the Japanese Empire's Kwantung army invaded Manchuria and murdered twenty-three million Chinese. Fourteen years of aggression followed; Japan finally gave up their quest for world domination in 1945 after America dropped nuclear bombs on Hiroshima and Nagasaki. The bombings were brutal; America has taken a lot of flack for being the only nation to ever use a nuclear weapon in war. History has mostly forgotten why it was necessary. Hitler wreaked similar havoc in Europe and eventually got a similar beating, without the use of nuclear weapons. After Japan's surrender to the United States, Mao Tse-tung re-engaged the battle for China, and in 1949 drove President Chiang's weary and corrupt armies from the mainland with no American opposition.

The 1930s and 1940s were an insane time on Planet Earth. Human aggression pushed mankind to the brink of annihilation, led by the cult ambitions of a few world despots and their idealistic armies. But it all ended in 1945 with the defeat of Germany and Japan. A few remaining and less powerful despots cleaned up undisputed territory. Eastern Europe and much of Asia re-arranged and re-oriented themselves with new allies, new boundaries, and new nations. China rebuilt under communist leadership and shut itself off from the rest of the world.

Weary of war and contemptuous of communism, the United States ignored Mao Tse-tung for forty years. But during the next three decades the world shifted. By the late 1970s Chairman Mao was dead and his predecessors, namely an entrepreneurial leader named Dung Xiaoping, were desperate to move a nation of one billion souls into the future. Dung Xiaoping's pragmatic vision included moderate politics and healthy economics. Xiaoping reached out to President Jimmy Carter, and in 1979, showing incredible foresight, a rarity in international diplomacy, President Jimmy Carter realigned the global balance of power by formalizing relations with the People's Republic of China. "The PRC is here to stay," he declared, "and our friends on Taiwan will have to adjust." In one bold move, the United States severed a sixty-year-old friendship with Chiang Kai-shek's Republic of China hunkered down on Taiwan and realigned with the largest communist government in history.

My visit to Hong Kong happened in 1977, two full years before Jimmy Carter's historic decision. China still silently existed behind a Bamboo Curtain. Only a few people on the planet knew what was coming.

After a week in Hong Kong we flew to Manila, Philippines. Wes planned to preach in an open-air evangelistic meeting in the heart of the city. That week in Manila, preaching to hundreds of hungry people on the streets of another bustling Asian city, confirmed my calling to Asia. On the flight home, now enflamed with vision for the multitudes of Asia, I read through the four Gospels. On page after page I saw Jesus interacting with multitudes! He had compassion for them. He taught them, He healed them, He fed them and was constantly surrounded by them. Everything he did during three years of public ministry, including his intimate connections with the twelve disciples, happened against a backdrop of great crowds of people!

When I arrived home Beth greeted me with a warm hug and lingering kiss, a welcome reception for this young, audacious traveler. Hardly out of the bone-chilling February air and into our kitchen, I gave the announcement: "We're moving to Asia!" Except for a few pithy stories in this chapter, I'll spare the reader all the details of our preparation, a process that absorbed two-and-a-half years of our lives and two additional scouting trips to Asia. Beth courageously followed me, with appropriate wifely cautions.

I met Wayne Crooke in Hong Kong on my second trip in April 1978. We had been introduced by a Zion Chapel elder and engaged a conversation about Asia via an exchange of letters. Wayne enthusiastically invited me to come to Hong

Kong and help him pioneer his crusade ministry in Thailand. Heady stuff for a young visionary! I took off work at Coachmen Industries for the second time, flew again around the belly of the earth, this time all by myself, and met Wayne at the Hong Kong International Airport. He was standing at the gate waving a big sign with the words "Welcome Doug Gehman!" scratched on white poster paper.

Wayne was a skinny man, ten years older than me, with thick jet-black hair and a bad case of Vitiligo, a skin condition that looks like sore, peeling sunburn. After a brief hello – Wayne wasn't one for long pauses – he grabbed my bags and led me through the crowded terminal to his old red car. We drove through Kowloon traffic while Wayne rambled about his vision, about Asia, about open-air meetings, and "dead-head" missionaries. The dead-head missionary reference, a curiosity at this juncture, was to become a tiresome mantra with Wayne. I sat beside him in the front seat, fighting jet lag. This man is intense, I thought. The skin condition added to the severity.

Wayne parked on the street and helped me drag my bags up three flights of stairs to the family's third floor apartment. Carolyn is the antithesis of her husband – genteel and composed – but no pushover I quickly learned. She was waiting for us in the small kitchen, snacks and drinks ready. Through the years Carolyn's quiet strength has been Wayne's saving grace. Wayne readily and appreciatively acknowledges the fact.

Their two girls, daughter Cheryl and niece Jodie, eleven and twelve years old, were in bed, or supposed to be, but curiosity about the arrival of new guests was keeping them up and awake. Another single man, Tom from North Carolina, arrived before me. After introductions, everyone retired for the night, and two days later we three men flew to Bangkok. Overall, except for the powerful cultural impact on me, the trip was an uneventful introductory foray to Thailand. We conducted a single forgettable crusade in Hua Hin on the coast south of Bangkok. Pastor Nippon graciously assisted us, with encouragement from his Swedish Pentecostal missionary sponsors. A constant flow from Wayne's lips about deadhead missionaries who "never leave the Capital and just sit in an office all day pushing papers around on their desks," apparently didn't apply to the Andersons. I wasn't a deadhead either I guess, because I was in Hua Hin preaching with Wayne. And he invited me back.

So, with an invitation to return, I made plans. In October I returned to Asia for a third time, this time with Beth and our one-year-old daughter Cori. Wayne met us again at the Hong Kong International Airport. Ray Jennings was in Hong Kong, Wayne told me. He came from India to spend a few months with his protégé. Wayne and Carolyn had served for a year on Ray's team, sometime in 1975 or 1976. We knew about Ray Jennings. Our church supported him. Our pastor read his letters – enthralling stories of preaching to multitudes – to the church. To now meet and travel with this living legend was an honor. Wayne's goal was to repeat in Thailand and Taiwan what he had experienced in India with Ray Jennings. He needed Ray's help to make it happen. We traveled and preached in Taiwan and Thailand for three months, but preached only to hundreds not thousands, a frustrating disappointment to Wayne Crooke. I figured Ray Jennings hadn't figured out how to transfer to Thailand and Taiwan the anointing he had for India.

On arrival in Hong Kong, Wayne booked us into in a creepy, no-star hotel in the heart of Kowloon. He later admitted the choice of hotels was a deliberate test of our resolve about missionary service. Wayne wanted to see how we survived a seedy experience. The tiny room on the tenth floor of an old high rise building in Kowloon was not much larger than the dingy double bed we were expected to sleep in. In the middle of the night we were awakened by a knock on the door. I sat up and sleepily leaned across Beth to open the door. The room was so small I could open the door without getting out of the bed.

"Don't you open that door!" Beth hissed. "It's the middle of the night!"

Oh, yeah. Right.

"Who is it?" I groggily asked, staring at the door and rubbing sleep from my eyes.

An old female voice replied in heavily Chinese-accented English, "I want to talk to you."

Beth shook her head. "Don't you dare open that door!" she hissed again. My foggy brain was still waking up.

"I just want to talk to you," came the plea again. Who is this woman and what does she want? Maybe the hotel is burning down!

"Please come back in the morning..." I said. If the high rise was on fire, Beth was going to need more evidence. After a few minutes, with Beth protesting and the voice pleading through the door, the knocking stopped. I lay back down, and drifted into fitful sleep. We never found out what the lady wanted, and the hotel didn't burn down. The next morning we rode the elevator to the street and there encountered four SWAT police, fully armed and decked in combat gear: black boots, black helmets, black flack jackets, and automatic weapons. Our little white family passed them in silence, dragging our luggage through the lobby while they jabbered on their radios.

Scolded by my wife about the dreadful accommodations, Wayne admitted to the devious plan a few days later. He apologetically endured Beth's light-hearted ribbing about the hotel room and midnight room service. We passed Wayne's test. At the end of three months, after we had preached in dismally attended open-air crusade meetings in south Taiwan and in Bangkok, as we prepared to fly home just before Christmas, Wayne invited us to return to Asia to work with him.

20 The Thoeng Event

Nine months later, in August of 1979, we packed up our belongings and flew to Taichung, Taiwan for a two-year commitment to work with Wayne. We settled into a tiny, two-bedroom row house in a long row of identical houses, several blocks away, and a couple of socio/economic rungs down, from the Crooke residence. I'm not complaining. We were young, new interns; they had been on the field for a decade. We had to prove our calling and commitment, to our church, to the Crookes, and to ourselves. I was just happy to BE in Asia. The poverty and the primitive domicile was not a problem. Basic safety and cleanliness were enough; content we were to live in utter simplicity. We couldn't afford a car, so I bought an old bicycle. I mounted a bamboo seat behind the handlebars for our two-year-old daughter. Beth, pregnant with Number Two, sat behind me on a padded seat over the rear wheel. When Jeremy arrived four months later, he rode along too, strapped to Beth's back or chest. That bicycle transported our family for two years to nearby stores, market, church and social activities.

The Crookes bought their first new vehicle in Taiwan, a Taiwan made diesel van. Quality workmanship was not a distinguishing feature. The vehicle started falling apart the day we brought it home. Besides the fact that it transported the Crooke family, AND US, all over Taiwan for two years – something for which I should perhaps be more grateful – two stories remain in my memory about this van. When we bought the vehicle, it was registered in the name of the sponsoring ministry under which Wayne's family had entered the country – the Finnish Pentecostal Mission. By law, and for registration to be completed, the van had to have the Mission's name on its sides. We drove the van from the registration office to a local sign company to get the name painted on the van. Wayne instructed the painter to wax the side of the van heavily and THEN paint on the signs. With an odd inquisitive look he complied, protesting that the paint wouldn't stick. Wayne insisted anyway, and waved his money in front of the man's face. Shaking his Chinese head, the man completed the job in bright red paint (a favorite among Orientals), took the money and we returned to the Vehicle Registration Office. As soon as we left, Wayne turned a corner, parked the van on the curb, and wiped off the signs. "We're not with the Finnish Pentecostal Mission," he said, "and I'm not putting their sign on my van. They just gave us a visa. This van will say *South East Asia Crusades*." The Finnish didn't mind.

The second memory involved the van's temperamental mechanics. On a trip to Taipei, the van engine shut down and left us sit on the highway. Nothing Wayne did could coax the diesel engine to re-start. After a few frustrated minutes a couple of Chinese men stopped and offered to take a look. Wayne spoke very little Chinese and these two spoke no English. They pulled the engine lid open – the engine is under the front passenger seat – and started fooling around. Diesel engines don't have spark plugs. The fuel is ignited in the cylinders by an infusion of oxygen and incredible pressure. The two men decided that the diesel engine wasn't getting fuel, so the best way to start the engine was to open the air intake and poor fuel in. Sounds dangerous but in fact the technique will work, if fuel starvation is the problem. They had no diesel fuel and had no container to put it in either. So, they went searching along the side of the highway and found a discarded plastic bag. Into this they syphoned diesel from the fuel tank. They started pouring the fuel into the air intake and instructed Wayne to crank the engine. The moment he turned the key, the high compression of the engine sucked the plastic bag and all its contents right out of the hands of the volunteer mechanics. It disappeared into the air intake manifold.

Wayne exploded. "THE PLASTIC BAG! THE PLASTIC BAG!!! IT WENT INTO THE ENGINE!!"

"It doesn't matter," one man said in Chinese, using hand gestures to support the lackadaisical response. "It'll go through and come out the back."

"WHAT ARE YOU TALKING ABOUT!" Wayne shouted in English. The men of course understood nothing but the emotional display. "GET OUT OF HERE!" Wayne more or less pushed the men out of his van and waved them off. They left without resistance. I'm pretty sure they knew what they had done. I don't remember how we finally got real help, or how the van was towed to a garage, but it happened before the sunset. When the repair shop tore open the engine, they found melted plastic bag on the cylinder head and wrapped around the valves. I think it cost Wayne $1000 to get the van right again.

Before we met them, Wayne and Carolyn had been tested and hardened in the fires of brutal missionary experience. In the late 1960s they lived on the Celebes islands in Indonesia, subsisting, according to Wayne, on "twenty-five dollars a month." Wayne perhaps under-stated their resources, but they *were* dirt poor. That reality inflicted indescribable hardship. They endured until tragedy struck. Their second child, an infant daughter less than one year old, succumbed to a tropical disease, probably Dengue Fever, because medical help was too far away. Broken and grieving, they buried their little girl in the Indonesian earth and went home to Virginia.

Tested by fire. On the route to every mountaintop, there are cruel valleys. Two years later the Crookes went to India to work with Ray Jennings. Wayne fell in love with Ray, and adopted him as his spiritual father. Ray's open-air evangelistic style, his overflowing faith, his heart-broken passion, his fervent prayer life, his determination and perseverance against all odds, and most of all the multitudes God gave him, were healing balm for Wayne Crooke. Ray lived what Wayne Crooke had until now only dreamed. Wayne resolved to do in South East Asia what he experienced in India. When we met Wayne a year later, he was flush with preaching to hundreds of thousands of people in India. Who could blame him? Missionary colleagues who had not seen India, who had not stood before such crowds, and had no connection to the energy of the masses and the palpable power of God in such places, gave him no encouragement. They were the deadheads that Wayne disparaged.

Wayne never was a man of diplomacy; he had no decorum to hide behind, and no refined way to express his frustration. "God is going to visit Thailand and we will preach to tens of thousands!" he boldly declared, "despite what these deadheads think!" The boasting and the edginess earned him scorn from some and inspiration from others. But Wayne cared for neither. He rejected the opinion that Asian people were gospel hardened idol worshippers. Prayer, patience, determination, and preaching with power would bring change to Thailand.

I had just gotten off the airplane from America, so what did I know? I had formed no opinion about deadhead missionaries or the determination of Wayne Crooke, this fountain of faith and vitriol. Wayne Crooke was an enigma, an intense missionary evangelist with splotchy skin. "People are hungry for God!" Wayne declared, "And we are going to bring the Gospel to them! Out in the villages! With signs, wonders and miracles!" Proving the deadheads wrong was not Wayne's primary agenda, but it helped. Scorn, if it doesn't kill you, can invigorate a vision. Wayne thrived on scorn. His favorite missionary was C.T. Studd, that British aristocrat who in the 1800s gave up a privileged life to become a missionary to China and Africa. Studd was the king of Christian contempt. His book, "The Chocolate Soldier," set the standard for sanctified scorn. Christians, like soldiers, are meant to be heroes, Studd declared. God's people are appointed to deny themselves comfort, luxury and safety, to courageously go and win battles against the devil. Studd had no patience for wimpy Christians who melted like chocolate in the heat of conflict. Wayne loved C.T. Studd. Reaching Thailand was Wayne's appointment, and he was going to do it no matter how many devils and deadheads stood in his way.

Wayne's background helped. The product of a broken home, and the hardening accomplishment of becoming an Army Ranger paratrooper, this Texas man was leather inside and out. Wayne was proud of his endurance in tough places and tough assignments, and enjoyed being tough on subordinates. Hence the Kowloon hotel test. We survived a two-year assignment under Wayne Crooke, loving the experiences his visionary leadership provided, while cringing at the rough edges of his personality. For a time, the leather taxed our friendship and respect, and I decided to lead differently, but we learned a lot from Wayne Crooke. His bold faith and stubborn determination was admirable, and, while the toughness was sometimes extreme, Wayne was one of the most generous and compassionate people we knew. He would go out of his way to serve or help people. He could be incredibly kind-hearted and gentle. In short, like many great leaders, Wayne Crooke was a paradox; a powerful man of faith and vision encased in rough human skin.

The scriptures declare, "Faith is the substance of things hoped for." This was our experience with Wayne Crooke. He had a dream, a vision, a hope to preach the Gospel to tens of thousands of Thai people. For three years he tenaciously prayed and trudged through a forest of disappointments, inferior equipment, insufficient funds, indifferent pastors and deadhead missionaries, and resistance from village leaders and Buddhist monks in both Taiwan and Thailand. He didn't quit. He wouldn't quit. He persevered through all of it, with our family tagging obediently along, and finally, in April 1981 in a little village called Thoeng, Wayne got his answer. God finally gave Wayne what he wanted.

I'll spare you, dear reader, the litany of that forest – we walked with Wayne through all of it - all over Thailand, traveling like a scruffy band of gypsies in a broken-down, patched-together, 1960s British-built Ford van. We lovingly – sometimes hatefully – called the white albatross "Lazarus" because of the regular need to raise it from the dead with replacement parts. Into Lazarus we packed people – our family, Wayne and sometimes his wife, several Filipino missionaries, and a Thai interpreter or two – plus luggage and equipment: boxes of florescent and quartz lights, wiring, tools, speakers and amplifiers. Much of the time the equipment and luggage traveled on the roof, because the van was packed with human cargo. A healthy vehicle would have struggled to carry the load. Poor Lazarus died over and over from age and sheer exhaustion.

One meeting in April 1981 changed everything for Wayne Crooke. What happened in Thoeng can be attributed to only two things. I need to emphasize this point. Every "move of God" has two components. One of course is God. The other is human, and this is where the story gets complicated. Thoeng happened not simply because God acted, although in our sincere desire to give Him credit, we tend to talk about such things in this singular way. But the fact is, Thoeng happened because of Wayne Crooke, his faith, his prayers, and his stubborn perseverance. Thoeng happened because Wayne Crooke wouldn't quit. He kept marching forward, he kept praying with determination, and he refused, scornfully refused, to believe any voice but God's! For three years in Thailand, and a dozen before that!

Ray Jennings taught Wayne how to pray. Ray and his team prayed two hours every day during crusade ministry. Two hours! We gathered in the morning to pray before breakfast, from 6:00 to 7:00, and then again before lunch. Ray prayed alone in his room, behind closed doors, throughout the day. One cannot live in such an environment of concentrated prayer and faith without experiencing the connection to God's power in evening meetings. People who don't pray cannot comprehend it. I still can't explain it. But it is real. On Wayne's team we prayed the same way, for three years. When the breakthrough arrived, it came unexpectedly to an unexpected little village. The ONLY thing that was different in Thoeng was its location. The village of Thoeng was in North Thailand, our first such foray into this region. Prior to Thoeng we had concentrated primarily on the Central and Eastern Provinces. Perhaps the people of North Thailand were more open than other areas of the nation. But, without the disciplines of Wayne Crooke – the patience, the prayers, and the stubborn determination to never quit – we would not have survived to arrive there.

When we arrived in Thoeng, Wayne dryly commented, "If I had known how small this place was I would never have agreed to a ten day meeting! Maybe two or three days, but not ten." To say our team accommodations were meager is a generosity. We moved into an old wooden schoolhouse, built five feet above the ground on stilts. The school had three large classrooms and nothing else. No electricity, no running water, no toilet facilities, only a simple wood structure. It was a barn on stilts. Our family moved into one classroom, Wayne into another, and the entire Thai and Philippine team moved into the third. We strung a wire from a neighboring house so each room had a single light bulb. We built a bamboo-walled bathroom outside. The "shower" was a fifty-five gallon drum of water for dipping baths. The toilet was a hole in the ground. At night our family – Beth and I and two children – lay on mats on the floor, fearing to turn off the light bulb because large rats crawled on the rafters above our heads.

The day before the meetings, like we had done a hundred times before, we built the platform, dug the holes, placed the poles, and rigged lights and sound around the platform. On the first night three hundred people came, a large crowd for my experience, especially in this remote village. But after three years of disappointments, we weren't expecting much. The second night a crowd of six hundred very energized people gathered. Surprise again. We preached the same messages, telling the same stories from the life of and ministry of Jesus. Typically I preached first, a ten-minute introductory message. This was the Ray Jennings's format, designed for two purposes: to warm up the crowd before the main message, and to give young men like me some experience in leading and preaching. I loved those ten-minute messages! I followed Wayne's example and developed my own style. We never spoke against other religions, we never got deeply theological, we just told stories about Jesus from the Gospels – blind Bartimaeus, the leper that was cleansed, the woman with an issue of blood, Nicodemus, the Calvary story, etc. – and we always declared that Jesus was alive, risen from the dead, and present in power to save and heal.

After the second night, the crowd started growing exponentially: 1000, 2000, 5000, 8000, 12000, 15000. I'm rounding the numbers here. On the ninth night over twenty thousand people gathered on that humble field under those pitiful florescent lights.

Why did this happen? I have no explanation. About mid-week, when crowds had grown to nearly ten thousand, people started coming early to claim space on the grass near the stage. Someone hired trucks to bring people to the field. Trucks rolled in one hot afternoon, packed with people, fifty or more souls in a load. We had no idea where they were coming from, but beginning at three o'clock in the afternoon, they came, unloaded their cargo, and left to pick up another load. The people – old ladies, children, families – sat quietly in the hot tropical sun, holding newspapers or umbrellas over their heads, waiting for the meetings to start.

By mid-week several hundred people had begun staying overnight on the school grounds. Some camped out on the field, others moved into the head-high space under the school. We could hear them below us, and if we put our eyes to the cracks between the floorboards, we could see them. Several old ladies tried to move into our room one night. They just walked in, carrying their bags. Our Thai team members shooed them out! We felt a little selfish, using an entire classroom for only four people, but enough was enough!

Our private toilet and shower space became public facilities. We ran out of water constantly and frequently found human excrement in the oddest places! The prickly experiences reminded me of the problems Jesus faced when He ministered to the multitudes. Multitudes! Pushing, shoving, climbing onto house roofs, sitting in the trees, backing him into a lake, pressing Him to teach them, sometimes for days! The crowds wearied Jesus and His disciples to the breaking point. They sometimes almost trampled Him under a thousand pairs of eager feet, so hungry they were to be near Him. Jesus and the disciples had to escape to the mountains for rest.

Thoeng made the Gospels come alive! The yearning of the multitudes! The problems of the multitudes! The sincere interest, the genuine hunger, and the exasperating human aspects of large crowds of people! Nothing in my life before prepared me for Thoeng. I'm sure it transformed the lives of many Thai people. It certainly changed my life. For Wayne Crooke, Thoeng was a reprieve, a vindication, but mostly it was simply an answer to earnest prayer. And, in the end, Thoeng threw open the floodgates in Thailand.

In the years after Thoeng, Wayne preached to large crusades regularly. All over the country, from north to south Wayne enjoyed a wave of God's visitation on Thailand; its impact lasted about four years. In that time he preached the Gospel to more people than anyone else in Thailand's history. For a brief season, the ministry of South East Asia Crusades shook this staunchly Buddhist nation. In the end, ironically, the success was the ministry's undoing. In 1985, the Thailand government, under pressure from Buddhist leaders, shut Wayne Crooke down and threatened to kick him out of the country. Wayne fought back bravely, and made a gracious case with the powers that be, but the battle was not winnable. Thailand was not ready to become a Christian nation. Defeated, and broken again – this time it was not the death of an infant daughter, but the rape of a dream – Wayne retreated to Si Ratcha, their home on the coast of Thailand's Gulf, for rest and prayer. For six months he licked his wounds, and then, not to be defeated, he determined to do SOME good in Thailand. He started reaching out to his neighbors and to the community. Wayne's team started a house church. It grew and within a few years the new church bought land and built a sanctuary, much of the money and material donated by wealthy Thai converts. The church became one of the largest churches outside of Bangkok, not big by American standards, only a few hundred, but it stood in my mind as a testimony to Wayne's resilience and faith.

Wayne Crooke died this past year. He was sixty-six years old. He had been a part of our lives for thirty years, and a lover of Asian people for over four decades. Wayne died of a massive heart attack, struck down after a morning walk near their home in Chiang Mai. This was not Wayne's first bout with heart problems. Quadruple bypass surgery saved his life once before, and became the catalyst for a spiritual renewal that focused him on a new land. While he recovered in a hospital in Japan, God called him to Burma.

The call re-ignited an old flame. God's voice to man has a way of doing that. After heart surgery, and while he recovered, Wayne and Carolyn visited us in Florida and Wayne told his story. He wept about the hurt of Thailand; he wept too for the new hope God was giving him, and of a passionate love for a new land. Wayne declared he would give the remaining years of his life to the people of Burma. A short time later the Crooke family moved to Chiang Mai. Wayne died on October 14, 2011, still living in Chiang Mai, near the Burmese border, still preparing to bring the Gospel to the people of Burma.

21 The India Team

After the Thoeng Event, in May 1981, we returned to the United States and headed to our family's homes in Indiana and Pennsylvania. Anticipating our arrival in Lancaster, Mother and Dad made plans for us to visit grandparents. Dad's folks had sold the old farm near Stevens while I was in college and moved into a red brick split-level house outside of Denver, Pennsylvania. Grandpa Eli met us as we pulled into the driveway. After handshakes and hugs, Beth and the kids went inside, and Dad and I lingered in the driveway with Grandpa. We hadn't seen each other for two years. Since college, Grandpa and I had experienced life like this, in short visits, honorary nods to a family patriarch, restricted in frequency by time and distance, six hundred miles from Goshen, ten thousand miles from Taiwan.

At this meeting, I was grown up – at least in my own estimation, all of twenty-four – now married with two children, and busy in international ministry, the Thoeng Event holding preponderance. Grandpa wasn't up to date on his grandson's personal history or global exploits. He would not have fully understood either, not from this isolated position in the heart of Amish country. In his memory, and from this paradigm, Dougie was still an intractable teenager.

"How do you justify that mustache?" Grandpa asked. We were standing in the driveway, still shaking hands. The women had gone inside the house, and family greetings were lingering in the air. Grandpa's brilliant blue eyes, set in a kindly face, pierced through me. He let go of my hand and waited for an answer.

"Geez, Grandpa, whatever happened to foreplay?" That's what I *wanted* to say, but wisely kept my mouth shut, too much respect for this sage, my progenitor. But, the question *was* abrupt, even for him. An awkward silence followed. I now realized Grandpa *had* been staring at me since we got out of the car – it was my mustache he was staring at – and could not hide the disapproval. Out it came.

My mustache! How do I justify it? Are you kidding me? Why do I need to JUSTIFY it? These words also remained behind closed lips, in silent space where adult wisdom trumps childish imprudence. I broke the uncomfortable silence and mumbled something like, "I.... uh, well, uh, I don't know, Grandpa." I really wanted to respect my grandfather, but he wasn't making it easy.

Dad saved the day. "I think the Mennonite aversion to mustaches goes back to the Lutheran persecutors in Switzerland. The Lutherans wore beards and big mustaches, and killed Anabaptists because of our opposition to the practice of infant baptism. Since then, most Mennonite and Amish men don't wear mustaches. And, Amish men grow beards but still shave off the mustache hair."

"Wow, Dad! Thanks for the reprieve! I didn't know that little piece of history. Did you make that up?" Again, thoughts not words. I breathed a sigh of relief, grateful for the intervention. An odd silence again loomed, but just for a moment. Grandpa looked at his son, then at the recalcitrant teenager. He shrugged and turned toward the door. "Let's go inside. Supper's probably ready."

We followed Grandpa into the house, which was indeed filled with the rich smells of Grandma cooking. Grandpa Eli was never mean-spirited. Even in this inquiry, he took my hand, gave it a manly shake and asked the question, looking at me with a meek, almost hurt expression. He exercised extreme patience compared to my effrontery, showing up at his Mennonite house with facial hair like so many ancient persecutors. I'm not sure Grandpa changed his opinion about my mustache – traditions do not die easily – but he let it go for the evening, and the family gathered around a bountiful table, preceded by a long Grandpa prayer that laid out the complete plan of salvation, including Jesus' sinless life, His substitutionary death on the cross, His resurrection after three days, ascension into heaven, and promised second coming. While he prayed, head bowed, eyes closed, hands folded on his lap, the grandchildren, and a few exasperated adults, squirmed in their chairs around the bountiful table. At the "Amen" we dove in and enjoyed the plentiful meal, completed with heaping dishes of ice cream from the freezer. Life has its compensations.

Traditions have always been a curiosity to me. Grandpa Gehman was a student of the Bible and lived his life by strict compliance to its tenets – both in spirit and letter. The Bible says nothing about mustaches, at least in no prohibitive sense. But Grandpa's worldview was shaped by more influences than a book, even The Book. A few unshaven Lutheran persecutors saw to that. The drowning of family members and friends in Switzerland's Aare River can have a cruel impact on one's sensitivities. Such experiences become harsh memories that go forward for generations, handed down as stories first, then as tradition. A few centuries later, an *un-persecuted* and uninformed grandson and a mustache, unwittingly throws a wrench into sacred gears... and upsets his grandfather.

We frequently visited Grandpa and Grandma Stoltzfus that year too. The most memorable event involved a dress Beth wore to dinner, made from blue jean material embedded with silvery sequins on front and back. "I don't know why anyone would wear a dress made from blue jeans," Grandma protested at the dinner table. "Blue jeans are for the barn."

"Doug liked it and bought it for me in Bangkok," Beth retorted, with a twinkle in her eye. Beth was familiar enough with Grandma's direct style, it being the little redhead's style too – I've been adjusting to it for most of our married life – so neither female was offended.

"Well, I don't like it," Grandma shot back, while she served a steaming plate of dinner. She turned and headed back to the kitchen.

"Well," Beth said, "I don't like your dress either." Grandma stopped in mid stride and for an icy moment the room went deathly silent. Then Grandma laughed and said, "I guess you wouldn't." And that was that. Everyone chuckled and returned to Grandma's bountiful table.

Through the remainder of the year we traveled throughout the east, south, and Midwest. We stopped in Goshen to spend Christmas with Beth's family and visit Zion Chapel, and then in January 1982 flew to Los Angeles. Dale was living in the San Fernando Valley and was studying at Dick Grove's School of Music. After a week on the west coast, which included a visit to The Church on the Way (where Dale played piano on the worship team), hang out time with his band friends in backyard cookouts, and a couple fun days at Knott's Berry Farm and Disneyland, we flew to New Delhi to join the Ray Jennings Team.

John Whalen sprang into our lives on the night we arrived. This ruddy, sandy-haired twenty-something single white male from Hawaii had also recently joined the Team. I introduce him here because he made an immediate impression – literally bouncing into the guesthouse parlor where we were gathering with our new teammates – and because in the years to come he would become an inseparable part of our lives.

John was white, a noteworthy detail only because he was from Hawaii. His European name notwithstanding, being from Hawaii, John's race cannot be assumed. Most of the one-and-a-half million residents of the Hawaiian Islands trace ethnic origins to South Pacific islands and Asian nations. Only about twenty percent are "haoles" (of the white race). Today, most of the people of the Hawaiian Islands are the children of immigrants. Ten percent derive their blood lineage from the indigenous Hawaii race, and only about eight thousand are pure Hawaiian. Two hundred years of inter-marriage has now created an infinite number of ethnic mixes. John was one hundred percent haole, born in Boston, raised in a career Navy family, and as Navy life frequently goes, the Whalen family started on the east coast, moved to San Diego, and eventually landed in Honolulu.

John's real dad died when he was very young, and his mother remarried a Navy man. She raised her boys – two from the first marriage, a third from the second – with an iron but loving fist of Christian discipline. The boys grew up following Jesus and living right. The strict boundaries, a maternal wall in John's youth, became internalized in adulthood. By the time he graduated from high school, John had committed his life to Jesus. He took Bible classes and became active in his home church. In 1982 the Honolulu-based Grace Bible Church sent John to join Randy Matsumoto on the Jennings Team in India. Randy, a Japanese American born and raised in Hawaii, was a couple of years older and had come to India two years earlier.

So John entered our lives in New Delhi. He bounced into the small missionary guesthouse lounge dressed in cutoff jeans, a ragged t-shirt and dirty tennis shoes. "What's going on!?" he announced. It wasn't really a question. He danced back and forth on his feet like his body had more energy than it could contain. His blue eyes darted around the room settling on us, the newest addition to the team. Exhausted and fighting the dull buzz of jet lag, we needed sleep not social interaction, but I was eager to meet our teammates and get plugged in. When John entered the room, Beth and I were fighting fatigue with black coffee and exchanging pleasantries with some of the team members. Carl and Barb Ropp, Ray's assistant team leaders, sat beside us. Other team members wandered in and out of the room, offering welcomes to the disheveled newcomers. John spied the large jar of Jiffy Peanut Butter on the coffee table, our American gift to the team.

"Peanut Butter! Get down! Cool!" This not yet introduced young man grabbed the jar and turned it over in his hands, examining the labels. "Did you bring this?" The question was directed into the air; John's eyes stayed fixed on the jar.

"Yes."

"All right! Is it, like, for Carl and Barb only?"

"No. It's for the team."

"Cool. Get down! Gonna be a feast tonight!" He put the jar back on the table and sat down in the circle, still fidgeting with youthful energy.

Peanut butter may seem like a lame gift, but the reader is advised that common American snack foods were not easily acquired in India in 1982. The western foods that could be found were attainable only at great cost after painstaking search in special stores catering to the international business and diplomatic communities. "Be Indian. Buy Indian" was a national slogan at the time – and for the most part it was proudly observed – so Indian businesses were not inclined to accommodate the palates of former colonists and their white friends. The reader probably remembers from high school history class, in the not too distant past, America nursed a similar attitude toward the British and one of their products. Our nation's preference for coffee is in part a derivative of the Revolutionary War and our now-famous dumping of another caffeinated drink into the Boston Harbor. British colonization of America ended in 1776; it took a little longer elsewhere. Great Britain ruled Hindustan for over three hundred years, a patronage that was terminated in 1948 when three hundred and fifty million Indians, inspired by Mohandas Gandhi, leveraged independence from the war-weary Empire. The popular uprising gave birth to the sovereign states of India and Pakistan. In an odd fluke of political planning, influenced by religious ideology – to give India's Muslims a home of their own – and demographics, Pakistan was created as a country in two places: West Pakistan and East Pakistan, land areas where most of the Muslims already lived. Years later, in 1971, East Pakistan became Bangladesh. But that's another story.

Before heading back to England, British-appointed cartographers divided Hindustan into pieces – called India and Pakistan. These map-makers were sequestered in windowless rooms for only a few months, drawing lines on maps, with little on-site verification, partitioning the entire sub-continent into Muslim and Hindu territories. By this official act they sealed the fates of millions of people. Millions of Hindus and Muslims who lived in the wrong territory for their religion migrated to their newly formed nations, moving families and belongings, often walking down the same roads in opposite directions hoping to find a place of refuge and freedom to worship Allah or Krishna. The two thus formed nations of India and Pakistan became independent states at zero hour on the fourteenth of August, 1947. This cataclysmic fact of history is documented in the book "Freedom at Midnight." It is a compelling read.

In the movie "Cocktail," Brian Flanagan, an upstart character (played by Tom Cruise) has an affair with an older woman. When the romp is over, she appeals to him, "Let's not let this end badly," to which Flanagan retorts, "It ALWAYS ends badly! If it wasn't bad it wouldn't end!" The quip could also apply to colonial rule. We threw British tea into the Boston Harbor, and then went to war with them, killing redcoats in America's first experiment with guerrilla warfare. Ultimately George Washington drove the British off our primitive soil, and a century later the new nation made peace with our former colonizers. Indian's angst with British colonists has followed a similar trajectory. Only the symbols are different.

Tea symbolized the America's revolt against its British colonizers; their place on the global clock is India's. The world's twenty-four time zones, a British invention, transformed seafaring, and made circumnavigation of the globe possible with pinpoint accuracy. Parallels establish north-south bearings. Meridians, running from pole to pole, divide the entire globe into twenty-four sections. Today, with few exceptions, the nations of the world set their time, on the hour, using one or more of these longitude meridians. No so India, Pakistan, Sri Lanka and a few other formerly colonized nations, who set their times on the *half* hour. There is no real reason for the half hour designation except to snub now independent noses at former British colonists. The adage, "The sun never sets on the British Empire" was true for a very long time. British hegemony was the pride of the English-speaking world. It did a lot of good! It advanced democracy and the rule of law. But, after 1948 some formerly colonized people came to view the British Empire as an unforgiveable and unforgettable scourge. To this day, India's national clock is set five hours *and thirty minutes* ahead of Greenwich Mean Time.

When we landed in New Delhi in January 1982 – twelve hours and *thirty minutes* ahead of Pacific Standard Time – we were carrying one of George Washington Carver's precious peanut creations. By this time we had lived in Asia long enough to appreciate one reality of overseas existence: food cravings. Before we left Los Angeles, we bought a super-sized jar of Jiffy Peanut Butter for our deprived teammates in India. It was a big hit. The PB disappeared within days.

John, a decidedly committed American, tolerated Indian food and obediently consumed what was set before him, but there was never any doubt about his preferences. When it came to drinks, "Dr. Pepper is LIFE!" he declared. LIFE could not be found in India, so John begrudgingly drank local alternatives, India's copy versions of Coca Cola incongruously named "Thumb's Up" and "Campa Cola."

Beth and I immediately connected with John and the other single guys on the team, the self-proclaimed "Brothers Incorporated." They weren't young enough to be our sons, but we took a peculiar parental interest in their well-being and friendship, and they responded to the new married couple and their two kids. The realities of team life threw the three young men together in a kind of forced companionship… for work, travel, and co-habitation. Randy and John knew each other from Hawaii so they had some common connections from the start, a fact that relegated Bill Katz, an army veteran and Bible School graduate from North Carolina, to odd man out. He accepted the minority status in the triage without complaint and endured constant chiding that he returned in kind. Christian convictions and missionary status restrained typical male meanness among this group of bachelors, but there is no place on earth where three young men who are forced to work and live together, will fully behave themselves and be nice to each other. Even the mellowing influences of marriage, children and middle age cannot cure male brutality.

"Get over here, Willistine, and help us!"

"My name is Bill! And, don't try to order me around!"

"Okay, Bill, with a *little* b."

"Knock it off!"

"I mean it Willis!"

And so it went.

"Wilma!" shouted like Fred Flintstone arriving home from work, was a favorite. Wilhelm was another.

Bill's braggadocio about army experiences and athletic victories (he was a long distance runner) encouraged the abuse: "You are such a JIVE WALLA, Willis!" This particular insult was a curious invention of The Brothers Incorporated. Jive of course means something close to "worthless bragging," and walla is a widely used Hindi word, meaning "skilled craftsman," like "Tin Walla" or "Leather Walla." So Bill was a Jive Walla. No matter how he tried, Bill could not dodge the broadsides, and his rebuffs never matched the duo. As a disseminator of insults and jive, John was Walla Master, the undisputed world champion off-the-cuff absurdity.

"ME!!! I'm so stinking tough its ridiculous!"

Randy was runner up.

One day, after a barrage of name distortions, Bill handed John the coup-de-gras:

"I'm not going to BE all of these names!"

247

Thirty years later we still talk about that one, and now it is recorded in this book. Today, the Brothers Incorporated live on both sides of the continent, John in Tucson, Randy in Los Angeles and Bill in North Carolina. Facebook facilitates regular connections... and ongoing jive. With everyone in middle age, the insults are few and the memories are rich. Perhaps we're all tired. Recently, John's wife (a blonde-haired, blue-eyed Swede) prepared a Punjabi meal for the family. John took a picture of the plate, uploaded it to Facebook, and started this banter, in Punjabi English and Hawaii Pigeon:

John: For you, Bhai Randy. Murgh Masala, home-made by my blonde Punjabi.

Randy: Punjabi! I always thought she was Rajastahni!

John: Good food coming, brother!

Bill Katz: Definitely!

Randy: My Mrs. been makin' some Indier food too. She made shappatis. It was much food putting, much full coming.

John: Wah, bradda! Afterward we can revive the 'Onion Club.'

Randy: It's still for Men Only right?

John: I suppose... Although, if da wahines can show dey got da kine, you know, den, no shame, ah?

Randy: Oh no, Bhai John! They mustn't know about the Onion Club! Let them think that it's like a vegetarian book club or something!

John: Yo, probably right. Noble traditions like the Onion Club betta lef no change.

Randy: Man, I really miss those dudes from the Onion Club.

John: No can fo'get da classics, braddah! Or should I say, "Bhai Ji"?

Randy: Where'd Willis go? Doesn't he remember the Onion Club? Maybe he eatin' bananas. He much like da banana. I tink of him when I eat tem.

Little has changed, even in middle age.

John's off-the-cuff style got him into trouble with Ray Jennings. Ray was the drill sergeant disciplinarian, founder and leader of the team and ministry. Who could blame him for the toughness? He had sacrificed everything to pioneer this ministry. He spent twenty years on the field, preached to millions, and buried his first-born son Phillip in Pakistan after a bridge climbing accident. He had little time for foolishness. But, poor John. This Boston-bred, California-conditioned, Hawaii-raised Navy brat could not turn off the wit. It leaked out of him like oil from a bad gasket. John was Adrian Cronauer, Robin William's radio announcer character in "Good Morning, Vietnam!" and Ray Jennings was Sargent Major Dickerson who disparaged his jokes. John's impulsive sanguinity grated against Ray's stern austerity. Months of working and living in close proximity to one another over thousands of road miles, dozens of open-air meetings, in scores of flea-bag hotel rooms, over a million marginally sanitary meals in dirty, poorly lit restaurants, there was no stopping the dissonance. John tried and Ray forgave. John learned to bite his tongue and keep his mouth shut. The two men – leader Ray and apprentice John – endured a two-year-long tenuous relationship. In the end, like a gracious Papa to a wayward son, Ray invited John to return for two more years and John accepted. But in 1984 Ray's wife Dorothy contracted cancer. Ray cancelled all crusade plans in India and stayed in Virginia. The team disbanded. When I got the news, I called John and invited him to join my team. Within a month he flew to Thailand.

I'm not making any judgments here about either man. Oil and water are necessary. The fact that they don't mix, that Ray's and John's personalities chafed, says nothing about either man's character. John loved the mission field, he loved preaching the gospel to the masses, and he honored and respected Ray as founder and leader. And Ray, the father of nine children and in our eyes the patron saint of India, was big enough to make allowances, even while he demanded that

John toe the line. Like all men, Ray and John were flawed, imperfect men who sold out to Jesus Christ and His global purpose. John was the newcomer. And Ray's story of faith and obedience is absolutely heroic, rivaling the best in missionary history.

22 Ray Jennings

Our family worked with Ray Jennings for only one year – 1982 – but the impact this man had on my life was utterly profound. His influence started many years before, when we lived in Goshen and Pastor Vic Hildebrand read his letters from India, written by hand and sent directly to Zion Chapel. The leadership and vision of Ray Jennings made The Thoeng Event possible for Wayne Crooke. Wayne Crooke himself would never dispute that fact. Ray's influence and impact happened to Wayne Crooke just like it happened to us, at an earlier time when Wayne's family spent a year in India with the Jennings' Crusade Team.

Ray was born and raised in the Pacific Northwest. When we came to know him through his letters, his family was living in Afghanistan. In the early 1970s Ray and Dorothy Jennings and their nine children – nine children! – packed their suitcases, left Hampton, Virginia and flew from Washington, DC to Germany. There they bought a Volkswagen van, loaded it with everything they owned in the world, and drove four thousand miles south and east across Europe, through Czechoslovakia, Austria, Hungary, Romania, Bulgaria, Turkey, Iran, and into the Asian sub-continent. After a month on the road, they arrived in Kabul, Afghanistan, where they rented a house and set up a home base. The Jennings family then lived in the heart of radical Islam for nine years until 1979 when the Russians invaded Afghanistan and forced them to leave. From their home base in Kabul Ray pursued his vision to preach the Gospel to India while wife Dorothy befriended the local Muslim and expatriate communities in Kabul and raised their children. To get to India, Ray drove east five hundred more miles through Pakistan, from the untamed western frontier town of Peshawar, through Islamabad, and then to Lahore on the eastern border to India. He made this trip over and over, spending months away from home. And, in time he preached the Gospel to millions.

"God, give me India!" Ray prayed and wept this prayer on his knees for hours, day after day, month after month, year after year.

When we joined the team in 1982, a decade after he started the ministry, he was still doing it: praying and preaching. That year we witnessed the most amazing demonstrations of spiritual power we have ever seen. Over and over we set up the team's simple equipment and stage in some dirty field in some unknown village in Utter Pradesh, Rajasthan or Punjab. With national workers we advertised throughout the area and then started preaching at night. A couple hundred people usually came the first night, a sparse crowd in a sea of grass. We told stories from the life of Jesus and then invited people to accept Him into their lives. We prayed for them, asking God to heal their sicknesses and diseases. And God, by some unquantifiable action, did what we asked. And the crowds rolled in. By the end of the week, the sea of grass had transformed into a sea of humanity.

"The living God, who made all things, is in this place tonight!" Ray would begin. "He loves you and has made a way for you to be saved! The God who made all things... the sun, the moon, the stars in the heavens... He created you with the breath of his mouth, and He cares about your life! He cares for your family! He cares for your soul! And, He has sent His son, Jesus Christ, to make a way for you to know Him and be healed." Ray was just getting warmed up. He would go from this introduction, emphasizing the power and presence of the living God, to stories from the life of Christ. After each story he would call the people to have the same faith in Jesus. "Like Blind Bartimaeus, you must call on the name of Jesus! God's word promises that 'Whosoever will call on the name of the Lord will be saved!' He will hear you when you call on Him!"

India has thousands of villages. In twenty-eight states and eleven union territories, seventy five percent of India's one billion souls – seven hundred and fifty million people – live in villages in quiet impoverished anonymity. Ray visited hundreds of these villages over the years. In January 1982, our family joined the team and visited the village of Budaun in Utter Pradesh. Three thousand five hundred people came the first night of the Budaun Crusade. This was a large crowd in my experience, even compared to The Thoeng Event. Only four days later, twenty-eight thousand people gathered to hear the Gospel. At the call for prayer the crowd mobbed the stage. They were not angry. Their only emotion was eagerness to get close to Jesus, or perhaps His messengers. The people – men, women and children – surrounded the stage, squashing themselves against all sides of the platform. Our position above them on a head-high, twenty-by-twenty wood-plank platform hardly protected us from the onslaught. The platform groaned and swayed under the human pressure. We, the team – including me and Beth and our two little children – stood in the middle of the stage and hung on to each other, fearing the whole thing might collapse.

Local police shut down the meeting on the fifth night because a group of radical Hindus threatened reprisals. Hoping to avoid civil unrest, the police did what peacekeepers do: they took the path of least resistance, revoked our permits and asked us to leave the area. We packed up the field the next morning and drove to the city of Bareilly two hours way. The scene repeated in Bareilly. Two thousand gathered on the first night; five nights later crowds grew to over fifty-five thousand. And again, the police shut us down, after radical Hindus made threats. This time the CID – the Central

Intelligence Division is India's equivalent of the American FBI – visited us, asking questions and taking names and passport numbers. We packed up and headed north to Amritsar in Punjab State.

In Amritsar, while we prepared the next meeting, we received a letter from the Pastor of the Bareilly Methodist Church. He thanked us for coming to his city and shared a story: A man with leprosy came to the field the day after we left, he wrote, but the stage and lights were gone. Nothing remained but a muddy spot on the ground where the platform had been. Disappointed, the leper took a scoop of mud into his hands, then "called on the God of the Christians." He was instantly healed, the pastor wrote. Of course we never met the leper, and couldn't verify the story.

When we joined the Jennings team in 1982 big crowds had become a common occurrence. But his ministry had not begun that way. He had started twelve years earlier traveling and preaching in churches, trying to satiate a deep passion to proclaim the Gospel to unsaved masses. He plodded, driven by a raw vision to reach India's millions, preaching in every pulpit he could. But church preaching was restrictive. Non-Christians don't come to church services. The Hindus and Muslims he wanted to reach would never darken the door of a Christian church. Ray got frustrated. He hadn't come to India to preach to Christians! He realized that if he stayed inside the church he could never reach the multitudes. Ray prayed. He read the Gospels over and over. Jesus of the Bible was a Man on the street, a Man of the people, especially the simple, country folk. Jesus spent most of his time outside the big cities, in the villages and market places and along the shores of Galilee. The common people, multitudes of them, loved him. He taught them, He fed them (even by miracles of food multiplication), He healed their sick, and consistently, even through the weariness of the work, had compassion on them. Everything Jesus did during three years of public ministry, even the more personal work with His twelve disciples, happened against a backdrop of crowds of people.

So Ray read the Gospels and prayed, and one day God spoke to him, in a "still small voice," not unlike the experience of Elijah the prophet (I Kings 19:11-13). God whispered these eight little words that forever changed the direction of his ministry and set him on a path to preach to millions of people: "Go to the open fields, like I did."

So inspired, Ray and his son Phillip bought microphones, an amplifier and large speakers. They bought florescent lights, a roll of wire, and wooden poles to hang them on. They found a field – the location has been long forgotten – and Phillip dug holes and planted the poles in rows into the ground. He strung wires and hung lights. They built a stage and connected the loudspeakers and amplifier. They asked a church in the vicinity to help them spread the word, and invite everyone to attend a "Free Healing Meeting." The invitations said nothing about Christianity, Ray didn't want to stigmatize the meeting with a religious affiliation before he had a chance to tell the people about Jesus. Ray got on his knees and prayed with tears – prayer and weeping had become a norm for Ray Jennings – asking God to give him India.

In conference meetings in America, Ray sometimes chided leaders for their "Bunny Rabbit Prayers," those selfish little prayers about personal concerns and people we know. God will answer Bunny Rabbit Prayers, Ray said, because He cares about all of those things too. But, Ray said, "God is looking for someone to ask Him for NATIONS! 'Ask of me,'" the Bible says, "'and I will give you the NATIONS for your inheritance; the uttermost parts of the earth for your possession!'" This was Ray's message, his passion. He challenged God's people to pray, really pray, to get God's heart for the nations, and ask Him for something bigger than ourselves. When we joined the team in 1982, Ray had been employing this simple pattern for over a decade, and over and over again God had powerfully answered.

The city of Amritsar, in Punjab State, is the Sikh capitol of the world. What Mecca is for Muslims and Jerusalem is for

Jews, Amritsar is the Sikhs' sacred city. In April 1982 we conducted a two-week meeting in Amritsar. The Sikh's welcomed us. The police did *not* intervene. We preached every night for two weeks. Crowds started small in Amritsar, only three hundred people on the first night, a small crowd in a sea of grass. But each night more people came. The crowd grew rapidly, sometimes doubling, then tripling and finally exploding exponentially. On the fourteenth night, over one hundred thousand people gathered on the soccer field in the center of the city.

It is a profound experience, watching the people roll in hour upon hour to a meeting like this. One can only stand on the sidelines watching a miracle unfold. Human effort alone cannot make this happen. If there ever was a move of God, these gatherings are it: people coming, as led by the Holy Spirit, through the catalytic mechanism of a simple community grapevine. Human personality, human leadership, effort and ego, are not enough. Human influences are wholly secondary when God starts doing what He does.

Watching crowds roll into a field is profound; preaching to them about God's love, His Son, and the salvation He freely offers, is beyond description. Ray allowed us, the young guys on the team, to preach for ten minutes before he brought the main message. I preached several times in Amritsar, once near the end of the two weeks when crowds had overflowed the boundaries of that soccer field. As far as the eye could see, out into the darkness, beyond the reach of our lights, the people stood and listened. My wife taught the "children's meetings" before the main service. On the final nights she sometimes stood before sixty thousand people, speaking to hundreds of children who found their way to the front – a tightly packed crowd of children against the backdrop of tens of thousands – telling the stories of Jesus with flannel graph.

Ray cared nothing for the fame he could have had, and would not allow any self-promotion – no pictures, no interviews, no cameras. He didn't care about documenting the meetings, and prohibited everyone from taking pictures even for personal use. Ray told his stories to supporters and prayer partners by dictating simple letters, hand-written on blue aerogrammes by his loyal assistants, Jacob and Miriam, an Indian couple who traveled with the Team. Those blue aerogrammes are the only documented history Ray ever created, words written in longhand on a blue sheet of paper and then folded by his hand. Zion Chapel received those blue aerogrammes, and our Pastor read them to the church on Sunday mornings.

Young people today know nothing about blue aerogrammes. They were the standard for cheap international communication for decades, and only became obsolete after the advent of email and the Internet. Ray's aerogrammes had a rare and precious value. We knew they originated in a village in India, had traveled around the belly of the earth, and arrived directly to our mailbox, from the hand of the author to the recipient. That intimacy is unknown in today's digital culture.

In his own words Ray described the open-air meetings: "I like to walk to the field from our hotel. I go early to beat the crowds, and then find a place on the sidelines under the shade of a tree, near an entrance. I want to watch the people arrive. They start coming at three o'clock sometimes, and by five they are pouring in, passing me as I stand there, not aware that I am the visiting white man preacher. They don't care about me. They only care about getting to the field to hear the Gospel and receive prayers." Ray loved the anonymity, and the fact that Jesus was more important to the people than anyone else. He described the crowds as a "sea of humanity" that stretched as far as the eye could see. His letters expressed deep gratitude for his friends and partners who prayed for him and supported the ministry with financial gifts. Ray always addressed the aerogrammes personally, "Dear Pastor Vic and the members of Zion Chapel..." and his letters always closed with: "Your brother who loves you very much in the bonds of Calvary for the millions of Asia, Ray Jennings." For me, the letters were mesmerizing. These compelling stories started on blue aerogrammes read to the church in Goshen, Indiana. In 1982 they became our living color reality in Budaun, Bareilly and Amritsar. Through them God burned into us a passion for millions without Christ.

In 1983, President Indira Gandhi asked Ray to come to New Delhi to conduct a crusade and to meet her in her home. Our friends on the team, including Randy Matsumoto, met President Gandhi. Randy, who now lives in Southern California with his family, proudly displays on the wall of his home a commemorative photograph of that meeting. In the picture Ray Jennings, bald and overweight (he fought a battle with obesity for years), stands with his team beside the leader of the second most-populous nation on earth. A year later, in October 1984, President Gandhi was assassinated by her Sikh bodyguards, shot to death as she walked in the garden of that same home, a conspirators' final solution to a cultural grievance. Earlier that year armed Sikh separatists, fleeing authorities, took refuge in Amritsar's Golden Temple. After a lengthy standoff, Army Rangers raided the Temple and killed the separatists. The action, while legal and necessary, outraged the Sikh community, who could not forgive President Gandhi for the desecration. Five months later, Indira Gandhi paid for the insult with her life.

1982 was one of the hardest years of our lives. Beth and I happily served under one of the most visionary and courageous leaders the world has *never* (no typo here) known. Underfunded, incredibly idealistic and full of vision, we dragged our two children, ages two and four, all over India and Pakistan, through dangers, dirt and dysentery, with guts and glory, and no home of our own for the entire year. Looking back, we were crazy. Our kids got lice, they suffered heat rash and we all endured borderline heat exhaustion and sunstroke. During Ramadan the summer of 1982, temperatures in Lahore, Pakistan hovered above one hundred fifteen degrees for a month. Candles melted into pools on the kitchen table. There was no relief from the heat, day or night.

We encountered numerous dangers too, including a violent intrusion into our rented house, but we survived them all, and saw God! Looking back I would not trade a day of it for all the tea in China. Cushy convenience and security has its benefits, and I'm frankly glad for it in mid-life, but there is no substitute for sacrificial experiences on the edge, especially when the work one is doing is rich with purpose. Too many Americans know only narcissistic existence, stimulated and entertained to utter numbness, and have never experienced this kind of life. Our wealth has given us the stuff of dreams, but robbed us of meaning. It is a shame how we have squandered our affluence.

23 Anabaptist Prejudice

With few exceptions, the Jennings Team was comprised of military veterans who had served from bases like Virginia Beach, Norfolk, Fayetteville or Raleigh. John's family hailed from San Diego and Honolulu. Into this military mix entered a Mennonite Pacifist from Lancaster County, Pennsylvania. Wayne Crooke was my first close encounter with "gun-ho" exuberance, which at the time I discounted as yet another odd feature of a quirky personality. Participation on an entire team of gun-ho veterans, however, was impossible to ignore. The dichotomy between my pacifistic ideology and their militancy thrust me into a theological crisis.

The United States military machine is not unfamiliar with Anabaptist pacifism. It established an official "Conscientious Objector" exemption as far back as the Civil War. The designation was created to exempt from bearing arms a broad swath of pacifistic religious and philosophical persuasions including members of the Anabaptist community. In the Second World War conscientious objectors were required to serve in the Civilian Public Service. Nearly twelve thousand men, including my father, chose this alternative. For two years my father served at a military hospital in the Mennonite's "1-W" branch, changing bedpans and assisting the medical staff.

261

The military vets on the Jennings Team roused many issues of my faith and Mennonite conditioning. For the first time in my life I realized how biased I was toward a particular theological and cultural orientation. Prior to Wayne Crooke and the Jennings Team I was exposed to other theologies and cultures, including the armed-services-as-duty paradigm, but nothing had yet challenged the engrained prejudice. The Team provided the challenge.

"Nuke them all! Let God sort them out!" Bill liked to quip whenever headlines and international events provoked him. It was grating pomposity to my non-violent ears. I knew he was just venting, but I also knew Bill would without hesitation take up arms and go to war against a declared enemy. I, by contrast, would *not*. I came to realize, for all the good qualities of Anabaptist pacifism, I was unprepared to resolve conflict, especially the kind that involved physical threat. Not so my military veteran friends. If there was a personal threat, they knew exactly what to do. Their Christian faith undoubtedly tempered behavior and controlled emotions, but there was no ambiguity about what action to take if circumstances required response. I was oddly conflicted, uncertain about yet attracted to the opposing view.

I went on a quest for answers and found a book entitled "War: Four Christian Views." Edited by Robert G. Clouse, the book is a symposium on war by four authors – Hermon A. Hoyt, Myron S. Ausgburger, Arthur E. Holmes, and Harold O.J. Brown – who present their cases from different Christian positions about war.

- Hermon A. Hoyt takes the non-resistant position, meaning a Christian can participate in the military machine, but should not take up arms and kill directly.
- Myron S. Augsburger, the Mennonite, is the pure pacifist: no involvement in a killing machine.
- Arthur E. Holmes presents the classic doctrine of the "just" or "defensive" war: if we are being attacked, Christians have a God-given responsibility to defend themselves and their loved ones.

- And, finally, Harold O.J. Brown makes a case for the "crusade," where Christians hunt down and eradicate evil from the earth.

After each case is made, the other authors comment and critique their colleague. The book is a stimulating read. It impacted me deeply and shed helpful light on my prejudices. Among my team friends, and the authors of "War," I was in the company of good people. That we differed on the subject of the killing of other humans – because, let's face it, that is precisely what war is – made the issue all the more compelling. In the end I concluded that while I may never wholly abandon the faith of my fathers, I could value the perspectives of others on this important subject. So today, my oldest son, having grown up in the Gehman house and come of age in a Navy town, is an attorney Captain in the Air Force JAG. So, our Anabaptist roots are spreading out a little.

In the fall of 1982 Pastor Sam Webb arrived in India from another military town, Honolulu, to join the team for a week. This tall Texan moved from Houston to Honolulu in the early sixties with his Oregon-born wife Nancy, a vivacious life-loving blonde. When we met them, Sam and Nancy had called the Hawaiian Islands home for twenty years. They lived in Guam in the 1970s, sent from the church in Honolulu to plant Guam Bible Church, and returned to Oahu in 1979 to become Senior Pastor of Grace Bible Church in Honolulu. In that role Sam came to India to visit the church's missionaries: Randy Matsumoto and John Whalen.

Sam adjusted to our paltry team existence without complaint. Calling our life *paltry* was a kindness. We were living in squalor when Sam arrived – not only because most of us were under-funded, but also because the villages simply had nothing better to offer. "When in Rome" is a cruel cliché for travelers to third-world countries. We rented a decrepit house and outfitted it with decrepit furniture, enough to survive for a few weeks, pretty much a big camping experience. We slept on mats on the floor, cooked our meals on a propane stove, bathed from a bucket, and lighted the house at night with candles, or, on the rare occasions when the electricity was available, with a single dim bulb in each room.

Sam didn't complain, unlike some pastors who can be tiresome prima donnas. Sam didn't seem to notice the meagerness of our lives. Even his towering height, so out of place in India, didn't distract from the contentment. That he stood head and shoulders above most of the team members – like I said, a tall Texan – gave him an air of gentle authority. The height was a benefit in Asia. One could always find Sam in a crowd; his head sort of rose above the milieu. He quickly earned my respect in India's simple surroundings. A million other such places we visited together in later years continued this legacy. Sam always maintained a distinguished grace: His wavy hair was always in place, his deep bass voice always resonated diminutive authority, he never complained, and he always had an insightful word when it was needed. Sam taught our daily team devotionals that week. We sat in a circle, some on chairs, others on the floor, on cushions or pillows, or the edge of a bed. The tepid desert air – this was Uttar Pradesh in August – permeated the house, even at eight o'clock in the morning. Wiping sweat and turning Bible pages, we listened while Sam shared from God's Word.

Randy Matsumoto was one of the team's designated drivers, assigned to drive the Mercedes passenger van. On one outing, Sam sat in the front with Randy. One has to live in Asia to fully appreciate the forthcoming exchange between Randy and his pastor. Randy was driving "Indian style," an aggressive-defensive mix of fast, slow, swerve and horn. It is not for the faint of heart, and is the only way to make progress down the road. Traffic flows like water toward the low point. One must get into the flow and stay with it or risk being run over by a larger vehicle. The danger comes in both directions. Trucks, buses, cars, and rickshaws aggressively fill vacant spots in the flow. Pedestrians, bicycles, push-carts, and animals, especially India's sacred cows – they are all sacred, a peculiarity of Hinduism, and they are everywhere – must also be avoided. Killing a cow, even by accident, is serious business. Randy was driving in a careful, bold style, flowing and swerving and honking and yelling out the window. Sam made a comment about Randy's driving, and Randy retorted, "Pastor, this is India." *That* didn't go over very well. But, in fact it was India.

Sam invited our family to visit Hawaii on our return to the United States in December. We made the changes in our itinerary and a few months later landed in Honolulu. The two weeks in Oahu with Sam and Nancy Webb and the Grace Bible Church network began a love affair with the Islands and a deep family bond with the Webb family, a friendship that has shaped our lives for thirty years.

INTERVAL

Mother went to the shore this weekend with her friends. These four women – Pearl, Anna, Dorothy and my mother – have been making the trip every year for decades. They are seventy years old and more now, four septuagenarian Mennonite blue hairs out for a weekend of good clean fun at the beach. None of the women drink, smoke or indulge in other such vices. They find their distraction in being together. Pearl the party girl, a self-appointed sanguine role she has successfully executed since this group of females met sixty-five years ago, has the same energy she possessed when four little blonde and brunette country girls with braided hair, in long skirts and white stockings, met on their family's farms.

Their friendships have survived through adolescent adventures, teenage dating and boys (when it was allowed, and sometimes when it was not), and then marriage, children, grandchildren and now great grandchildren. Pearl was Mother's maid of honor, and Anna and Dorothy were her bridesmaids, and so forth. Life and friendship continued when children arrived. I grew up knowing Pearl, Anna and Dorothy... and their families. None of these women or their husbands are related by blood to the Gehman family, not in any known past. The common bond is the Mennonite Church and Lancaster County farm culture.

A handful of years ago, Mother called and told me about another such girl-trip to Ocean City. "We all went to the shore" – she has called Ocean City "the shore" for as long as I can remember – "for three days last week," she started. "We came home Thursday."

"How was it?" I asked, trying to sound interested, but frankly I could not image how a trip to the beach with four old women could be interesting to anyone beside themselves.

"I got sunburned!" She seemed a little annoyed by the fact.

"That's what people do at the beach, Mother," I said. "They get sunburned." This was going to be a long phone call.

"No, no. We never get sunburned. We don't go out in the sun."

"So why then do you bother going to Ocean City?" I really didn't know this detail about their beach adventures.

"Oh, we just hang around in our hotel rooms and go shopping on the boardwalk. If it's daytime, we wear our hats. Besides, Anna doesn't like the sand. I don't like it much either. It gets all over you."

"So, how did you get sunburned?"

"Well, we decided to go swimming in the ocean. It was Pearl's idea. You know how she is."

"Oh, yeah, always the adventurer." I began picturing this little escapade in my head.

"So we get into our bathing suits and traipse down to the water. It's June but the water is COLD. Anna and I didn't want to go in, but Pearl insisted. 'We've come this far,' she said. So, we wade in up to our waist. The waves were rolling, not real big, but enough that we had to jump when they went by to keep from getting our hair wet."

"What was Dorothy doing?"

"Oh, she followed us, she always follows us. She's the least fussy one."

"Why didn't you just dive into the waves?" I joked.

"That would've been a sight, four old Mennonite women playing in the ocean. We were self-conscious as it is, just bouncing in the waves like a bunch of whales. At least me and Pearl. Anna and Dorothy have kept their weight down." I was imagining the scene. Even in the twilight years, women think about their figures.

"It was a beautiful day, and we're all standing around in waist-deep water with the waves coming in. Pearl is trying to keep her hair dry, because we were going out for dinner at a fancy restaurant later. She didn't have a hair cap on, so she's trying to keep her head out of the water, but the waves are knocking us around, and she keeps telling jokes, and then she laughs at her own jokes and gets a mouth full of water. You know Pearl."

Yes, I know Pearl. Mother is painting a pretty good verbal picture of the scene.

"Well, we're all laughing, mostly at her. The jokes really weren't that funny. She just gets tickled at herself, and then she starts giggling and we laugh at her. We must have been a sight! A bunch of old women acting like teenagers. Anyway, Pearl told a Little Suzie joke and we all laughed so hard that the next wave rolled right over us. Pearl went completely under!"

"So, she got her hair wet?" I asked.

"Oh yes! We all did. Pearl came up gagging and coughing and said, 'Well, there goes the hair!' She also said she peed in her pants but no one would know because it was in the ocean. That made her start giggling again and she almost went under again."

"Sounds like you were having a good time, Mother."

"You know Pearl's Little Suzie jokes?" Mother went on, "They're kind of dumb. But Pearl laughs so hard at her own jokes we all just get to giggling too."

"Yeah, I understand, Mother." I smiled on the other end of the line. Memories of Pearl's jokes and always-jovial presence wafted through my sub-conscious. Everybody needs at least one Pearl in his life. "So, what was the joke?"

"Well, Little Suzie couldn't sit still in Sunday School. She just squirmed and squirmed in her seat, and was making the Sunday School teacher so mad. Finally, he said, 'Susie, why can't you sit still? Do you have ants in your pants?' But Susie just laughed and laughed because she knew he had a *fly* in his! Pearl got the mouth full of salt water after that one."

All the women in this little group of friends, including Mother and Pearl, married young, in their early twenties. Pearl's husband Mel left the family farm and began working at a lumber company. Eventually he became a partner in the business. They did very well financially, but, as Mother pointed out to me once, "They never let it go to their heads," which meant they were having too much fun sharing life with friends and family to be uppity.

A few years ago Pearl bought an old lady wig from a party costume store. She dressed up like a homeless woman with clothes acquired at a second-hand shop in Bird-in-Hand. This was typical of Pearl, planning her fun far in advance! One afternoon she put the wig on, powdered it with white talcum, donned an oversized hat, fixed old glasses onto her face, and splotched her cheeks and lips with makeup, old lady style. She exited through the back door of her house and walked around to the front and rang the bell. Mel answered the door and was greeted by a bent-over old woman.

"Can I help you?" he asked.

"I want some money," the old lady mumbled. Pearl kept her head down, and had to work hard to control her voice and not burst out laughing.

"What?" he asked again.

I want some money." She repeated.

"Just wait here and I'll go see what I can do," Mel said sternly. He left the door partially open to keep an eye on the strange woman, wondering where exactly the old bird had come from. They lived in the country, far from town! Pearl followed him into the house; Mel turned and scolded her. "I told you to wait at the door! Please go back and wait outside." Unable to control the giggles, Pearl pulled off the wig. She probably peed her pants too. She repeated the trick at all their neighbors' homes, and on her friends, including Mother.

When our family was home from Asia one year, everybody – even Dale was in from California – drove to the Lapp's home in southern Lancaster County for dinner. Afterwards everyone sat around in the living room, exchanging jokes and stories, mostly about pranks we had played on friends and family members. Pearl, a master ice breaker, started with a selection of corny jokes and funny stories about family escapades. One story followed another, each teller trying to outdo the previous tale. Finally, Dale jumped in. "Well, I have one that beats them all," he said.

"A couple years ago," Dale began, "when I was still living at home over on Roseville Road, I came home from work and went into the kitchen. Mother had prepared dinner. I got home late, so she left it on the counter. I fixed a plate of potatoes, roast beef, and corn on the cob, heated it in the microwave, put butter and salt on the corn and then went outside to the back patio picnic table to eat it. I finished the potatoes and the steak, but was too full to eat the corn. Bunky (the family Labrador Retriever) was lying under the table, so I let him lick the butter and salt off the corn on the cob. Then the phone rang in the house, so I put the cob back on my paper plate and went inside to answer. While I was inside talking on the phone and looking out the window, Mother comes around the side of the house. She sits down at the picnic table, and begins to pet Bunky. Then she picks up the corn on the cob. I thought she was going to give it back to Bunky, but she starts eating it!"

At this point Mother puts her hand to her mouth, her eyes look like big, round saucers. "Oh, no!" she gasps.

Dale continues the story while the group guffaws hysterically. "I'm standing at the window, somebody is talking into my ear on the phone, and I'm going... 'Uh, uh... No! No!' while Mother chomps into that cob! There's no way to stop her! She's just going at it. So I gave up and watched her eat that whole cob of corn. 'Oh well, she'll never know,' I thought."

"No, you didn't!" Mother cried, clasping her mouth. "That's awful!!"

"You're right, Mother! I didn't. You did! You ate the whole thing and laid the finished cob back on that plate and then brought it into the kitchen!"

Mast and Anna still live and work their farm, but the other families have retired and downsized. Dorothy's family turned their family farm into a golf course, and run the new business with their sons. Pearl is still "up to her old tricks," Mom reported in a phone call recently.

"Pearl and Mel went on a two-week motorcycle trip with four other couples their age. All are over seventy years old! They're in Atlanta today. Sunday at Charles Stanley's Church. Monday they'll drive to South Carolina to hear the Lewis' family sing. Pearl knits on the back of the motorcycle while Mel drives. She stuffs the yarn in her blouse. The last trip the ball of yarn flew out, and down the road it went. People in passing cars were pointing at them. Pearl hurriedly wound it back up, she said. She also reads and sleeps while Mel drives! One time they stopped for a bathroom break, and before Pearl could get her helmet on and climb back onto the bike, Mel took off without her! He was five miles down the road before he realized Pearl was missing – and that only because one of the other cyclists pointed to the empty back seat. He went back to pick her up. She was still standing there in the parking lot!

"He'll never hear the end of it!" Mother exclaimed. "She'll never let him live it down! Anna and I think they're both crazy. We'd rather stay home than sit in the hot sun on a motorcycle for hours on end. They even ride in the rain!"

24 Psalms Twenty-three

In December 1982, after a year of vagabond existence in India, we continued a vagabond existence for nine more months, traveling throughout the United States. In August 1983 we finally arrived in Los Angeles at the ragged end of thirty consecutive months of inter-continental drifting that had started when we left Taiwan. When we finally drove through the Mojave Desert past Cajon Pass and into Los Angeles, our quintessential family had been living in hotel rooms and sharing space with family and friends for nearly two-and-a-half years.

The planned launch from the west coast back to Asia was to begin two MORE similar years in a second India assignment with Ray Jennings. Somewhere between the Grand Canyon and Las Vegas, however, Beth melted down, and when we arrived in Los Angeles it was all over. I wrote to Ray Jennings saying we were not returning to India. While we waited for a reply, I learned that Ray wasn't returning to India either; his wife Dorothy was losing her battle with cancer. Within a year the team disbanded.

After spending a week with Dale in Van Nuys, we climbed aboard a Greyhound bus to San Francisco and caught a flight to Malaysia. Thirty-five hours later, friends met us at the Kuala Lumpur International Airport and helped our weary little band settle into another forgettable hotel. Preoccupied with vision, I still didn't register my wife's deteriorating emotional condition. The kids were doing fine thanks to our ability to maintain an appearance of normalcy in their presence. Children have incredible resilience. As long as Mom and Dad are standing up straight, as long as smiles and kind words are coming out of their faces, and food is appearing at regular intervals, children will live happily in a cardboard box. Beth had enthusiastically co-led our family for thirty months of hard travel. Upon arrival in Kuala Lumpur she could no longer smile; she could barely stand up. Beth loved our gypsy existence... until she didn't anymore. Her emotional tank suddenly ran dry and that was that.

"Get me a house NOW!!" was the only way she could convey the exhaustion.

Those five words – I don't remember anything else in the conversation – are seared on my psyche, and are now written here for the permanent record, a reminder to the male gender about our proclivity toward spousal neglect. Appropriately redirected, I called Wayne Crooke. They were living in Penang. Wayne, always ready to serve, offered to help us find a home, a lifeline for a drowning family! I jumped on an airplane and flew to Penang four hundred miles to the north. Wayne and Carolyn met me at the airport and within a few hours we found a fully furnished cottage in Tanjung Bungah, nestled beautifully on a hill overlooking the Indian Ocean. I flew back to Kuala Lumpur the next day, loaded the family into an air conditioned transit bus – we were too low on cash for airfare – for an eight-hour ride north to Butterworth.

The city of Butterworth is located on the western shoreline of Peninsular Malaysia, directly across from the island of Penang. At that time, a fleet of monster-sized vehicle ferries connected the island's principal city of George Town and the mainland. Today a bridge has replaced the ferry system, but in 1983 the ferries carried cars, trucks, buses and people between Butterworth and George Town every hour.

We rode the bus to Butterworth intending to taxi four people and seven over-sized bags onto a ferry and then to our new home. About an hour outside Butterworth, with daytime slipping into twilight, the bus broke down. A murmur ran through the crowded bus, the obvious question on everyone's mind, thought and spoken in four languages – English, Tamil, Cantonese, and Bahasa Malaysia: "What is going on?!" For ten minutes, while the bus's air conditioning steadily lost the battle against the tropical heat outside, and rush-hour traffic whizzed by on the four-lane highway, fifty passengers patiently squirmed in their seats. Most Asians are an incredibly patient people and polite to a fault. Americans are not known for these qualities and have earned the accolade "Ugly American" for our tendency to speak our mind, and move heavy obstacles. Most of the time we are a pain in the neck, but in crisis the attributes serve the situation well.

"What is going on!" I whispered to Beth, grinding my teeth.

"I'm sure they are working on the problem?" Beth, always the patient one, and always countering my angst, was trying to be hopeful. "What else can we do?"

"It's getting dark," I protested. "We can't sit here all night along this highway!" I got off the bus, fuming about our misfortune, weary beyond measure, and genuinely worried for my wife and our children. I opened the side baggage compartment doors, and began dragging our suitcases off the bus. Twenty-five pairs of Chinese, Indian and Muslim eyes stared at me through the side windows. The driver came down to protest.

"You cahn't do tees sir! You must lait on ta bus."

"I have a wife and two children," I countered. "It's getting dark, and we are NOT going to sit along the side of this road all night!"

"A leepareman is coming. We must lait."

"How long do we wait?" I demanded. "It will be dark in fifteen minutes. I have two small children on this bus.

275

The driver backed off. Asians understand the family argument. My white foreignness probably helped too, in a confusing sort of way. The passengers who had been watching through the bus windows began disembarking and following my example. Beth and the kids joined me. I asked Beth to guard the pile of suitcases while I waved down a taxi. I had no idea if a taxi was even possible on this highway, but I was determined to make SOMETHING happen. It is amazing what can be accomplished when a human being is determined to change the status quo. I stood by the side of the road as speeding traffic whizzed by and waved at anything resembling a taxi. Other passengers joined me and we all waved. Apparently, nobody wanted to "lait on the bus" anymore. Within minutes a large flatbed truck veered onto the shoulder and ground to a churning halt fifty feet away. I ran to the side door and told the driver I needed a ride to Butterworth with my family, and could he help me out? I would pay. The driver stared at this odd-looking white man, and nodded a kindly yes.

Thirty other passengers grabbed their bags and followed us. I threw everything onto the back of the truck – a flat bed with wooden rail sides and open back – and helped Beth and the kids climb aboard, then assisted a few others, older men and women and a few young ladies in dresses and high heels. Everyone found seats on suitcases and travel bags. I waved at the driver through the cab's back window, he ground the gears, roared the diesel engine which puffed blue smoke out of the tail pipe, and crawled into heavy traffic flowing north toward Butterworth. An hour later the driver pulled over at a major intersection on the outskirts of the city, and signaled to me that this was the end of the line. I gave him a healthy tip, and off-loaded everything including the grateful ladies and gentlemen all of whom I think went home with a new appreciation for ugly Americans. We hailed two taxis and negotiated the price. Beth and one weary child climbed into one taxi with a few bags and I did the same in another, with a promise of fare and a generous tip to both drivers. When you are on the outer edge of extremity you just have to do what needs to be done.

We arrived safely to our new home on the hill in Tanjung Bungah, Penang Island and crashed. The year in Penang was Beth's little heaven. Even after fifteen years of accumulated experiences in Asia, Penang remains her fondest memory. As she puts it, "Penang was my 'Psalm Twenty-Three year.'" Thirty-five years of marriage to a wonderful woman and I am still an obtuse male. I don't completely get the whole Penang "little heaven" thing, but for Beth the Psalmist's *green pastures* and *still waters* is an appropriate description for Tanjung Bungah. Beth rested, and I made my first trip to Sri Lanka. While I focused on Sri Lanka, she connected with the wives of Royal Australian Air Force Officers stationed on Penang.

Malaysia was more strategic than pastoral for me – a vision to explore opportunities in the region, and to make forays to Sri Lanka. Formerly called Ceylon and located off the southern coast of India, Sri Lanka is only fourteen hundred miles to the west of Penang, an easy three-hour airplane ride. Malaysia is a complex mix of ethnicities, cultures and religions: Islam, Buddhism, Hinduism and Christianity, four world religions cherished in the individual hearts of Malays, Chinese, Indians and pseudo-Europeans, all co-exist together in relative, howbeit legally enforced, harmony on the Peninsula. The government strictly regulates religious activity, especially the proselyting of Muslims, to keep the peace. Christians can witness about their faith to Buddhists, Hindus and other Christians, but are forbidden, at threat of jail, deportation, even death, to talk about Jesus to a Muslim. Ironically, Muslims, who comprise fifty percent of the population, are free to propagate their faith to anyone. Few seem interested; the propagation seems focused on educating their children and keeping them inside Islam. For the most part, Christians are the only people on the planet who are excited about sharing their beliefs – for reasons of God's love and grace in the present, His offer of salvation through Jesus

Christ, and His judgment in the future. Muslim devotees by contrast seem indifferent, sometimes even happy, about sinners heading for damnation.

Christianity has gone viral on the peninsula, including Singapore, where demographics and religious legalities are similar to Malaysia. Forty percent of Malaysian and Singaporean Chinese are now Christians. Indians, who traditionally are Hindus, are not far behind in rates of conversion to Christianity. The governments of Singapore and Malaysia do not care what religion is practiced among Chinese, Indians, and Europeans, but they passionately guard the heritage of the "Bumiputeras," the indigenous Islamic "Sons of the Soil." The arrangement, especially in Singapore, is not purely ideological. Only half of Malaysia's citizenry are Bumiputeras; a smaller percentage of so-called indigenous people live in Singapore.

The compelling pressure comes from two sources: an internal political need to keep the peace among Malaysia's Islamic ideologues, and an external overbearing neighbor, Indonesia, where two hundred million more Muslims live. Indonesia has more Muslims than every other nation on the planet, except for India. That considerable demographic weighs heavily on the region's political policies. Indonesia is the largest provider of food, fuel and natural resources to Malaysia and Singapore. It is also a huge consumer of exports from those countries. Nobody wants to bite the hands that feed them, so Malaysia and Singapore dutifully play nice.

Despite the restrictions, Malaysia is a beautiful country, prosperous and hospitable. Penang welcomed us and gave our weary family a year of rest. We bought a 1963 Ford sedan for $600, from thousands of choices, delightful old automobiles for sale and exchange by car dealerships catering to RAAF personnel. For a year, we drove our little lime green Ford all over northern Malaysia and south Thailand, making friends with locals, ministering in churches, and generally recharging our batteries. But, by the spring of 1984 my love affair with Malaysia was wearing out. Our unofficial "tourist" status forced us to leave every three months, which was a tenuous and expensive interruption to tranquility. After a year of visa runs to Thailand and Singapore, we decided to move north to Thailand. Wayne and Carolyn Crooke had moved to Si Ratcha right after we arrived in Penang, and upon hearing about our plans, they offered their home, rent-free for three months, while they traveled in the United States. They also offered to help us find visa sponsorship in Thailand. With these carrots dangling in front of us, we left paradise, sold our green Ford, and boarded a train for the thousand-mile journey to Bangkok. From there, Chonburi Province on the east side of Thailand's Gulf Coast is a short bus ride.

Wayne and Carolyn's home in Si Ratcha was a large waterfront compound with three houses. Wayne's team members rented the other houses, so our new home came equipped with a social life. Our old friend from India, Bill Katz, had joined Wayne's team, bringing his North Carolina wife Mitzi along. Other newcomers, the Bailey family and their two teenage boys, completed the team and brought American culture, including twenty years of military service, with them. On our arrival, Army Veteran Lon offered me some home security advice.

"I keep this behind my bedroom door," he said, tapping a baseball bat into one hand. "Any intruder will find out what we have for him." Tap, tap. Five years in Asia, and we had not been robbed. I didn't own a bat and the idea of arming myself with one had never crossed my mind. Mennonite pacifism had quietly followed me around the globe and here it was again, a reminder of how different I was from Army veterans like Lon Bailey. I doubted Lon had encountered any nighttime robbers in Thailand – he hadn't been here long enough – but every veteran of war (and whatever else had shaped his past) knows the bad guys are out there. Lon wasn't taking any chances.

I can't entirely blame Mennonite pacifism for my naiveté. The little towns of eastern Pennsylvania in the 1960s and 1970s were not known for high crime rates, regardless of your religious affiliation. In those days, most people didn't even lock their homes, day or night, absent or sleeping. Thailand, by contrast, was rabid with crime, mostly petty theft and break-ins. The culture had evolved to protect itself. Almost every property boundary in Thailand has a ten-feet-high concrete wall, complete with glass shards embedded at the top to deter would-be thieves. Every window is barred, and every door locked and grated with iron. Pickpockets, those mischievous little pests on buses, trains, and crowded streets, are hard to avoid. We learned quickly how to protect our belongings. With all the hardware and concrete at our new home, I didn't see a need for a bat, but really, I didn't blame Lon for the extra layer of protection.

We enjoyed the summer in Wayne's house – no baseball bat needed – and in early August loaded our newly acquired van, and drove through Bangkok to the west side of the Gulf. Trixie, the name Beth gave to our Mitsubishi Colt van, was old when we bought her, but she was all we could afford. She had no air conditioning, and the engine compartment under the front seat blew a searing barrage of noise and heat onto the driver and front passenger. Trixie offered a singular quality: convenient transportation. She was faster than a bus. Travel inside Trixie rated high on misery and low on comfort but we got there faster. On the first day out of Si Ratcha, we drove the entire distance around the northern curved shores of Thailand's Gulf, through Bangkok and finally to Hua Hin, eight grueling hours in heavy traffic. We arrived weary, dirty and suffering from heat exhaustion. After cold drinks and cold showers at our hotel, everyone revived enough to walk into town for dinner.

The villages of Thailand, including this little beach town, have the best night markets in the world! Exquisite selections of Thai food are served right on the street around a rickety table and four chairs: Oyster omelets, grilled chicken with sticky rice, fried bananas, stir fried Thai noodles, hot and sour soup, fried whole fish over rice, sun dried squid, grilled chicken and pork kabobs with peanut sauce, sticky rice and mango, and "WORMS!" Worms – the name our children gave to this dessert – are pieces of fruit-flavored gelatin, shaped like their namesake, and served in a bowl of chilled, sweet coconut milk. Our children could not pass a stand selling this delicacy, offered in a zillion colors and shapes, without shouting "WORMS!" at the top of their lungs. If we returned to Thailand today, my four children, now married and parenting, would remember and shout out the word. I'd bet my life on it!

Hua Hin is famous in Thailand. Honored as the King's summer beach home, the resort town is cleaner and more family-oriented than Pattaya. Prostitution is officially illegal in Thailand, but like all illicit activities around the world, governments and the people they represent, make compromises and come to terms with things they cannot fully control. The Thai people wink at prostitution in Bangkok and Pattaya. Not so in Hua Hin where a higher standard is observed in deference to the king. As the guardian of all that is good in Thai culture, he represents a moral line in the sand. If there is any prostitution to be found in Hua Hin, it is carefully hidden away.

We stopped in Hua Hin to visit a Swedish missionary family – Bertil and Casja Anderson, and their five children – and to scout the town as a possible home. If Hua Hin didn't fit, we would drive south to Haadyai on the southern border to Malaysia, another six hundred miles down Thailand's long "elephant nose." Italy is famous for its boot shape. Thailand's border forms the shape of an elephant's head. Haadyai is at the tip of the nose, Hua Hin is at the elephant's mouth. We made the elephant's mouth our new home, and lived there for seven years. We built our team in Hua Hin, added two more children to our family, and John Whalen, who came to work with us later in the year, found his wife.

25 The Phone Call

The ringing that woke me from a sound sleep on Sunday morning, October 14, 1984, came from a glaring lime green rotary telephone in our new Hua Hin home. It was our first telephone in five years in Asia, so even at six a.m. I didn't mind staggering out of bed and groping my way downstairs. Trying not to wake the children was an almost impossible affair in this Thai-style wooden house. The teak floors and stairs creaked under every step, echoing human stirrings through the entire structure. And, because we had no answering machine, the phone just kept ringing. It had to be one of our parents. Who else would call at this hour? I stumbled through the living room and picked up the receiver.

"Hello," My voice was still raspy from sleep.

"Doug. This is Dad." The line crackled, almost drowning out Dad's voice. We both paused to let the line clear. The phone, even this old thing, was to me a miracle of modern technology. Ten thousand miles of wire connected me directly to my father. A tiny copper strand stretched across two continents and an expansive ocean separating them, from one house in Pennsylvania to another in Thailand.

"Can you hear me?"

When I answered the phone, the sun was rising in Asia, casting a warm orange glow on the waters of the Gulf of Thailand out our east windows, a new day in Hua Hin. That same sun was setting on the east coast of the United States outside Dad's kitchen windows. Across from him, their hands folded on the table, were my grandparents, Aaron and Katie Stoltzfus.

"Yes, I can hear you," I said, trying to keep my voice down, "but there's a lot of interference." We waited for the crackling to subside. John Whalen, our new team member, was asleep in his downstairs bedroom five feet from me. Shackled to the short phone cord, I couldn't move, even two feet farther away. "Hello? Are you there?" I whispered.

"Yes, I'm still here," Dad said through crackles. A brief pause and then he continued, "The news I have is that Dale committed suicide."

How does one describe the moment after receiving devastating news? To this day I can feel the impact of those words. They settled over me like a cold, heavy blanket. I leaned onto the bar by the phone, and put my head in my hand. The line kept crackling, and we had to wait, which helped because I couldn't think of anything to say. I stood there for a moment in the morning shadows, my head in my hand, a hissing in my ear.

We knew Dale was struggling with depression – for two months we were talking about it – but I never thought it would come to this. Dale was twenty-seven, living in Los Angeles. In 1980 he moved to Southern California to study piano and music theory at Dick Grove's School of Music, and quickly plugged into the Church on the Way, Pastor Jack Hayford's renowned six-thousand-member congregation in Van Nuys. The connection opened doors for Dale. He connected with the music scene at the church and eventually was invited to play piano on the Sunday morning worship team. He regularly rubbed shoulders with professional musicians and entertainers who lived in southern California, or were passing through. He was writing and recording his own music, and even collaborated with Pastor Jack in the creation of a Christmas hymn. I was proud of Dale. Having a creative, aspiring musician younger brother living in

California, connected to the "scene" there, was inspiring. Dale was going places. How could this happen?

"Are you still there?" Dad's voice dragged me back.

"Yes. I'm here."

"We decided you shouldn't come home for the funeral."

"No. I want to come home."

"Do you want me to call back in a couple of hours so you can think about it?"

"NO."

I couldn't say anything more. Words would not come. Dad was very patient and just waited. The words 'Dale committed suicide' were echoing in my head like a bad dream.

"I, uh, how..." I wanted to ask some questions, how Dale died, how he did it, what had gone wrong, but I couldn't get the words out. I wanted to ask about the funeral, but I couldn't get THAT word out either. It felt wrong to speak of these things, especially on the telephone! This was just too abrupt! I remember thinking that maybe I was dreaming, and if I could only wake up, it would all go away. But, I knew.

If we were closer, I would hang up and drive to my parent's house. But, TEN THOUSAND MILES and this crackling green telephone! Months passed before I could hear the phone ring without shuddering.

I tried to ask Dad how Dale did it, but the words came out as mumbling jibberish. Dad asked me to repeat the question.

"How... did... what... did... he...?"

"Do you want to know how he took his life, Doug?"

"Yes..."

"Well, it seems last night he cut one of his wrists... and then this morning..." Dad sighed and took a slow breath. "...This morning... he drove his van to the Hilton Hotel and jumped from the roof." Dad had been remarkably composed, but now his voice was quivering. My mind pictured that awful scenario. This had to be brutal for my parents.

"How is Mother?"

"She's in California… She just flew out there this morning to spend the week with him. Art and Charlene met her at the airport with the news…"

I groaned. She missed him by a couple hours.

"She'll fly home tonight. Charlene says Mother is actually doing very well. A group of Dale's friends have been with her at the Remingtons."

"How is Judy?"

"She cried pretty much when I called her, but she is doing all right now. I wanted to go over to tell her, instead of having to call, but things have been crazy here and I needed to stay near the phone. She's coming over soon. Grandpa and Grandma Stoltzfus are here." Dad continued, explaining that, even though Mother was in Los Angeles, he got the news first.

Dale died around 8:00 a.m. Pacific Standard Time. A grounds keeper heard the impact, discovered his body, and notified hotel management. The police came, identified Dale from his driver's license – it was in his pocket – then went to his apartment in Reseda. His roommate, Paul Van Haligen, answered the door. Paul called Art and Charlene Remington, Dale's "Mom and Dad in California." Art called Dad. Because Los Angeles is four hours behind Pennsylvania, Dad picked up the phone at 2:00 p.m. Eastern Time.

"Fran is at LAX right now," Dad told Art. "She's waiting for Dale to pick her up! Can you go find her?" Art said they knew and were going immediately.

Dad explained a few more details to me, and then we said goodbye. I promised to call again after I made flight arrangements. Dazed, I went upstairs to tell Beth. She rushed to the kitchen to make breakfast while I packed. Two hours later I boarded a bus for Bangkok. In the afternoon, Beth called me at the hotel, saying she and the kids were coming with me. Zion Chapel was sending money. Pastor Steve shared the news with the church and people immediately gave the funds to bring us all home! Beth and the kids met me in Bangkok a few hours later and by the evening we were on our way.

The thirty-five hour flight to New York was torturous. Our lack of details about Dale's struggles, and now his abrupt death, created insufferable grief. Around us, people were indifferent – in the airport, in the planes, everywhere – but who could blame them? They knew nothing of our sorrow. For the first time in my life, I experienced how uncaring the world can be, how no one notices a stranger's anguish. I wondered how often I had been insensitive to grieving people around me.

Dale had talked openly with Dad and Mother about his battle with depression. In August, I called home to ask about Dale after he wrote me a letter that included this sentence: "Maybe I should drop everything here and come spend a month with you in Thailand. It would probably do me good." The words raised an alarm.

"Pray for him," Mother said. "He is really depressed."

"I got a burden for him after that letter. That's why I called."

"He even said he's been having suicidal thoughts."

That scared me, and it didn't make sense. Dale seemed eternally confident and upbeat. Something exciting was always happening with him in California! He loved Pastor Jack, he loved the church, the staff, the musicians, and talked constantly about what he was learning, what he was doing, and the people he was meeting. Opportunities were opening for him in music, on the Sunday morning worship team, with "Class Action," the church's post-college-single's ministry. He was forming a worship group called "Selah!" I was proud of him and a little envious. Dale was no longer the punk kid brother. The previous year He came home for Christmas and was invited to play a piano special at Neffsville Mennonite Church. I usually got *that* invitation, to speak. He arranged a piano and cello duet with his friend Andi Hess, a medley of "Sing Hallelujah to the Lord" and an original score by an Australian composer Dale had met when he was in Sydney earlier in the year. The medley combined the reverence of "Sing Hallelujah" with a lively bridge that lifted the song to a beautiful crescendo. When Dale and Andi finished, a normally reserved Mennonite congregation burst into applause. Applause in a Mennonite church!

"Mother, God spoke to me about Dale. He should come to Thailand and spend a month with us. I can help with the ticket. Can you talk to him when you go to LA? He needs to be with family. At the very least, he should come back to Pennsylvania for a while."

"Why don't you call him," Mother suggested. "He is staying with Art and Charlene Remington... You remember Charlene. He didn't want to be alone. I have their number."

"Can you call him? Ask him to call me right now. I'll wait by the phone. It is so much cheaper to call from America." Dale never called. I didn't understand the urgency, and was trying to save money. Big mistake. I have since learned about depression and suicide. Family and friends of the struggling person usually choose denial over action. Denial is easier, but is dangerous. Now, my brother was GONE. I didn't blame myself but I lament my inaction.

As we flew home, I thought about how to honor my brother at his untimely memorial service. Thankfully Associate Pastor Daniel Brown, with whom Dale worked closely at The Church On the Way, was coming in from Los Angeles. He was perhaps the best person to talk about Dale's recent life. Maybe he could shed a little light on this incomprehensible death.

Police always investigate suicide cases for homicide. At Dale's apartment an officer listened to his answering machine, a stream of calls from friends reaching out to Dale, offering counsel, saying they were praying for him, inviting him to join them on outings, and asking him to call. John Wohl, Music Pastor at The Church On The Way, called to remind him he was scheduled to play piano on Sunday morning and asked if they could get together to discuss other projects. The police officer began to cry. Nearly twenty calls from Christian friends! The officer told Paul he had never seen a suicide victim with so many friends. Most are lonely, friendless people. He couldn't understand how a young man with so many friends could take his own life.

We were asking ourselves the same question.

26 "He's with Jesus"

"Will Dale Gehman please meet your party at the American Airlines Baggage Claim." The pleasant female voice echoed through the terminal at Los Angeles International Airport. Mother sat alone near the conveyor belts in Baggage Claim. It was 1:00 p.m. She had removed her brown sweater, necessary in Lancaster's autumn, but too warm in southern California. Yellow sunshine radiated into the dismal steel and tile arrival hall. Enjoying its warmth, she didn't mind waiting. Dale was meeting her here, but after two hours, she wondered if there was a mix up.

"Dumb me," she thought. "I probably gave Dale the wrong time." Her flight from Philadelphia had been interrupted in Chicago because of fog. The plane diverted to St. Louis and she was transferred to USAir. After waiting in the USAir Baggage Claim for an hour it occurred to her that Dale had gone to the American Airlines terminal. She collected her things and boarded a shuttle bus, but Dale wasn't there either, so she waited again. After another thirty-minutes she asked the attendant to page Dale.

"He probably went to USAir looking for me," she told the attendant. "But I can't keep running back and forth." The pretty ground staffer said she'd page Dale every ten-minutes. The terminal bustled with weekend activity, but Baggage

291

Claim was virtually deserted. Mother sat quietly, watching the lady behind her desk. She remembered the last time she had seen Dale, a similar scene at an airport, in Billings, Montana. That was over a year ago, in August! The family – Doug and Beth and their kids, plus Fran and Bob – were on a road trip west across America. Dale took off work and flew to Billings to join the gang for the last ten days. They camped through Yellowstone National Park, Wyoming's Grand Tetons, the Utah deserts, and Grand Canyon National Park. While everyone enjoyed sightseeing and the natural beauty of America's west, Mother simply enjoyed her children and grandchildren. The little things – and just being together – were enough.

She loved Dale's way of saying hello, and looked forward to hearing his cheery greeting today. It was always the same: "Mother Dear!" followed by a hug and kiss. In Billings, he came off the airplane wearing blue jeans, an open flannel shirt over a t-shirt, and... wool-top house slippers! "They're comfortable," he said.

Fran smiled, remembering, and wondering if Dale would still have the same cheery manner today... and maybe those crazy slippers too. Of their three children, Dale was the most affectionate, even in adulthood, maybe because he had not yet married, maybe he just needed more hugs. During high school, when most teenagers distance themselves from parents, Dale still liked to hug his Mom. After graduation, when he wandered far from God, he came home every time with "Mother Dear!" and a hug, and usually a gift. Once he brought her a one-pound Hershey's chocolate "Kiss" – no special occasion. She expected something similar today, but was very worried about his depression.

A few years before, in 1979, he had battled depression. After two years on the road with a band of nightclub musicians, Dale quit and came home, burned out. Gaunt, nervous, unable to eat or sleep, he moved back into the house and tried to make sense of a raging storm inside. The only way he could express it: "I want to get into a better kind of music." He stayed with Mother and Dad for several months, trying to figure things out. His piano and musical equipment gathered dust in the garage. He would not play again, he said, "until God gives me peace." During those months, one of Dale's childhood friends ended his life with a gun. Dale commented, "I wonder where he got the guts to do it," a worrying statement for Dad and Mother. He worked odd jobs, first for a local builder, and then for a greenhouse business. His Christian bosses talked with him and tried to answer his questions.

One morning he reached a breaking point. "Mother!" He shouted from his room." Come here!!" Mother found him on his knees crying. "I need help," he said. "I've got to get my life straightened out." Mother knelt beside him, talking and praying with him for a long time. "He was so distressed," Mother shared later. "He cried and cried, letting out the despair... like a child. I had to help him through everything, leading him to confess his sins and showing him how to talk to God. He was at the end of himself." The day birthed a new beginning.

Sitting in the Los Angeles airport, Mother wondered why Dale was battling depression again. She hoped that during this week – talking, shopping, sight-seeing around Los Angeles – she could perhaps help him again. She would certainly help him clean his apartment. He was always busy, so he would appreciate a Mother's touch. She worried that overwork may be part of the problem. He had recently returned from a month in Scotland with a group of young people from The Church On The Way. Meetings every night, and daily outreach activities had worn him out he said. He admitted to being depressed in recent months. They had talked two days before this trip, and when she asked him how he was and he replied simply, "So, so." He wasn't very talkative, but Mother brushed it off thinking, "I'll be with him in two days, and then we can talk all we want."

Before Mother arrived, Dale moved back to his apartment. He spent Friday evening at home. Dale was in bed when his roommate Paul returned at 1:00 a.m. Their apartment had only one bedroom, which Paul used. Dale slept on a foldout bed in the living room. The living room doubled as Dale's "studio." His piano, Hammond organ and Leslie, synthesizers, amplifiers, and recording equipment filled the small space. His friends often chided Dale about his haphazard style, how he arranged his music and sound equipment at home and everywhere else, including practice and performances. Tangled wires sprawled in every direction, amplifiers, mixers, junction boxes, and recording equipment were scattered and stacked precariously. A friend drew a comic sketch of the disarray, Dale in the middle surrounded by keyboards, his feet and hands reaching in four directions!

Dale was awake when Paul came home. They exchanged a few greetings and Paul went on to bed. He heard Dale leave the apartment a few minutes later, but thought nothing of it because Dale often went for walks or a late-night run when the Reseda streets were quiet. This night, however, Dale walked to his blue Ford van, got in through the side door, and crawled into his sleeping bag. He then cut his left wrist with a knife. He had written a note, probably earlier in the evening, trying to explain:

"Dear family and friends, I know this will come as quite a shock to you. Believe me, not wanting to hurt anyone has been my main sustaining factor. I have been suicidally [sic] oppressed for over three months. It has been as though I was drowning, but couldn't swim, only able to get my head above water on a few brief occasions, but then to sink back into a deep, dark sea again. Most of you probably had no idea, because I generally have felt better when at church, because of the love I have felt from and for you. The rest of the time has been like a nightmare that never seems to end. There have been many nights that I have laid on the floor and wept bitterly, as so many of your faces have gone through my mind, and I realized how special each of you are to me. Rationally, there's no big reason to be depressed, yet I can't seem to shake it, and I'm very tired. I have received much

prayer and love and counsel, and have received each bit of insight with anticipation. However, I'm convinced that no one can comprehend what this is like, unless they go through it. God forbid that they ever do. Surely it is a disease to the soul, as cancer is to the body. I only hope and pray that I can be remembered as someone who once may have brought some love and joy into your lives, rather than one who's life ended tragically. Please forgive me, Jesus.

"Jeff & Miriam, Glen & Melia, Art & Char, Bobby, Paul, and all my dear friends. You are all so very special. God richly bless your lives!

"Mark Sanders, 'Selah,' and 'Class Action,' I'm sorry to let you down. I feel responsible. Please continue to worship our Lord as you have. This shouldn't weaken just because I have.

"To all my friends in Pennsylvania, at Neffsville Mennonite Church, Jay, Bill and JoAnne, Joe and Lynda. I love you so very much. Please cling to the good times that we've shared."

He finished with a personal note to Mother, trying vainly to ease the pain and make her understand:

"Mother, I know this will be hardest on you. I was excited about you coming, but then the last few days have been so bad that I feel it would be even harder seeing you. Please be strong... I love you and Dad very much."

Dale woke up at 7:00 a.m. on Saturday morning, still very much alive. The bleeding from the cut on his wrist had coagulated. He crawled into the driver's seat of his van, drove through Reseda to a nearby Hilton Hotel. He parked, entered the hotel lobby, and rode the elevator to the tenth floor. One of the janitorial staff saw Dale walk into the lobby, and later commented to the police that he thought the young man looked disheveled. On the tenth floor, Dale took the stairs to the roof and climbed over safety barricades. His wrist had begun bleeding again from the physical exertion, leaving a trail of blood. Standing on the edge of the roof, ten floors above the ground, he stepped off.

Paul was the first to get the news. When the police arrived at the apartment they said they must search through Dale's belongings. Paul let them in and began looking for Art and Charlene's telephone number. On the refrigerator and saw a note in Dale's handwriting: "Paul, I'm in the van. Call Dad." Paul couldn't at first find the Remingtons' telephone number. While he looked, Art and Charlene were leaving their house for a weekend in Phoenix. They had driven a few miles when they turned around, remembering something they needed back at the house. Paul finally found the number. He dialed. The phone was ringing when the Remingtons pulled into their drive.

Charlene ran into the house to answer. "Hello?"

"Charlene, this is Paul. Can I talk to Art?"

"Art is busy right now, can I help you?" They were in a hurry to get back on the road.

"No, I want to talk to Art."

"Okay. Just a minute."

Art got on the phone, "Hello?"

"Art, this is Paul...." He paused. "We lost Dale last night. The police are here. And Dale is supposed to pick up his mother at LAX in fifteen minutes."

Art also received the call from Dad. He made a few other phone calls and then left for the airport. With Paul's help finding telephone numbers, they called Pastor Ed Bontrager of Neffsville Mennonite Church in Lancaster and asked him to contact Dale's Dad. "The family probably needs a pastor right now," they told him. "We are going to the Airport to meet Fran." On the way to the airport, they tried to deal with their own overwhelming sense of loss. Dale was like a son. But even in the grief, God gave them peace that Dale was with Him. "We never questioned that fact," they later reflected.

Charlene Chapalere was a widow with two grown daughters. She had taken Dale into her heart like a son since she first met him. Dale often came over for meals, or to visit and swim in the pool. He brought friends. When Charlene started dating Art (they married in June, 1984), she told him, "I have two daughters and two sons."

"I know you have daughters, but… sons?"

"My sons are Dale Gehman and Paul Van Haligen."

Dale and Art began spending time together, and the two quickly became friends over pick-up basketball, family picnics and Dale's group "Selah." Dale wrote a piano sonata for Art's and Charlene's wedding. One night he took them the church's Prayer Chapel and said, "I want you to hear something. If you like it, I can play it at your wedding." Charlene loved *Song for the Celebration*; Dale played it in their wedding ceremony.

That was only two months ago! Charlene could hardly believe this was happening today. She wanted to cry. She wanted to shout at Dale, "Why did you do it!!?" Entering the airport parking garage, they asked God for strength. They found Fran waiting in the baggage claim area. She recognized Charlene.

Charlene said, "You know me?"

"Yes, Charlene," Mother replied, wondering why they were here.

"This is my husband Art."

"Where's Dale?" Mother was thinking, Dale probably had gotten called to work and asked Art and Charlene to meet me. Charlene stood silently, not answering.

"Where's Dale?" she repeated. For a brief moment, Charlene stared gently at Fran, searching for the right words. For an hour on the way to the airport, they had prayed, "God, please, we need to talk to Fran in a private place with no people around. And please, give Charlene the right words."

Mother grabbed Charlene's arms with both hands. "Charlene, WHERE IS DALE!?"

"Fran, please sit down," Charlene said. "Dale won't be coming to pick you up today. He's with Jesus."

Mother later reflected that she had no premonition of Dale's death. For two hours she expected to see him and to hear him say, "Mother Dear!" Charlene's words contained the harshest news any Mother can hear, but the words "He's with Jesus" poured comfort and peace into her soul.

Grief is a brutal human emotion. Around the world, in every nation, people grieve when a loved one dies. The loss of a son or daughter is incalculably painful. Culture cannot dictate how people feel, but it does prescribe how we express our grief. Modern media broadcasts wailing Middle Eastern women, mourning the untimely deaths of loved ones in war. Typically, German Mennonite culture is not so expressive.

"Oh my," Mother responded. "I can't even cry."

First reactions are a strange thing. Trauma can numb the mind. Later, when the initial crisis passes, shock subsides and the psyche surrenders to a flood of memories, reflection, loss and tears. My father, a pillar of strength through the first days, burst into tears when he saw Dale's body at the funeral home. I was numb traveling home, meeting my parents and the family, helping with arrangements, sitting through the funeral and sharing the eulogy – but the next day, when Dale was buried and I realized he was gone forever from our lives and I would never see him again, the dam broke and I cried all day.

Mother slumped into an airport chair. After a long pause, she looked at Charlene and asked, "How did he do it?" Charlene didn't want to talk about those details. Not here. Not now. "We can talk about all of that later, Fran, " she said. "We'd better go." They walked with Fran to their car and drove back to Granada Hills.

27 Memorial

While events unfolded at the airport, telephone messages spread to friends and church leaders. Associate Pastor Jim Downing was at the Remington home when they returned. Charlene led Mother to an over-stuffed gray chair in the living room and brought her a cup of coffee. They urged her to stay overnight, but she insisted on returning to Pennsylvania "as soon as possible. I need to get back to Bob," Fran said. Art called the airline to make flight arrangements on a redeye to Philadelphia. Friends began to arrive. They crowded into the small Remington living room. Pastor Daniel Brown arrived and sat down next to Mother and took her hand. The group talked about Dale, his impact on each of their lives, and their recent attempts to help him. Seeing the warmth and companionship among Dale's friends and "family" in California, Mother leaned to Daniel and said, "It would be so nice if you could come to Pennsylvania to talk about Dale in the funeral."

"I'm already planning to do that," he replied, "if only to support your family."

Jeff and Miriam Leggett, Paul Van Haligen, Charlene's two daughters, and other members of "Selah!" lounged on chairs, sofa, cushions, and the carpet. Most stayed all afternoon and evening. Although everyone was in shock,

Mother noted how no one was overcome. Each offered encouraging words, and talked about their friendship with Dale. Others, who couldn't come that day, forwarded written condolences to our family.

Art was on the phone making arrangements. In late afternoon, leaving the group at their house, he and Charlene drove Fran and Paul to Dale's Reseda apartment to collect a few personal things. "I will never forget the feeling, walking in there and seeing his apartment in shambles," Mother later remembered. "Dale usually kept an immaculate house, but it was in chaos, dust everywhere, things lying around the kitchen, nothing put away. There was a pile of dirty laundry in a corner. I told Paul to throw it away." Dale's piano, Hammond organ and Leslie, and other musical equipment, sat ominously silent. A drafting table and stool – Dale used them for music composition – were nearby with an unfinished project taped to the board. His Bible was on a lamp table. Mother took it. From his wardrobe, Mother selected one suit for the funeral and burial. She sorted through his belongings, asking Charlene and Paul to take things and give others away. They left after about thirty minutes. Paul went with them. "I'll never live there again," he said. Art and Charlene invited him to live with them until he could find another apartment.

Back in Granada Hills someone brought food – pizza, drinks and cookies. When Mother returned with Art and Charlene, they gathered in the living room and sang together. Everyone wanted to talk about Dale, about his talent and leadership, and other qualities. Mother sobbed as "Selah" sang Dale's songs, worship music he had written during the past year. The songs contradicted the realities of this day. After the funeral, months passed before any of Dale's friends or family could listen to those songs. Jeff Leggett grieved the most. He and Dale were inseparable for five years, and since Jeff married Miriam a year before, Dale had become an extension of their family.

"He was one of the few people we know who could walk into our home without knocking," Miriam said. "No one cared either when he helped himself from the refrigerator, or invited himself over for supper!" Dale and Jeff did almost everything together, from church activities to work projects to basketball. In recent months the two had closely conferred over the creation and direction of "Selah!" Dale on keyboards, Jeff on bass, and another friend, Glenn on drums, comprised the instrumental foundation of "Selah!"

After Dale started battling depression and suicidal thoughts, he and Jeff made a pact. Dale promised to call Jeff first, no matter what. Jeff last saw Dale on Thursday evening, twenty-four hours before he died. Dale never called, which for Jeff was a brutal betrayal. He shared at the Memorial Service on Tuesday, October 16, at The Church On The Way:

"This must be the hardest thing I have ever had to do, to come before you today and talk about someone that I loved so much. But I am comforted to know that Dale Gehman walked uprightly before God, with a pure heart. He developed into a man of God who wanted nothing more than, each day of his life, to search after God with a passion that was just never satisfied − he wanted more everyday.

"When I first met him, in a Christian band, he had just an ordinary vision about music, that it was just music and that it was a good tool to tell people about Jesus. And I watched him develop over a period of around four years, by studying the principles of the Word of God, to find out the actual power of worship, what it can do to transform our lives and transform our world, through us and through the obedience of going before our God and just knowing Him better by being in His presence. And I just watched him develop like that and to see the things he shared with all of us – and the vision that he had. He went to Australia and met some people involved in worship in a new way, in a creative way, going before the Lord each day new, creatively, going before your God and being in His presence and basking in that. Dale brought that back to us, and set us on fire for that.

"To see him develop from something that is just ordinary – a tool to tell people about the Lord – and to take it to a place, because the Lord gave him that desire and vision to use that thing, to just get

to know the Lord better. It was an incredible thing in my life. It changed me. I'll never be the same. For knowing him...to go out and walk and talk, play basketball, racquetball, just to be with him – the Lord was always foremost in his mind. He could have a great time, but yet there was something about him – he sought after God with a passion that I've never seen in many people.

"And when this happened, my mind couldn't comprehend this because of knowing his passion for God, and knowing he studied the Word of God with a passion...

"Knowing this could happen to him, then none of us are safe from a devil who seeks to destroy everyone in this room. If a man who loves God with all his heart, and believes His Word with all his heart, can be overtaken by the darkness, then anyone can.

"One of the things I've seen here is that we need each other. And we need never to be isolated and stand alone. And when times of darkness come upon us, we need to reach out to the brother and sister in our lives and grasp hold of their hand, and ask the Lord, who will be there with us – in the strength of the numbers will keep that darkness from engulfing our lives. So this just re-enforced this on my mind – we need each other and no one can stand alone.

"The Lord impressed on my heart a scripture that seems to fit this situation. It's in the book of Isaiah, fifty-seventh chapter, verses one and two. It says, 'The righteous perish, and no one ponders it in his heart. Devout men are taken away and no one understands, that the righteous are taken away to be spared from evil, and those that walk uprightly enter into peace, and they find rest as they lie in death.'

"And my brother walked uprightly everyday of his life. And I know he has entered into that peace of God – he's before the Throne this very moment – and he will find rest in his death. I believe he wants us to keep our focus on Jesus Christ, our risen Lord and Savior, and dedicate our lives to our Lord for what He has for us – each and everyone – and press on to the fullest potential that God has for us. I believe that is what he would say if he were here: 'Press on to what God has for each of us – our fullest potential.'"

In the Memorial service, Pastor Brown summarized the perplexing reality of Dale's untimely death:

"We are bewildered. We are confused. And that really is the emotion that Dale most expressed in the letter he wrote. He hoped, in the letter he wrote to me, that there would be some gracious way to explain what he had done.

"Dale knew that he had done wrong. You see, the hardest thing about talking of this situation is that it would be dishonest for us to not address the fact that Dale took his own life. And while we have the great comfort to know that Dale is with Jesus, and that upon his death the Lord received Dale... we cannot overlook the fact that what he did was wrong.

"You might feel that at a memorial service to remember his life, it is inappropriate for me to discuss the fact that Dale did that which was not in the heart of God. But you see, Dale knew that it wasn't in the heart of God. You say, 'What happened? He led us in worship!' It reminds me of the Psalm where David says, 'My soul, why are you in despair within me? I used to lead the people of God in worship! I used to be at the head of the procession that glorified you! And yet I find this despondency in my heart.' But David went on to say, 'Still hope in the Lord, for you shall yet again come to praise Him.'

"Dale was received by the Lord. But there is something inside of me that grows indignant, because of how the enemy overwhelmed one of our brothers in a moment. You see, the temptation that he experienced to opt out of God's plan for his life is the temptation we all experience. People say, 'How could he do that? He was a man of God!' Well, how is it that you and I can opt out of God's plan for our lives? Yes, Dale committed suicide. But how many of us in our own way and particulars of our life, spiritually are committing suicide? We know the Lord says, 'This is the way, walk ye in it... Yes, it is a difficult road. Yes, it is hard. But I promise I will be with you to deliver you, to make things work and make them right.' How many of us commit suicide by growing bitter; by saying, 'I'm tired of waiting for the promises of God.' You see, as much as Dale Gehman loved Jesus, there was this area of temptation where he grew weary of relying on the promises of the Lord. He felt there was no longer any hope. But you see the Bible says that it is only by our faith that we can hope to gain a testimony...

"Please understand, that I loved Dale. But I ask you, what kind of a testimony has this been? Oh, God is able to turn it to profit. But you see, Dale tried to engineer his own deliverance. And deliverance by man is vain. You must know that God had deliverance for Dale. But God's deliverance didn't happen this past Saturday morning. And what deliverance, I would ask you, does God have for you? You have endured for a period of time, and you say, 'Lord, it doesn't seem like your promises are coming true to me. It doesn't seem like it will ever get better. It doesn't seem like there is any way out.' And have you too been tempted to engineer your own deliverance? I am grieved... that the enemy might take this situation and recommend to some of you that taking your own life or engineering your own deliverance – whether it's taking your own life physically or hardening something in your heart – the enemy might suggest to you, 'Well, it's an acceptable way. Because, look, Dale's with the Lord and look how his friends mourn his passing. And things are hard for you. And why not take this way out.'

"You see, how do you explain the welcome of the heavenly Father? How do you understand how the angels were right there to take Dale home and that when he came before the Lord there was no reproach – there was nothing of God holding Himself back and saying, 'Well, I don't know.' How can you understand, on the one hand the aggressive embrace of God to pull Dale in and yet at the same time the heart of the Father that would say to all of us, 'Deliverance is from Me,' says the Lord. 'You cannot engineer it yourself.' How can I explain to you the welcome that Dale has known, with the grave danger that some of you experience yourself now, thinking of this as an option? How can we understand the great all-encompassing forgiveness of God, a God who still has a way and a path that He wants us to walk?

"Without faith you don't get a testimony. I would be quick to say that Dale Gehman's life was a testimony that was perhaps stronger, more vocal, more pronounced, than many of our lives might ever become. You see, we have to honor him for the integrity of his heart of which we heard earlier, for the diligence with which he sought the way of the Lord, for the earnestness with which he said,

304

'Lord I want to be what you want me to be.' We must honor him for that.

"He had a lot of faith. But at this one point.... we don't know all the explanations. But let us decide that as there has been one brother who has given in to temptation – we still would honor him for all that he has been to us – but let there come something of an anger in our heart, not against Dale, not against God, but an anger against the powers and the principalities that rule this world wanting to rob us of our life, wanting to overwhelm us. Do we not know that it is only by the mercies of the Lord that everyone of us is not overwhelmed all the time? And how the enemy comes in like a flood and it is the Lord's desire to raise up a standard. But my friends we must run to that standard. To run and hang onto the Lord, knowing that though the flood does come, the Lord's standard is higher and higher and higher. Dale knows that now. No reproach from the Lord. No reproach from us. But, something inside of me wants to say, 'Enough!' Something inside of me wants to say then, 'Look at all the death out there in the world!' And want to do something about it.

"And I think the word to us is right: Let us join together. Now as the struggle is before us – the things that still have to be done – and let us run with endurance the race that is set before us. Let us know we have a great cloud of witnesses surrounding us, and let us lay aside every encumbrance that so easily tries to hang onto us. And let us say, 'Lord, though it wasn't right what Dale did, and though it was not in your heart for him to take his own deliverance into his own hands, yet Lord, he was an example to me of a man who worshipped you. He was an example to me of a man who walked in integrity. And with those examples, and learning what I have learned from my brother's mistake, I say to you Lord, I want to run with endurance the race that is set before me.' And can we expose the lie of the enemy who suggests to some of us that there is another way out. And let us be quick to say, 'Lord, Your will, Your way, Your purpose be done in my life.'

"Oh, we honor Dale. Oh, we love him. We love the God who allowed us to have touch with his life. But again, I ask you, How have you taken your own life? You see, what Dale cut off from us *was a lot of blessing that could have been. There are a lot of songs that Dale is writing in heaven that we won't get to hear until we go. That we could've heard. But isn't the same true of your life? Aren't there blessings that God wants to pour through you to others, that because of something you have done, or are doing, or are thinking about doing, will never happen? God meant for us while we are still on this earth to serve Him and to serve one another. and to withstand any temptation to draw us away from that service to others. And so let that be your resolve.*

"Can we pray together..."

The Funeral was scheduled for Thursday, October 18 at Neffsville Mennonite Church. About three hundred people attended. I gave the eulogy. Prior to the service, a family friend, Mrs. Landis, met me in the foyer, gave me a hug and said, "I think God said, 'Dale, you came a little early, but welcome anyway!'" It was a helpful lift during a tough day.

Friday, October 19, the day after the funeral, our family had breakfast with my parents. With the week's activity behind us, now in the serenity of my parent's home, the new reality flooded in. I started crying and cried all day. It felt good to weep. Like a cleansing stream, the tears began to wash away the hurt and bitterness. They didn't leave quickly. I ached for two years. We stayed in the United States for two months and then returned to Thailand before Christmas, to a burglarized home.

28 A Year of Grief... and Comfort

While we were in America, our house in Hua Hin got robbed. John forgot to shutter the kitchen windows one night, and two robbers entered the house and stole all of our electronic equipment – right from under the noses of two sleeping dogs and one sleeping human. The next morning John discovered the missing television, a radio/cassette system, and other valuables. The loss of possessions hurt, but the forfeiture of our security was an added burden to our over-wrought psyche.

By coincidence, I called the morning after the robbery.

"Hello." John answered the phone.

"Hey John. This is Doug."

"Hey! How are you guys?"

"We're OK. How is everything there?"

"Uh, well, the police are here... The house got broken into last night and they... uh, took a bunch of stuff."

"What! What stuff? Are you OK?"

"Yeah, I'm fine. But, they took, uh... some of the electronics..." John went down the list. "I slept through it all. Crazy thing is, even the dogs slept through it. Never woke up. Weird. I think it was two guys, because they carried off the television and your radio, and then dropped my radio when they were going over the wall. I found it outside this morning."

"How did they get into the house?"

"They came in through the kitchen windows."

"Didn't you lock them?" I asked, trying to hide my angst. I had warned him about security before we left.

"No, I forgot."

I held my tongue. I didn't want to scold John from ten thousand miles away and through the blur of my brother's funeral. The police finished their lame investigation and left. We never got anything back. Our security went out the window and over the wall with the thieves. If you have never experienced a break-in, you can't understand. It's a terrible violation. When we returned to Hua Hin, I installed alarms on the exterior doors. It helped, but we weren't sleeping anyway. A week later I awoke to shrill buzzing. I jumped out of bed and began stomping around on the upstairs wood floor and out into the hallway, determined to scare the burglars out of the house. While I stomped Cori called to me from her room, "Daddy! Daddy!" I ignored her, determined to rid the house of the burglars first. Finally I went to her room. "What is it Cori?"

"Daddy! It's my bed alarm."

The "alarm" was her bed-wetting buzzer. Embarrassing… for both of us. This was going to be a tough year. The death of a family member is not an easy experience or a smooth recovery. Psychologists have identified five distinct stages of grief. To know the stages does nothing to eliminate them. One must walk through the valley of the shadow of death. Knowledge only makes the wrenching journey a little more tenable. For two years, I got lost. I wasn't mad at God, and I didn't act out or run away. I did my duty and kept living. But I was very sad… and a little angry… mostly at my brother. Nobody pushed him off the hotel roof. Ironically – and Jeff Leggett pointed this out to me – on that final horrible day, God gave Dale a second chance. Dale cut his wrist, but six hours later the wound had clotted and he was still alive. One would think a reprieve like that would save a desperate person. But apparently Dale was determined to do himself in.

Suicide may be the final act of a besieged soul, but surviving friends and family remain, and now besieged with grief, they must pick up the shattered pieces. In their misguided quest to escape pain, suicidal people minimize everything and everyone else. Their final desperate act is utterly selfish. I have told my friends, when I meet Dale in heaven, I am going to punch him for cutting his life short, wasting his talent, and foisting on his family and friends such an unimaginable load of grief. Well, twenty-five years have passed. Maybe I'll punch him; probably I won't. I'm not angry anymore. I still miss him and still begrudge him the waste. I think about the girl, whoever she is, whom he might have married – my would-be sister-in-law – and the children they would have produced together – my would-be nieces and nephews – who would be celebrating weddings and having children of their own in California, or Pennsylvania, or maybe Lagos or Shanghai. Dale stole a lot of life – and a lot of joy – from Mother and Dad, from Judy, from me, and from a host of other people. Our families, our children, and friends like Jeff and Miriam Leggett were denied lifelong companionship. And God only knows what contribution he might have made to the planet. On that auspicious fourteenth day of October 1984, Dale snuffed out a whole family line and an entire legacy. It did not have to happen. THAT still makes me angry.

A couple of weeks after Dale's death, Pastor Jack Hayford needed to help the Church On The Way process their shock and grief. He preached a two-part sermon called, "The Sin of Suicide." You have to know Jack to appreciate the implications of those messages. He was gracious, but he held nothing back about the negative effect, both for the deceased who must answer to God, and the community left behind who must grapple with the pain. Suicide is sin, as final as murder, not unforgiveable or beyond mercy, but with serious consequences. Medical science in 1984 was not what it is today, but it wasn't the dark ages either. Dale could have gotten treatment. He had options. What a waste.

But God had a plan of redemption. On that dreadful October 1984 morning after I hung up the phone and I bolted up the stairs to tell Beth, God had already started the plan. Beth came downstairs to make breakfast. Crying over coffee preparation in the kitchen, the Lord spoke to my little redhead: "I am going to give you another baby, to bring joy back into your lives." Beth minimized the nudge initially, but, as women do, she tucked the thought away. Two months later, while we were in America, she began to feel what women feel. Of this very special time, Old Order Mennonites say, in their typically reserved fashion, "She's in a family way" or "She's staying home from church." (The two forthright women in my life – my mother and that red headed Irish Methodist I married – were never that coy). A visit to a doctor confirmed Beth was pregnant, due in mid-July.

We returned to Hua Hin in time for Christmas. By late June 1985 I was scheduled to go to Sri Lanka again, my third trip to the island. With Beth's due-date approaching we discussed travel plans. After missing Jeremy's birth six years before, I was not going to make the same mistake again, especially at this anguished time in our lives. Beth had forgiven me for the previous absence, but I had learned my lesson. And any way, a grieving soul prefers a warm home and familiar bed over conquest and adventure. I offered to cancel Sri Lanka, but this time Beth countered. "You need to make this trip, honey. The baby will wait and you'll be home in time. Go!" We reviewed schedules and due dates, and the math seemed to work, barely. So, off I went for two weeks, leaving behind an eight-and-a-half month pregnant wife with two kids. Looking back, I am again persuaded that we were insane! But, in this instance, the insanity was consensual.

The realities of international communication in the 1980s were not what they are today, with e-mail, the internet and cell phones. A few privileged souls owned a mobile phone in 1984, but the "portable" devices were the size of a brick and were available in only a few places like New York and Los Angeles. Sri Lanka had never heard of a cellular telephone. The technology and its supporting infrastructure was still a decade into the future.

To call Beth from Sri Lanka, I had to walk to a post office, pay for an international phone call and wait two hours. The ten-minute "private" conversation with my pregnant wife transpired inside a wooden phone booth within earshot of fifty people. For two weeks that July I engaged this laborious routine twice a week at a cost of about thirty dollars per call. Finally, on July thirteen, after fourteen grueling days away, I caught a flight back to Bangkok. On arrival at Don Muang International Airport at five-thirty in the morning, Beth was waiting for me. There she stood at the Baggage Claim exit, all red faced and flush from the tropical heat, weary after a near sleepless night. Crowds of people and their suitcases flowed around her, a pretty figure in a flowery sun dress and bulging abdomen, a sight for sore eyes and a huge relief to a guilty conscience.

"What are you doing here?" I asked after a lingering hug and kiss.

"I came three days ago for my doctor visit and he told me to stay in Bangkok because the baby could come at any moment. I've been at the Lewises."

"How did you get to Bangkok?" I asked.

"I rode the bus, honey. How else?" She said it with such sweetness, I didn't have the nerve to tell her I had forgotten about the doctor visit. With men, some things are unlearnable.

"What are we going to do now?"

"We're going straight home! I haven't had a change of clothes in three days, and we have to get back to the kids. They're staying with the Staggs." Team members Ron and Lynn Stagg lived down the street. We boarded a bus for Hua Hin. Five hours later we picked up the kids, went home for a shower and fresh clothes, then loaded Trixie, and drove back to Bangkok. The next morning, July 14, Beth woke me up.

"It's time to go to the hospital, honey," she said.

"What time is it?"

"It's four o'clock. We've got to go."

Trevor Dillon Gehman was born ninety minutes later at five-thirty a.m. on July 14, 1985. In case you didn't notice: Trevor Dillon Gehman arrived nine months, to the day, almost to the hour, after Dale died. I can be anal about the details. I've done the math. I'll spare the reader, except for this: Dale's Death Certificate says he died on Saturday morning of October 13, 1984 in Los Angeles, California. At that moment, Pacific Standard Time, it was fourteen hours ahead in Thailand, which means it was nighttime on October 13, and we were in bed, if you catch my drift.

Like I said, God had a plan of redemption.

29 Grandpa Stoltzfus Dies

In 1986, we returned again to the United States for itineration and refueling. We needed a car to get around. Choices were limited on our missionary budget, and besides, who buys a car and sells it again in six months? I scanned the Lancaster New Era and found a 1973 American Motors Ambassador Brougham for the bargain price of $695. The old station wagon was a tank with a V-8 engine, full leather interior, wood grain side panels, high mileage, and room for our family of five. "It won't give you any problems!" the mechanic declared as he emerged from the garage, rubbing his greasy hands on equally greasy overalls. "I guarantee it." As we walked to the car parked on the far side of the lot, he offered a story about a trade-in. "It's in top shape," he assured me. He wouldn't, however, put anything in writing.

I slipped into the plush driver's seat and cranked the motor. It roared to life and then purred quietly behind the optional sound-abatement package. We took her out for a spin. On return I tried to negotiate the price. No soap. I peeled off seven one hundred dollar bills. He gave me five dollars back, with the keys and the title. Over the next six months, that Ambassador faithfully delivered our family to destinations from Pennsylvania to Florida to Indiana to Iowa and back again – thousands of gas-guzzling miles in cool, faded luxury. We weren't old young enough to care about our gypsy appearance in the rolling brown behemoth.

While on the road, Mother called and said Grandpa Stoltzfus was in the hospital, diagnosed with leukemia. Grandpa was ninety-one years old, retired for twenty years, and until this interruption was enjoying the twilight of his life with Grandma. They stayed active with church and a large community of friends and family. In retirement Grandpa needed a hobby, so, always a handyman – a talent of every farmer – Grandpa had started building grandfather clocks in his basement. The kits were not easy to assemble. They arrived in boxes of rough-cut pieces of raw wood, brass mechanical parts and diagrams. Grandpa sawed, screwed, nailed, sanded, glued and varnished the wood and brass into works of art.

During one session, he cut off three fingers on his band saw. He collected the dismembered fingertips, wrapped the injured hand in gauze and asked a panicked wife to drive him to the hospital. Emergency Room doctors reattached the fingers. Miraculously Grandpa regained the use of his hand and fingers, and resumed building clocks, a little slower and a lot more cautious. He never sold a single clock. He gave them all away, one at a time as he finished them, to family and friends. We stored ours in my parents' home, and then, when we returned to the United States, proudly displayed it in ours. It is still in my office.

A few weeks after the diagnosis, Mother called again and urged us to come to Pennsylvania quickly. Earlier in the week the doctors had sent him home to die, Mother said. At ninety-one, what more could be done? We drove six hundred miles from Goshen to Paradise, Pennsylvania the next day. When we got to the house, Grandma met us at the door. Mother had spent the day with them, she said, but had just left to do errands. We exchanged hugs and hellos, and then Beth took our two children aside with Grandma while I went into Grandpa's bedroom. His eyes were closed when I approached the bed. The attending nurse had just sedated him for the night, so he might not be very responsive she said. I took Grandpa's left hand and squeezed it gently. "Hi Grandpa," I said. "This is Doug. Beth and the children are here too, out in the living room with Grandma. We wanted to come and see you."

He lay on his back, eyes closed, breathing steadily, unresponsive. I was glad to be by his bedside and had things I wanted to say. It felt odd talking to him this way, but I pressed forward, first thanking him for everything I could think of – his example, his encouragement, being available to us, everything he had done for me as a child, and for our family since. Grandpa's nurse sat quietly in a corner chair during the monologue. I wasn't sure if Grandpa heard anything. I sighed and continued, "Grandpa, I prayed for many years that you would live to see the coming of Jesus...but now, it doesn't look like that is going to happen, so I want to pray for you and release you to go to be with Him in heaven."

I prayed a short prayer, and when I finished he stirred. It was a subtle but immediate response, one quiet event following another, not unlike the rustling in a church crowd after the benediction. Grandpa stirred, then, he winced and opened his eyes. He squeezed my hand ever so slightly, and, well, began to die. The nurse stepped forward and checked his pulse. "He's dying," she said. She left the room and returned with Grandma, who rushed in to the other side of the bed, grasped Grandpa's right hand with both of hers, and leaned in close. "Oh Aaron!" she cried, as tears rolled down her wrinkled cheeks. She hovered over him stroking his hand, and together we waited in sacred silence while he entered into eternity.

Our secularized scientific and educational communities tell us that human beings are nothing more than biological tissue, a fluke of millions of years, evolved from primal goo, a now intelligent life form, bound to a random blue planet. We are told that the human heart beats two billion times during an average seventy-five years, between birth and death, through passion and pain, and that the last beat of that heart ends our temporal, animal existence. Against such an ocean of knowledge and culture it is hard to argue for faith, for God, and eternity. But there I stood beside Aaron F. Stoltzfus, my Grandpa, in quiet awe as he passed through a meta-physical doorway, from earthly life to Divinity and His Realm, the end of frail physical existence and to continue an eternal one. The experience offered stark clarity to me that life is more than flesh and blood and death and earth. Can I prove this empirically? No, but neither can the evolutionists prove otherwise. God is inherently unprovable. We weren't around fifteen billion years ago, or even six *thousand*, to observe the goings on. Recorded history spans mere thousands of years. What do we really know? We childishly, and sometimes arrogantly, make broad assumptions and projections about the grand subject of origins. I'm not against the speculations, but all things being equal, faith and heaps of humility are much better options.

If, in my life, there was ever a holy moment, this was it. What a life Grandpa lived! What a legacy he was leaving behind. Standing by his bedside, I was overwhelmed. To be with him as he passed from earth's reality to heaven's was an honor beyond description. It's not within me to question or evaluate these realities. They simply are what they are. Faith has its own palpability, and is, as Hebrews declares, "the evidence of things hoped for." On this planet of broken relationships, busted families, mean behavior, and skewered priorities, too few give faith a chance. And suffer the lack of it. And too few experience Grandpa's kind of existence, and of his kind of legacy. Of such people Hebrews says: "...the world was not worthy..." I wish everyone could know someone of this ilk, because in measuring life, and in unveiling eternity, few men are his equal.

The funeral was held at Maple Grove Mennonite Church, one of the churches he helped found and pastor. Three hundred people came to pay their respects and say goodbye. I gave the eulogy and retold that bedside moment.

Seventeen years later, in 2003, I spoke again at Grandma Stoltzfus' funeral. She was ninety-five. She outlived all her friends, and still over one hundred and twenty five people attended her funeral! As I joined the children, grandchildren, great-grandchildren, and their kin and friends to say goodbye, I was again reminded of legacy. Standing before the crowd at her funeral, I said, "Aaron and Katie Stoltzfus lived their entire lives as a consistent, godly example before us. What I am today is a result, not only of my choices, but also of their influence. They prayed for me to follow God's call, and stood with my family and me as we followed it. What I am today is not just the fruit of my own choices. It is also because of the example and influence of Grandpa and Grandma Stoltzfus. In short, my grandparents made it easier for me to be a man of God."

That is a legacy!

ASIA II

I'm writing these words from the sofa in the Webb's home in Kailua, Oahu. Sam and Nancy are traveling on the mainland. It's a pretty nice arrangement... for us. I called Sam in July to say hello, and when he heard I was taking a late summer writing break, he insisted we come to Hawaii. "We're traveling for three weeks in Asia, so come and use our house and cars!" was the way he put it. We weren't going to pass up *that* offer, a free house and car in Hawaii, so we made arrangements and landed in Honolulu a month later. Their son James met us at the airport and helped us settle into the house, with all the amenities, including two surfboards.

I planned to write in the mornings, and surf in the afternoons, while Beth lounged on the beach. Three days into that plan I came off my surfboard in big waves at Ala Moana. "We haven't seen these kind of waves on the South Shore for ten years" was the news report. Indeed. I got thrown over the cascading falls, landed on my upside-down surfboard, and broke off a side-bite fin on my left calf. I'll spare the reader the gory details about the excruciating pain, the huge hematoma, and the paddle back to shore. The next day a doctor lanced the tumor and ordered me out of the water for the duration. So, here I sit, leg draped over the back of the sofa, writing memories about India, Malaysia, John Whalen, my brother Dale, and Grandpa Stoltzfus. Accidents are brutal, but they can be a gift! The down time – and I am DOWN, on the couch and unable to walk for two weeks – has given me a muse to write. Many of the stories on these pages are the fruit. Sam and Nancy return in a few days, and by then my leg should be healthy enough to limp around Honolulu with them and Beth to enjoy each other's company over Hawaii's marvelous Korean Bar-B-Q and Kua Aina Burgers, and forays to favorite haunts in Ala Moana and Kaka'ako Waterfront Park where we will gaze for an hour at Oahu's incomparably beautiful Pacific Ocean sunsets. And I'll enviously watch local surfers catch waves in the golden evening glow. Life, as they say, has its moments, even when one must experience them with a limp.

30 Sri Lanka and the Team

On an April day in 1987 John Whalen was driving our blue diesel "lorry" through Matale District on our way back to Colombo. The team was squashed shoulder-to-shoulder beside him on the bench seat, consisting at this time of four men: John, Bill and myself, with one addition: Roger Bontrager, a single man from Indiana who joined us for a year. Everyone in Roger's family – his father, mother and two siblings, all members of Zion Chapel – had visited or worked with us in Asia. Roger's older brother Terry served with us twice, first as a single man and then later with his wife and new baby. We'll get back to Terry.

On this return trip to Colombo after two weeks of open-air meetings and church plants in the hill country, we chose a different-than-normal route, through the northern foothills, with a singular purpose for the diversion – to climb Sigiriya. Sigiriya is a famous Sri Lanka landmark, the "Eighth Wonder of the World" thus dubbed by UNESCO. The massive rock monolith juts six hundred feet out of the surrounding dense green jungle; it has been an object of veneration for Sri Lanka's Buddhist culture for a couple millennia. On arrival we parked the lorry, paid the tourist entrance – double the price for non-locals – and started up the narrow, winding path to the top. The ascent is cluttered with obstructions: narrow paths, bulging rocks, seeping water, steep climbs, cliff-hanging steel-cage walkways, and other hazards requiring physical dexterity. Sri Lanka's tropical heat adds to (or perhaps takes away from) the exertion. We completed the ascent within an hour and arrived pouring sweat and ravenously thirsty. After three-dollar soft drinks – offered by entrepreneurial Sri Lankan vendors who had long before discovered that tourists, having no other options, will pay five times normal price for a cold drink – we completed a brief walking tour of the summit's gardens and temples and then started an even more precarious descent back down.

Along the steeply declining path we returned to a five-foot-wide stone staircase. It was bounded on both sides by two-foot-wide stone bannisters, all carved out of the rocky sides of Sigiriya ages before, transforming this part of the craggy cliff face into a comfortable stairway. The stairs and bannisters descended about twenty or thirty steps to a large platform and then the path turned left around the belly of the big rock, narrowing and descending along a ledge. The stairs and bannister were worn smooth from centuries of human traffic. Seeing the bannister, John shouted, "Hey cool!" Before I could stop him, he mounted the bannister to ride it like a sliding board. The platform below was at least twenty feet away. Unfortunately for John, he took off like a flash, way too fast and instantly out of control. His feet and legs flailed into the air, while he futilely grabbed at the rock bannister to slow down. At the bottom John launched off the bannister. Miraculously he landed on his feet, but only for a second, because his feet immediately skidded out from under him, slamming him to the stone platform on his rear end. We raced down the stairs and gathered around him.

"Are you all right, man!?" I asked.

"Yeah, I'm fine." John said as he struggled to get up, rubbing his backside, obviously bruised and dazed. He was sort of leaning over too, bent at the waist. "Man, that knocked the wind out of me." He started brushing off his trousers.

"Are you sure you're all right? You hit pretty hard."

"Yeah, I'm fine." John's face was turning gray, the color of the surroundings, and he started rocking back and forth on his heels.

"I think you better sit down."

"Yeah, maybe." With that, John collapsed to the gray rock, unconscious.

At the same moment, a group of three young European women, dressed in halter-tops and flowing flowery cotton skirts, were ascending the narrow path from below. They arrived as John toppled over, and quickly pushed us aside and gathered around him.

"Oh my God, he fainted!" one shouted. The words came out in thick, accent-laden English, sounding like, "Oh my gawd! Hay Fiyeented!" The women circled the prostrate and unconscious man and started fanning him with their flowing skirts, revealing to us and everyone else glimpses of tanned legs and black panties. John, who was lying face up on the ground, woke from the stupor with a full view of uncovered female thighs! He jumped to his feet, still staggering, awakened more from embarrassment than the fresh air being offered by flailing skirts.

After five years of working together, I had adjusted to John's impulsiveness. A few years earlier John had an unfortunate encounter involving fingers and a car door. Another involved a bet with our children, something about his ability to jump and tap his forehead on the living room ceiling beam in our Hua Hin home. He won the bet... with a lot of bloodletting from a split-open forehead. John had a penchant for embarrassing self-infliction, an impulsiveness that frequently trumped common sense. With an IQ that hovered somewhere north of 160, the combination had an endearing, and for John, humiliating, irony. The fingers and car door episode is worth retelling, but it will help if I provide a little context first. So, I must go back to my "pioneer" days in Sri Lanka.

Calling myself a pioneer, and comparing our escapades with the great heroes of history, the true pioneers, who risked life and limb to sail around the world in tall ships in their hoary quest to discover new lands and riches, is almost obscene. Unfortunately for contemporary pioneers, hoary quests are no longer possible. By the time I arrived on the planet all new lands had been discovered, explored, tamed and populated, and most of the treasures hidden within their earthen bellies had been found and exploited.

We modern missionary types use the word pioneer to describe the visionary who carries the Faith to a new place and a new people. But again, let's face it, by the time I landed in Colombo in January 1984, Christianity was present and had been established on the Island of Ceylon for a thousand years, perhaps longer. It is believed, with supporting evidence, that the Apostle Thomas (you know, the Doubter) visited the island during the first century. So, my use of the word pioneer refers to the fact that I was the first of *my people* to visit this island. In other words, my pioneer status is based solely on the fact that, on arrival, I didn't actually *know* anyone. Ah well, the word still has a nice ring to it, if it is a little hollower these days.

I researched the nation of Sri Lanka before that first trip in January 1984, made inquiries, wrote letters, and received several invitations to conduct meetings, two of which involved preaching in open-air meetings in the capital, a heady offer for an ambitious young missionary. Only one contact interested me, however, from a Tamil pastor in Jaffna. In the early 1980s things were not going well for Sri Lanka's Tamil people. I decided to forego the Colombo invitations, an example set previously by Ray Jennings and Wayne Crooke who were uninterested in sophisticated capitals and their sophisticated churches. Like them, I headed to the remote places and the neglected people, which in part meant Sri Lanka's Tamils in the northern villages near Jaffna Peninsula. The beginning chapter of this tome is a part of THAT adventure.

The Island of Ceylon declared its independence from Britain in 1948 (Ceylon was renamed Sri Lanka in 1972). In

1960, a Buddhist woman named Sirima Bandaranaike was elected Prime Minister of the fledgling nation. It is an interesting tidbit of history that the first nation to officially inaugurate a woman head of state was a small island nation in the Indian Ocean. So much for western civilization's presumed leadership in progressive thinking. Mrs. Bandaranaike won the election by courting the Buddhist religion and the Singhalese race after which she steadily passed laws favoring the Buddhist, Singhalese majority. For many years, this block of fifteen million people had been nursing a grudge against the minority Tamils who, although only three million, were more ambitious and progressive in business, education, and politics. Mrs. Bandaranaike leveraged the Singhalese angst to come to power.

By the time our team arrived in Sri Lanka in January 1984, Mrs. Bandaranaike's nationalist policies had escalated racial tensions to crisis levels and driven the country to the brink of bankruptcy. She lost the 1980 elections to J.R. Jayewardene, a former ally, now political rival, who had run his campaign on a more moderate platform. Jayewardene, also a Singhalese, promised political and economic reforms. Unfortunately, by the time he came to power, the damage was done. Trust between the races was at an all time low. Jayewardene could do little to heal tensions. In July 1983, six months before our first trip to the island, Tamil separatists ambushed and killed thirteen Singhalese soldiers in the northern city of Jaffna, a strongly Tamil area. The Singhalese population exploded across the island against the Tamil people. Riots and reprisals broke out everywhere against Tamil communities. When the dust finally settled a few days later, over ten thousand people, mostly Tamils, were dead.

When we landed in Colombo six months later we were greeted by a nation on the verge of civil war. Martial law was in force nation-wide. Armed military posts were everywhere on the streets, the press was censored, and curfews were in force. Desperate to save face before the international community and keep tourist and foreign investment money rolling in, the government tried to restore peace and get the factions talking to each other. But Tamil separatists and Buddhist religious leaders weren't having any. Tamil separatists intended to divide the island, they said, and form a new nation, Tamil Eelam, in the northern and eastern provinces. Buddhist and Singhalese extremists were calling for all out war. Negotiations failed over and over. Tourist and business investments dried up, and Sri Lanka plunged into deep recession.

The military established tent-city bases everywhere on the island, especially in Tamil areas, trying to maintain order and stop the violent attacks coming from both Tamil separatists and Singhalese militia. Nervous soldiers, mostly young Singhalese men armed with AK-47 assault rifles, stood guard on street corners, crouched behind heavily sand-bagged bunkers in the Capitol, and manned highway checkpoints throughout the island. To have open-air meetings in this environment was perhaps naïve. But after Thoeng in Thailand and Amritsar in India my passion and faith knew no bounds. I was ready to take on the challenge of Sri Lanka. If Thailand belonged to Wayne Crooke and India belonged to Ray Jennings, Sri Lanka was mine! Of course we needed police and military permits for public meetings. Miraculously we got them, most of the time, probably because the government wanted to demonstrate to the world, and visiting friends, that freedom of religion and other such liberties and normalcies of life were still actually functioning in the country, even while an alarming number of people were dying by bombings, separatist assaults on police and military compounds and in public places, and from mysterious night raids by armed bands of thugs.

The "Tamil Tigers," officially the "Liberation Tigers of Tamil Eelam" (LTTE), were the largest and most organized separatist group on the island. Other groups existed. All had formed during the latter years of Mrs. Bandaranaike's reign. Some separatist leaders started in politics and then, frustrated by blatantly racist policies against their people, abandoned the political process and took up arms. The separatist groups fought both the government and each other for control of territory and to be the "official" voice of the Tamil cause. Eventually the LTTE prevailed because their ruthless leader, Vellupillai Prabhakaran, wiped out other groups and then rounded up and assimilated the remnants into his Tiger organization.

Were the Tamil separatists terrorists or freedom fighters? It's a compelling question. One got different answers depending on whom was asked. In the beginning, I naively assumed two things: separatists are terrorists and governments are humane. For people caught between the pointed guns of government soldiers and armed separatists, the issues are not that simple. Tamil Christians, who are commanded by Scripture to honor and pray for their government leaders, found themselves in an almost impossible predicament. Frequently I heard Tamil Christian leaders, who in every other way were moral, law-abiding citizens, refer to leaders in Colombo as a "terrorist government." One Tamil church member in Jaffna, after a long diatribe against the government and their discriminatory policies, declared, "The Tigers aren't terrorists! They are freedom fighters!" I withheld response but made a note of the man's frustration. I disagreed with the "freedom fighter" designation for the Tigers and their leader primarily on the grounds that George Washington and the heroes of the American Revolution didn't go around killing men, women and children at community halls and bus stops. George Washington focused on armed British soldiers. Vellupillai Prabhakaran didn't qualify for the label.

We entered Sri Lanka at the height of this boiling caldron. Looking back from the perspective of mid-life, I really was nuts! We walked into a war. And the young men and women who followed me were just as loony. After our initial connection in Jaffna, we headed to Mullaitivu on the northeast coast, the heart of Tamil separatism, to conduct a second meeting. We secured police permission for the open-air meeting and while we set up our equipment in a dirty soccer field, national team members drove through the town in an old white van broadcasting the meeting with loudspeakers on the roof and scattering thousands of handbills. Opening night we cranked up our little borrowed generator and turned on the lights and sound. The local Christian musicians brought an assortment of broken down instruments and started playing and singing, mostly out-of-tune, but the noise was joyful and it drew a crowd.

After thirty minutes two hundred people were standing in front of the platform curiously listening to the dissonance. What came next was not in the program. Two green military Jeeps stuffed with soldiers drove onto the field and plowed into the crowd, who saw them coming and wisely got out of the way, parting like the Red Sea. The Jeeps stopped within several feet of the platform. A military official in green combat fatigues jumped out. His green trousers were tucked neatly into black boots, a green beret with official markings was perched at an angle on his head. He was packing a side arm. While the drivers stayed behind the wheels, a few of the soldiers in helmets and flack jackets and carrying Russian AK-47 assault rifles got out and stood guard, scanning the crowd, fingers on the triggers. The officer and guards walked to the stage and shouted at us.

"What's going on?" I asked.

"They say we must shut down the meeting." Pastor Ambrose said, looking very nervous.

"What!? Why?!"

Pastor Ambrose went down to talk with the soldiers while I remained on stage. I was both afraid – my second experience with automatic weapons – and outraged at their rude interruption. We had a permit! This was a legal and peaceful assembly. Pastor Ambrose finished talking with the leader and returned to the stage.

"We must close the meeting immediately."

"But we have a police permit!" I protested. "They can't just shut us down like this!"

"They say this area is under military control, and we did not get a permit from them."

"The police gave permission!" I protested. "We have it in writing!"

"They say the police don't have jurisdiction."

"Why didn't the police tell us that?"

Ambrose shrugged, a forlorn look on his face. "I guess the police and the military don't agree," he replied.

"Can we finish this meeting? There are people here!"

"No, he said we must close now and leave. We must do as he says." Ambrose looked nervously at the lead officer who was staring at us.

Disputes over jurisdiction are a common consequence of martial law. Wartime creates it's own issues. With no recourse – they had the weapons – and with a rapidly waning crowd of now terrified people, including our musicians and volunteers, we turned off the lights and sound, packed up our gear and headed back to the guesthouse. I decided we would go visit the police and military compound in the morning to sort this out.

That night it started raining. January is monsoon season, so we should not have been surprised. The next morning, with the rain still pouring, the electricity went out in the entire town, thus settling the matter of an appeal to the authorities. The downpour and the power outage continued for four days. On a sunny day, the Mullaitivu Guest House, our accommodations for the week, was gloomier than a cow barn and not much cleaner. In monsoon season it was deplorable. Mold grew like black carpet on the walls and in corners. Dust accumulated, a half inch thick, on out-of-reach surfaces – ceiling fan blades, wardrobe tops, and floorboard trim – anything off the normal cleaning path, if there was one. The walls in each room were ten feet high, and there was no ceiling above, only a roof. Exposed wood roof rafters stretched across the entire building, painted with black tar to protect against termites, supporting an ancient orange tile-covered hip roof. With no ceiling, guests in one room could hear the goings on in any adjacent room, and, if said guest was so inclined, he could climb up and *observe* the goings on neighboring rooms. We hoped no one was so inclined.

On the second day, rain still pouring, the guys waded through flooded streets and removed our equipment from the soccer field, which was now submerged in three feet of water. I stayed in my room to pray about our next move. In the adjacent room, Roberta Bontrager and her infant daughter Amber – the family had bravely joined our team for six months – waited while husband/father Terry led the field strike duty.

Midway through the morning a voice called out to me. "Doug!" a female voice echoed over the ten-foot wall. I didn't answer immediately. The voice sounded like Roberta's.

"Doug!" came the voice again, echoing over the wall.

"Uh, yes."

"This is Roberta. Can you come to my room?"

"Uh. Sure. Be right there."

I went out to the porch – there was no hallway, the rooms opened to the outside like a motel with a large covered porch. Hotel patrons, all males on this day, had gathered for food, beer, and idle chatter. They watched me emerge from my room and knock on Roberta's door. "Come in," came a faint voice from inside. Roberta was in bed, lying on her back, holding infant Amber on her tummy. Her face was ghostly white, and her hands, holding the baby, were curling into gnarled fists.

"Roberta! What is the matter!?"

"Can you hold Amba fa me. I haf to oos the bafoom." The request came out distorted because her white lips were twisted and slightly paralyzed.

Roberta was a nurse, so I figured she had some idea what was going on. I took the baby from her gnarled fists. "What's wrong Roberta?" I asked, alarmed.

"I sink I got food poisoning fuhm the westwant. Jus take Amba." I took the baby from her twisted hands while she slowly sat up. Roberta stumbled to the bathroom and remained there for a very long time while I walked the baby in circles praying. Retching noises wafted through the room, heightening my anxiety. I had visions of a young American tourist woman, dead on the black moldy floor of a ratty guesthouse bathroom on the eastern coast of Sri Lanka. It didn't help that rumors about massive monsoon flooding in the region had begun circulating among guesthouse employees. Roberta eventually emerged from the bathroom. Her color was a little closer to human and (thank God) her hands and mouth looked normal too. She explained, without the twisted lips, that she felt better after losing most of her insides from both ends. The words actually came out normally. Roberta was a refined young lady. She did her best to maintain poise and dignity through what was certainly an embarrassing ordeal, now told to a man holding her baby in her bedroom. Sometimes there simply isn't much decorum to preserve. I handed Amber back and returned to my room, hoping Terry and the guys would get back soon. I felt like going to look for them, but thought better. Roberta might need me if the convulsions returned.

The guys returned from the field and we packed up the soggy equipment. Two days passed, with rain pouring down. We spent the time in our rooms in quiet gloom, sometimes gathering in my room to pray, or on the porch or dining room to play cards, tell stories, and take our chances at the guesthouse food. We read books for hours, waiting, but mostly we languished in dingy light and moldy air. In this sad little town, with the pouring rain and downed electrical grid, there was no place to go. Every afternoon the guesthouse porch and dining areas filled with Sri Lankan men, clad in shirts and sarongs, smoking cheap cigarettes and sipping whiskey.

Many Sri Lankan men, especially in the villages, wear the sarong. The sarong is a large swath of cloth wrapped around the waist covering the legs to mid-calf or lower. The sarong can be both casual attire and official dress. Typically sarongs are white or a colorful plaid. On the day I assisted

Roberta I had wrapped a plaid swath of cloth around my waist, one I had a purchased from a local vendor. When I emerged from my room, the drunken men at the porch tables began jabbering in one of Sri Lanka's languages – either Tamil or Singhalese – I was too new to the nation to determine which – sounding something like, "Gumpala gilia bed sheet, magalaba ramalula bed sheet..." All I heard was bed sheet bed sheet bed sheet, and realized that the cloth I had wrapped around my waist was not in fact a sarong. How the men could make the distinction was beyond the divination of this uninitiated and now embarrassed white man, and was another reason why, after entering Roberta's room to hold Amber and pray for her retching mother, I chose to remain there. That was the last day I wore a sarong.

The rain stopped on the third day, and of course everyone on our team was ready to get out of town and head back to Jaffna. Not possible, I was told by the fat, bald-headed proprietor of our establishment. He seemed to know what he was talking about, even though his appearance, in greasy T-shirt and dirty white sarong, didn't convey much authority, and left us wondering where he got the information. Nothing in my experience in Mullaitivu to this point helped alter the impression that the entire town was a dirty rat hole populated by drunken men and power hungry autocrats. How the proprietor could know anything about what was happening even a few miles away seemed impossible, seeing as how there had been no electricity for three days and flood waters prevented travel. But his report was: Flooding throughout the northern and eastern provinces, hundreds of thousands displaced from their homes, all roads impassable. Maybe he had a battery-powered radio.

We waited an additional day and then, fighting claustrophobia and a myopic frustration with dark, dirty rooms, no electricity, bad food (thank God, besides Roberta, no one else got sick!), drunken neighbors and snappish military rule, I pressed Pastor Ambrose and his team members to find a van and a driver, and, if necessary float us out of

Mullaitivu. The van and driver arrived at 3:30 p.m., about three hours late but enough time to get to Jaffna before dark. Remember, this is wartime. On the trip back, we didn't want any trouble from separatists who had a reputation for robbing civilian vehicles at night. We left Mullaitivu loaded to the gills, people and suitcases stuffed inside the van and large boxes of equipment strapped to the roof.

Our transportation was almost comical, like a circus prop carrying a load of clowns into the ring, a big laugh for adoring fans. The van resembled something discarded at a junkyard. Every square inch of the exterior was dented, rusted, or faded beyond restoration. The headlights were gone, only the dark holes remained, giving the front a sort of skull-like appearance. The side sliding door was missing, and the gaping cavity was so gnarled that a new door could never be re-attached. Except for the windshield, most of the windows were missing. Roberta and Amber scooted onto the ripped-vinyl bench seat behind the driver and Terry positioned himself beside them, next to the gaping orifice, to keep his wife and baby from falling out. Pastor Ambrose and his team of four squeezed into the back seat. The pile of luggage behind them served as a massive sharp-cornered headrest. We stuffed handbags and boxes under every bench and into every available corner. Because I was paying, I was expected to sit in the front seat with the driver. It was not a significant improvement. If we were in an accident, or plunged into a flooded hole, the driver and I died first. Ambrose' brother Anthony sat between the driver and me. His polished appearance and an upbeat demeanor – both attributes were an asset in this soon to be unbearable excursion – helped temper the atmosphere. It needed tempering. The three of us sat above a grinding, smoking, wheezing excuse for a diesel engine. In my eroded state of mind, Anthony's smiling face was one of the few remaining high points on the island.

Off we went. After a few miles, a short distance by most measurements of travel – but then you probably haven't driven in the northern and eastern districts of Sri Lanka – the road disappeared into a sea of brown water. Anthony got out, removed his shoes, rolled up his trouser legs, and walked into the ocean in front of the van. He waved his hand and said something to the driver in Tamil, obviously intending to guide us forward on the roadbed and keep us from slipping off the submerged shoulders. The driver shifted into low gear and we proceeded forward at two miles per hour. Sometimes the road re-emerged from the water, and then Anthony climbed back in and we sped to twenty miles per hour. Then when the road dipped back into the ocean again, Anthony the Navigator resumed his work. One time the water got so deep it began flooding into the side door. We quickly backed up to shallower water-at-axle-level and stopped, then re-arranged the suitcases. Some were sent to the roof and others onto laps and available empty spaces. While we shuffled gear, the driver opened the engine compartment, disconnected the air-intake hose from the air filter, and raised it to a higher position. A diesel engine will run, even under the water, as long as a supply of fresh, dry air is available. Our driver obviously had previous experience with floods. The knowledge wasn't reassuring. Then off we went, descending into unknown depths, until the water was running through the van floor six inches deep, and Anthony was out in front up to his thighs!

By 6:30 p.m. darkness set in and we were far from Jaffna. The brown sea steadily faded into an expansive black ocean that blended at the horizon into a blackening sky. Gray monsoon clouds above – no stars, no moon – faded into blackness. I asked the driver to turn on the headlights. No lights, he said. I then remembered the empty sockets on the front of the vehicle – black holes in a dead skull. Trying to contain my frustration at this van driver's incredible lack of foresight – he was obviously interested only in the foreigner's money at the end of this fated journey – I pulled out my flashlight and pointed the beam into the black void. The pathetic yellow light scarcely illuminated Anthony's backside.

Never had I experienced such blackness. Monsoon clouds obscured every hint of celestial light. That we were far from civilization mattered little because the electrical grid was down; if there were any other human domiciles nearby, there was no manmade light anyway.

Westerners, especially city dwellers, take the night for granted. We are rarely in utter darkness. We live our entire lives bathed in light, available at the flip of a switch. The outside is so widely illuminated by streetlights, store lights and house lights that urban areas never actually experience darkness. Not so in most of the third world, where nighttime is dark time. Here we were in utterly rural Asia, along a flooded road in a remote corner of Sri Lanka, with cloud cover obscuring every celestial glimmer. Besides my dimming flashlight beam, there was not an observable source of light – human, natural, cosmic or divine – in any direction! We stopped moving, unable to see beyond the front bumper of the van. For a moment we all sat in gloomy silence with only the diesel engine purring in the blackness, and the faint sound of floodwater flowing around us.

"Well, what are we going to do now?" I mumbled to no one in particular.

"Why don't we dig out our quartz lights and fire up the generator?" Terry suggested from the seat behind me.

"What?" I asked from the sadistic gloom.

"We have the stage and field lights in the box on the roof! We can just rig it all up and plug it into the generator. We'll have plenty of light."

"Yeah! Great idea Terry!" The odd suggestion shook me out of the funk. "Let's do it!" Everyone climbed out of the van. Terry and a couple of the Sri Lankans leaped to the roof and unpacked lights, wires, poles and the little red kerosene generator. Within minutes they mounted two five-hundred-watt quartz lights onto poles. They strung the wires, and stuck the light poles, one through the left side window of the van, the other through the right side window. The poles projected out of both sides at forty-five degree angles.

335

"Fire it up!" Terry commanded. Someone on the roof pulled the cord and the generator purred to life. Our black watery wilderness instantly brightened like a nighttime high school football field. The road, visible but awash with floodwater, burst into view.

"Wow! Way to go, Terry!"

A flurry of back slaps, handshakes and Sri Lankan style atta-boys followed and then everyone piled back into the van and off we went. Rolling slowly down the road we looked like a Boeing 747 taxiing for take off! When the road finally rose out of the water we rose with it into a happier state of mind, sailing down the runway, lights ablaze. We were probably not going more than twenty-five miles per hour, but it felt like eighty. Within twenty minutes we arrived at a small village. As we chugged into town the generator sputtered and died, plunging us back into blackness. Everyone jumped out of the van again and one or two climbed onto the roof to check out the problem.

"Brother, we're out of kerosene," someone said.

"Don't we have any in the spare can?" I asked.

"No, brother. Empty." What an oversight.

"Is there a petrol station or a store nearby where we can buy some?" I asked.

"No, brother. Small village. No petrol stations." Besides, it was ten p.m. Sidewalks get pulled in at dark in these villages. Not to be dissuaded, the Sri Lankan brothers fanned out and started knocking on doors asking for fuel. They returned after thirty minutes with a plastic bottle, about one liter of kerosene, a merciful provision from a Sri Lankan Good Samaritan.

"Is that enough?" I asked, eyeing the bottle.

"Yes, brother. Jaffna close."

Soon we were on our way again and within an hour rolled into an electrified Jaffna! The first light I saw – it reached out to us in the distance – was an illuminated Christian Cross at an Anglican Church. It appeared almost angelic in the distance, like a heavenly sign from God. An ancient Star guided wise men on their journey to Jesus. They certainly felt something like what we experienced driving into Jaffna. Sadly, our plight and the deliverance was superficial compared to the tragic loss suffered by two hundred thousand Sri Lankans who were displaced by the flooding. A little perspective.

31 John and the Car Door

I promised to tell the story of John and the car door. So we finally get to it. The episode happened in an earlier time, during our second trip to Sri Lanka, in September 1984, but it remains one of the most comical and endearing experiences in my personal history. The nation was at war, bombings and their curfews happened at regular intervals, military presence was everywhere, and our team was in the heart of conflicted territory. John, recently arrived from India because the Jennings Team had disbanded, accompanied me on this second trip. He was a welcome addition. The Bontragers had finished in June and I needed a replacement. Open-air meetings were scheduled on the island's northern-most point, on the Jaffna peninsula, in Jaffna City and the town of Kilinochchi near Elephant Pass.

The field we chose for the first meeting was in the heart of Jaffna City, easily accessible to the general population. After five or six nights of preaching, crowds grew to nearly one thousand people. We finished the service one evening and waited for the crowd to disperse, then gathered up our stuff and packed it into a taxi, a black British-made Austin. Jaffna was overrun with these little black fifty-year-old right-side steering cars. Left lane driving is of course a lingering feature of British colonialism. The black British Austin, a relic of a bygone era, was reminiscent of 1930s automotive creativity. Henry Ford, the progenitor of the mass production automobile, was once asked why he didn't offer his automobiles in other colors. He replied, "You can have any color you want as long as it's black!" Mr. Ford was known for maniacal eccentricities, and this seems to be one of them, but in fact, on the point of the color of his cars, he was a pragmatist. Black paint dries faster. Time was money, and Mr. Ford wasn't going to muck up profits for something as trivial as the color of an automobile. The policy reached around the globe, and for a time, almost every car in the universe was painted black. Up into the 1980s Sri Lanka seemed to have kept most of them operational.

We packed all of our equipment – sound system, wires, boxes, literature – into the back of the car – the load reached to the ceiling – and I squeezed into the left bucket seat beside the driver, and then slid over the gap in the bucket seats, straddled the gear shift, and pressed shoulder-to-shoulder against the driver so John could squeeze in beside me. This little British car was not designed for three adults in the front, especially when two were American men. We were butt to butt to butt, shoulder to shoulder to shoulder. John and I had grown accustomed to such uncomfortable proximity in Asia. The driver, Sri Lankan to the bone, seemed oblivious, nothing outside Sri Lankan norm for him. The passenger door was still open and half of John seemed to be hanging out of the car. John grabbed the roof ledge to hold his torso on the seat, then reached across his chest with his inside arm, gripped the door handle and slammed the door shut.

A brief moment of silence followed. "We're in," I thought. The silence ended abruptly. John started screaming. "AH, AH, AH, AH! MY HAND! MY HAND!" John had forgotten that the car door had a metal frame around the window. The slamming of the door wedged his fingers between the door frame and the roof!

"AH, AH, AH! MY HAND IS STUCK! OH, IT HURTS! IT HURTS! I WANT TO SAY BAD WORDS!!!"

Pressed like a sardine between John and the driver, I could offer no assistance. The driver careened his neck to see what all the fuss was about while John frantically scratched for the door handle with his free right hand. Finally, the latch released and John exploded out of the car into the grassy field. Jumping and hopping around in the darkness, holding his smashed fingers, John bellowed again, "AH, AH! MY HAND! MY HAND! I WANT TO SAY BAD WORDS! I WANT TO SAY BAD WORDS!"

I could have been more compassionate, but the event simulated a Road Runner and Wile E. Coyote cartoon. I was the clueless bird in the car. Chortle. Chortle. It really was funny. Miraculously, and perhaps because of the age of the car, nothing was broken or permanently damaged. I climbed out of the car to check John's hand, and he eventually calmed down. Unlike almost every other male in the universe who has pinched his fingers, John never uttered a bad word. Man of integrity. I am certain he *thought* of them. We got back into the car, slammed the door shut without incident, and rode to our hotel in silence. En route, John nursed his swelling hand and mumbled under his breath. And I added another story to our epic opera, performed in the Asia theater of the absurd.

32 Frustration and Renewal

By 1987 two other issues that started as tolerable inconveniences, had become tedious, repetitive frustrations. First, the living conditions in Sri Lanka's remote villages offer almost zero creature comforts. Pampered Americans are famous for complaining about comfort, so I was determined to be different, and endured in silence for three years. In fact most of the world lives better than Asia's impoverished villages. The tourist industry isn't booming in such places – there's nothing to see – so the adventuresome visitor has limited choices in lodging. Mullaitivu set the dubious precedent on low standards in 1984. Occasional discomfort is endurable, even desirable when young men embark on expeditions to prove themselves. Guts, glory and the bragging rights earned from tough survival experiences are big motivators for youth on a mission. We man up for the duration and return home boasting about dirt, mold, lice, and roaches. The technique works for short excursions. Years of monotonous repetition of vermin infestation is another matter, and raises serious questions about one's own good sense.

The tipping point happened in Nawala Pitiya. Our host pastor welcomed us as guests in his large old British-built home. The mansion was a leftover parsonage from colonial days, ornate in its prime, but now a decaying cavern of falling plaster, moldy concrete, and leaking roofs. Our eight-year-old son Jeremy and I stayed in a small bedroom with an attached bath, apparently the main guest suite. The bedroom ceiling leaked like a faucet when it rained, dripping streams of water ran down the moldy walls. The blackened mold-covered bathroom was beyond description. Bill and Mitzi Katz stayed in a drier room, an accommodation to the lady on the team I presume, and John just got lucky in his dry one-person corner. I wondered: was the church without money, or did the board not like their pastor?

Ironically, the second tipping point in Nawala Pitiya was related to the first: Rain. Rain is the archenemy of open-air meetings. In open-air work some inconvenience and a few cancellations are expected. "God sends rain on the just and the unjust," Jesus wisely commented, so, open air preaching – a tradition of Ray Jennings, Wayne Crooke, and now me – required planning around the dry seasons, accepting the inherent risks, and praying for favor. However, after three years, the plan to cover Sri Lanka with the Gospel of Jesus Christ was being seriously dampened by precipitation. Rain had become a chronic and debilitating nuisance. Nothing we did – schedule changes, dryer regions on the island, prayer and fasting – made any difference. Disappointment turned to stress. Stress eroded to distress and then it metastasized to desperation and finally sarcasm. We joked about renaming our ministry the "Free Rain-Making Crusades." Gloomy, fighting cynicism, but not to be beaten, I was determined to press forward. What else could we do? We were obeying God here. I just did a lot of wondering why He didn't take care of this detail. We began experimenting with tents and covered pavilions. It made little difference, in terms of improving the results. People are smart enough to stay inside when it is raining. They're NOT making a drenching trek across town for a meeting.

Threatening monsoon skies greeted us on arrival in Nawala Pitiya. Rainy forecasts added to the gloom. We decided to move the meeting to a small shelter at the edge of the soccer field. When the meeting opened, we preached a damp message to a drenched group of poor souls mostly from the church. I hated giving up the outdoor venue; even this field-side half-shelter was a compromise. "The lost will not enter a church building!" was a mantra I inherited from Ray and Wayne. "We must take the message to them!" I just wasn't shouting it very loudly anymore.

Jeremy helped the nationals distribute handbills around town for the meeting, and when he returned one afternoon, a young female worker from the church took me aside and said, "Uh, Mr. Gehman, your son has lice. You probably should wash his hair." She was obviously embarrassed, having to inform the guest preacher about his son's hair. I'm sure she secretly assumed our American family lived like pigs in Thailand and brought the lice with us. I smiled and thanked her and then went to my room and shouted (quietly of course) at God, something about not doing this anymore! Jeremy got the lice from the church's moldy, vermin infested guestroom! How do I communicate THAT with our host pastor?!

We closed the meeting after two nights and left town. At this low point, I was determined to end the travesty. At the time our team was reading Donald McGavran's book "Understanding Church Growth." I was enrolled in a Master's degree program at Fuller Theological Seminary; McGavran was required reading in the church growth course. The book began shifting a paradigm in my thinking; I required the entire team to read it. "We are going to sit at McGavran's feet," I declared, "and learn from him." McGavran held to two imperatives: people group thinking and receptivity principles. The shortest explanation for these terms is:

• People Group Thinking: humans naturally assemble themselves in groups – usually around what they have in common, starting with ethnicity and language. Sub-groups form around other things like age, special interests, etc., but the big default tends to follow race and language identity.

- Receptivity measures the relative openness – of such groups of people – to new ideas, practices and beliefs. Specifically Christian witness seeks to quantify a people group's possible openness to the Gospel. Typically people in crisis are more open to change than others. Natural disasters, war, racial or cultural discrimination, economic hardship, and etc. contribute to openness to change and adapting new ideas and practices, even religious orientation.

During the first few years of my work in Sri Lanka, not understanding any of this, I used a "shot-gun approach" to ministry: go anywhere and preach to anyone. After four years of randomly fruitful ministry that included a year of seminary studies (by extension) I became familiar with the principles of people groups and receptivity and was able to sharpen my strategy. Our team began noticing patterns: the Singhalese were indifferent or even resistant, while the Tamils were highly receptive to our message. Whenever we ventured into Tamil areas, they came by the hundreds, sometimes walking miles from the hills and tea estates to attend our meetings. They listened respectfully to our preaching, and, rushed forward to receive Christ. I started to understand why this was happening. Tamils were the persecuted minority, and therefore welcomed a message about a loving God who cares for them in their impoverished and downtrodden condition.

The Singhalese, by contrast, ignored us. If a few curious souls ventured into our meeting, they stood aloof, arms folded or hands on hips. They listened briefly and left. Young men sometimes came forward and stood defiantly near the stage, mocking and shouting. They waited for the meeting to end and then argued with us, insisting that Sri Lanka was a Buddhist country. We never argued or debated with them. Our preaching avoided references to cultural practices, religious traditions, or commentary about Buddhist icons or idol worship. We only talked about Jesus – his words, his life, his actions. But for some Singhalese, even that was too much. To be fair to them, our foreignness, our white skin and English language, was an insult to their cultural sensitivities. We looked and sounded too much like British colonizers. From their bruised worldview, British hegemony and western religion were inseparably linked. Forty years of independence had not yet healed the wounds.

The Tamils had no such gripe with the West. Their offenses originated inside the nation, linked to the discriminatory policies of the Singhalese. So, in late 1987, after observing the openness of the Tamil people, despite the rain and the despicable lodging conditions, we decided to focus on the Tamils, and conduct crusades in Tamil areas. We also decided to begin planting churches after the crusades. This too was a major paradigm shift, from crusade crowds as goal, to church planting as goal.

Of course, to plant national churches we needed a national partner. Through an almost miraculous turn of events – a sponsoring church abandoned us and thwarted us onto another – God led us to a Tamil pastor, Pastor K. Yoganathan. He had a vision to plant churches among the hill country Tamils. He started the Hatton Church in 1979, and planted two more, in Maskeliya and Bogawantalawa. Our first joint crusade church plant together was in the hill country town of Kotagala, ten miles from Hatton.

Still very tentative about rain, I asked Pastor Yoganathan about the weather. "No rain," he said, not even looking at the sky. "It won't rain." I appreciated this pastor's positive demeanor, but was dubious. He was right. That week, rain fell all around Kotagala, but our meeting was dry, completely rain-free! Tamils crowded to the four-day meeting under clear skies, there were no Singhalese interruptions, and no police interference! Four delightful days of uninterrupted preaching that concluded on a Saturday night. We opened a new church on Sunday morning. One hundred people showed up for the first service. Over the next year our friendship with Pastor Yoganathan and his wife Sheila grew. Pastor Yoga – the name all of his friends used – was easy to like. He never pressed me for money. He talked often about his vision to plant churches in the hill country, and never whined about the challenges. I didn't offer to assist financially – too early for that – but just listened, and together we planned for more crusades and church plants.

The first year we planted four churches. Using our outdoor meeting model, we started on Wednesday or Thursday and ended on Saturday night. On Sunday morning we launched a new church in a rented house or storefront. Pastor Yoga got the required permits from local police – he was obviously respected in the area – and we were never interrupted. He rallied his workers, a lot of single young people, to do most of the work. They advertised around town, helped prepare the field, and provided music for the meetings. We paid the bills. And, we were never again rained out again. For five years we conducted open-air crusades all over the hill country, preaching the Gospel and planting new churches, and never had trouble with rain!

Living conditions improved too. Pastor Yoganathan had great connections with the tea estate superintendents and arranged for us to stay in their homes. These palatial mansions – called bungalows – were built for the "boss" of each estate. They were built on a hill or high point in the middle of each plantation. The superintendent bungalows were a remnant of British organization and excellence. Built by the British, Sri Lanka's tea industry today is owned and operated by the national government. Tea is Sri Lanka's main export to the world. Orange Pekoe tea is the pride of the nation. There are rivals, including India and China, but no tea in the world can match the excellence and variety of Sri Lanka's BOP – Broken Orange Pekoe.

Tea estate laborers, mostly Tamils, plant the trees, pluck the tea, operate the processing plants, and maintain the estate. They are not slaves, but life on the estates for the average laborer is simple existence. Besides meager wages, the government provides the Tamil labor force with basic housing, education for children, and medical care. Workers get stability and security but little else. Estate labor is not a career aspiration for Tamil youth, but most have few options because of their ethnicity and poor social standing.

By contrast, estate management, offered to the Singhalese, and a few educated Tamils, pays well. The head manager – the Superintendent – lives like a king compared to others on the estate. He and his family live in the main bungalow surrounded by pristine gardens on a pristine hill overlooking the estate under his care. There are over six hundred such estates in the hill country. An attentive staff of cooks, servants, and gardeners cater to the Superintendent. If he is married and has children, the wife and kids usually live in Colombo so the children can study in proper schools. They only return to the hill country on weekends and holidays. Most of the time the bungalow is an empty, lonely palace.

Yoga's superintendent friends welcomed the foreign guests! They were glad for some company for a few days and treated us like kings! At dawn every morning, servants brought "bed tea" to our rooms. Breakfast arrived at eight: eggs, bacon, ham, toast with butter and jam, steaming coffee or tea, all served in an elegant dining room on white china and white linen! Sometimes the servants prepared a Sri Lankan breakfast: "string hoppers" or "egg hoppers" with yellow curry and dal. Lunch was served at noon. Dinner was ready for us after the meetings. Tea was offered at four o'clock in the afternoon, always served on white linen and china. Servants did our laundry and returned it neatly folded and pressed!

It was heaven!

And, it never rained!

From 1988 into the mid-1990's our new experience in Sri Lanka was marked by profound fruitfulness and peace. We conducted outreaches, planted churches, and enjoyed fruitful ministry in the cool tranquility of the hill country, five thousand feet above sea level. We planted over thirty-five churches in that short time and reached thousands of Tamils.

In 1991, mid-point in this amazing run, my family and I had to go home. While the work flourished in Sri Lanka, our family, now four children and fifteen years in Asia, was wearing down and needing maintenance. Beth was unhappy. She was stressed from managing a growing brood of children and co-leading an expanding team and ministry. She worried over keeping our home, providing education for three of the kids, and being a good wife to a traveling leader. It's a tough story to talk about, and I struggled immensely with the conflict between answered prayer in Sri Lanka, the supreme success God was giving us, and my love for my family.

In June 1991 we decided to go home. It came down to a simple priority: family first. We made arrangements with the team, notified Pastor Yoganathan that we were moving our base to the United States, and then flew to Hawaii for a three-month break with Sam and Nancy Webb and Grace Bible Church. In August we flew to Goshen to put the kids in school for the fall semester. I'll spare the reader further details of the transition. It was extremely difficult. Our marriage was in crisis, the recovery took much longer than I expected, and the process veered us into new and unforeseen directions. For the next three years I returned to Sri Lanka regularly from several U.S. bases to conduct outreaches and plant churches. Our family entered a new kind of vagabond existence. We moved four times in three years, over distances that sometimes exceeded ten-thousand-miles, first from Thailand to Indiana (via Hawaii), then back to Hawaii for a year. In June 1993, we moved to Lancaster County for another year. Chapter One of this book starts during that year in Lancaster. My parent's helped us buy a house and we set our hearts on permanence in Amish country. Within six months I received four job offers, one of which took us to a new assignment in Pensacola. In July 1994 we packed all of our belongings again and drove a thousand miles to the Gulf Coast.

Transitions are not easy. Christian leaders carry heavy responsibilities. We lead, people follow us. Their loyalty is not skin-deep and is not associated only with the job. It's personal, it's relational, and their connection to us is based on trust. So when a leader makes a change in his or her life, the effect ripples through every relationship in the organization. Pastor

Yoganathan wept bitterly when I told him I would no longer be coming to Sri Lanka to plant churches with him. We were close friends and had made a powerful alliance that had reached tens of thousands of people. Changes are painful.

John too was deeply affected. He and his new wife Maria moved to Sri Lanka to help take up the slack with the ministry. But Sri Lanka was too unstable for Maria, a mother of two infant children. Maria was a tough Swedish missionary kid who had grown up in Thailand; she was familiar with life in Asia. But living in a war zone can be brutal; Maria could not cope with bombs exploding nearby – rattling the windows of their home. After a year, they left Sri Lanka and returned to Thailand, and a year later they returned to Hawaii. John began teaching in a Christian school.

By the time we moved to Pensacola in 1994, our team had planted thirty-six churches in Sri Lanka's hill country. In ten years of crusade ministry we had preached to several hundred thousand people, and helped bring ten thousand to Jesus and His church. Our plan was to plant a church every ten miles throughout the tea estate region. Without the interruptions, it would have happened. But, mortality sometimes limits us, God doesn't always explain Himself, and life isn't always fair. Through the changes, and the disappointments, I learned something. Our dreams, if they are borne of God, exist in a place that is bigger and more secure than ourselves and our abilities. Our dreams belong to God, and they are fulfilled by a Power that is greater than our own.

While I focused on my new assignment in Pensacola, and attended to the needs in our family, God put His own plan into motion. Other people, inspired by our story and the vision Pastor Yoganathan and I started, stepped in to reach the hill country Tamils. Young Tamil leaders, "Timothean" trainees when I first met them, started pastoring their own congregations. They stepped up to expand the vision, and began planting daughter churches. Other American churches, and leaders, and missionaries, many of whom had been introduced to Sri Lanka by our team, joined hands with Pastor

Yoganathan and moved the vision forward. The vision did not die. It thrived! Today, Pastor Yoganathan's three original churches has now grown to over ninety, and those first five hundred believers now worship in the company of nearly thirty-five thousand Tamil souls who have given their lives to Jesus Christ.

RETURN TO WHITE PICKET FENCES

Well, before we close this little tome, we must tie off a few loose ends. I recently read about a noted Hollywood actress who decided, at the pinnacle of her career, to withdraw from the public limelight. For two years she stayed in the shadows and spent time with her family. When asked why, she replied, "If you want to tell stories as truthfully as possible, you have to have a normal, boring existence." Touché'! My experience has been far from such celebrity, but I have been around long enough to understand the insight. Adventurers have a difficult temptation; we want to avoid boredom at all costs. But boredom is a part of the rhythm of life. Routine is the space between the high points. It may feel like a valley, but in fact the valleys are what ground and center us. They are our friends, reminding us where we came from and what we are made of. The biblical Sabbath, which was God's idea, could be called institutionalized boredom! It is God's gift to us, to refill our reserves, recharge our batteries, and re-create the energy we need to climb the next mountain or navigate the next storm. We need these breaks! Too many human tragedies are the result of insufficient refueling time.

Anyway, to the loose ends.

33 Acquainted with Grief

A few months ago Ron and Carolyn Manning's twenty-eight-year-old son was killed in a car accident. Charles was the oldest, and only boy, of the three children. Charles had recently gotten his life back together after a troubled journey through adolescence. His death was not the family's first heartache. The trouble started years earlier with Ron. From radiant beginnings when I first met him at Goshen College, then as a worship leader and teacher at Zion Chapel, Ron had followed a promising path into full time ministry. Eventually Ron became the lead pastor of a church plant. The position lasted two years and ended abruptly after a moral failure. Ron left the ministry and abandoned his family. After the divorce, Carolyn held the family together, returned to her teaching profession, and kept their life solvent while Ron ignored them. The family really suffered, and some of the kids lost their way, especially Charles. Carolyn endured years of loneliness. But when Charles died in that car accident on a dark, snow-bound Indiana road, the family's grief became indescribable. At the funeral, Ron helped carry the coffin, and read a letter to his dead son, asking forgiveness for all the pain he had inflicted on his family.

Life is fraught with painful roads down which we are sometimes forced to walk. We don't always choose these roads. Sometimes, simply because of the actions of somebody else, we find ourselves on them. Faith, however sincere, does not guarantee protection from these experiences. I know this, all too well. An October 1984 telephone call from my father was my introduction to unwelcome grief.

Suffering is not unknown in scripture, nor is it demonized. The prophet Isaiah wrote about the Messiah he saw in a vision. Bible scholars call him "Isaiah's Suffering Servant." "He is despised, and rejected of men, " Isaiah wrote. "A man of sorrows, and acquainted with grief." Isaiah was of course envisioning Jesus. At the beginning of His ministry, John the Baptist called Him "the Lamb of God who takes away the sin of the world." John foresaw a road that included tragedy. Jesus' suffering on a lonely hillside outside of Jerusalem, where Roman soldiers brutally hammered nails into his hands and feet and hung Him on a cross, almost defies description. By God's design, Jesus became acquainted with grief.

Grief is not someone we want to meet. He is not our friend, and we don't want to know him. Jesus prayed that the cross experience could be avoided if possible. But it was not possible. Sometimes Grief just comes knocking at our door and we have to let him in. We suffered terribly after Dale took his life. Later, the painful road Beth and I had to walk in our marriage, the one that brought us home from Asia, was almost unbearable. It took years to learn the cause: a chemical imbalance that thrust my precious wife into severe depression and harassed her with unpredictable emotions and hounding, angry thoughts, many of which she directed at me. Nearly twelve years passed before we found a cure. We walked out the grief of Dales' death, and then another in our marriage, one painful day at a time. The experience almost wrecked us, and I nearly quit the ministry. Suffering takes a toll, and changes us. But, in truth, we need to be changed! It is not easy, and we struggle on this difficult journey toward redemption.

I don't want to suffer any more grief! It is not fun. It is not easy. It just hurts. It hurts. It hurts. Yet, I have learned two things. First, I no longer fear suffering. I am acquainted with grief. I know what grief looks like, smells like, *feels* like. And I now know it can never deprive me anything of real and eternal value. Second, I can now empathize with others who suffer. I don't know if empathy is a spiritual gift or just the natural by-product of difficult experiences and the healing God brings to our souls. But, because I have suffered, I can understand what other people go through. I can't take away another person's pain, but I can be a friend walking beside them in it.

Empathy isn't learned in sociology class at college. It is acquired, step by painful step, on the rocky road of experience. Empathy is what Jesus did for thirty-three years. His acquaintance with the human plight is the essence and the miracle of the Incarnation. It is also the absolute verification of Divine Love. Jesus condescended to men of low estate. He was tempted in all points like we are. He wept. He suffered. And then, He died on a brutal Roman cross. He became sin for us. He took upon Himself the world's guilt and shame. Jesus can relate to us because He is a man of sorrows and is acquainted with grief. And we love Him for that!

So, when we suffer, when we walk through grief, we can turn our backs on God and shake our fists in His face, or we can choose to let God draw near and, in time, heal us and redeem our circumstances. We can keep our head up and not allow pain to press us into making bad decisions. We walk forward, even on a road that seems to lead to nowhere. We don't quit! We gather our loved ones around us and weather the storm! Someday, somehow we get through, and THEN we become better people, and we become more effective in helping others. Only those who suffer, and overcome, can truly empathize and tell the victor's story! The world desperately needs such examples! The Apostle Paul wrote to the church in Corinth, saying, "Our light affliction, which is but for a moment, is working for us a far more exceeding and eternal weight of glory." (2 Corinthians 4:17). James said it another way: "Consider it pure joy, my brothers, whenever you face trials of many kinds, because you know that the testing of your faith develops perseverance. Perseverance must finish its work so that you may be mature and complete, not lacking anything." (James 1:2-4).

The end of Jesus' suffering and death was resurrection. We don't always get resurrection immediately, but Jesus' resurrection gives us hope that ultimately we too will prevail. That is the power of the Christian faith! It is the essence of the most powerful story the world has ever heard!

34 Dad Dies

Dad died on our twenty-third wedding anniversary. Ironically, it was technology – the thing he loved – that killed him. As an electrician early in life, and later as a research and development technician for RCA, Dad was exposed to asbestos. Asbestos was not a known carcinogen in the early days of Dad's career, not in the legal, government-controlled sense. Companies knew of the dangers, but they were under no legal compulsion to protect the public or their employees from the toxicity. Asbestos was commonly used to insulate electrical components, and as a heat barrier in other applications. At RCA, Dad used asbestos sheets to build ovens to test heat tolerances in solid-state circuits. Over the years he breathed in lethal doses of the dust.

The asbestos molecule has a unique fish-hook-like shape, with a barb. When asbestos dust is inhaled, the molecules embed in the lung's membrane tissue. Over the years the irritating, carcinogenic characteristics do their nasty work. In 1998, when Dad was sixty-nine years old, he was diagnosed with Mesothelioma, asbestos cancer. He died less than a year later, on April 17, 1999. Mother, Beth and I were at his side.

Nine months before his death Dad wrote these words:

My sister Arlene has been pressing me to write a few things down about this current medical journey, because as she says, "I want Robert to tell his own story." So here goes...

I started this year, 1998, with what I thought was a bad cold, coughing, backache and shortness of breath. So, I finally went to my chiropractor and his x-rays showed what he thought to be fluid in my right lung cavity. He sent me to an MD who sent me directly to the emergency room of St. Joe's where they tapped three quarts of fluid, relieving me of all symptoms (cough, backache and shortness of breath) but this didn't stop the doctor. After x-rays, a CAT scan, lab tests of the fluid and a sample of my bronchial tubes there was no evidence of cancer, infection, injury or heart problems. They convinced me to accept an exploratory operation through my right rib cage which revealed cancer, mesothelioma, which they said was caused by asbestos exposure. This was April 1, 1998.

Yes, I worked with asbestos forty years ago for a short time. The surgeon told my wife how long I have to live and he told me that I have a seventy percent chance to live one year after an operation that removes my right lung, followed by chemo and radiation and a forty five percent chance of living two years. I turned down further treatment and asked to be prepared to go home. They put me on home care with a Hospice nurse, and I was discharged after ten days, ten days in hospital ten days homecare.

People ask me, "How long I have to live?" I tell them I don't know, I don't want to know, and my wife will not tell me. :-) All I know is I am ready to die, enjoying life and planning to live. I am feeling much better than I did six months ago and I am back to mowing the lawn and doing other home maintenance work, and walking two miles, etc. I just had an examination June 18th by my lung specialist. He said there is a little fluid in my right lung cavity but not enough to affect my lung. I have no breathing problems. I wish I had more energy but ... I am 69.

360

Now for the Inside Story

You may already be asking, why I would go to a chiropractor when I have shortness of breath. Well, I must confess I have some distrust of the medical profession and furthermore I didn't have an MD, I very seldom needed one, I was never in the hospital up to this point and I did not have a physical since Uncle Sam forced me into it in 1952. So I asked my chiropractor which MD I should go to and he recommended Dr. Mershon of Cornerstone in Lititz.

At this point I will have to make something clear. In 1952 I passed my physical and was drafted into 1W service, but I was emotionally unstable and I was in a new job, a new place by myself after just being married looking for a place for me and my new wife to live while serving 1W and I was calling for God's help. It soon came. I heard a voice saying, "It is the Spirit that gives life... My words are Spirit and Life." John 6:63.

This became my guiding light, my philosophy of life. I began reading the Bible starting in the beginning, Genesis 1, where I saw how God wanted or planned for us to eat fruits and veggies. So, I became an avid gardener and fruit and veggie eater. I never stopped eating meat but I can easily do without it. Pastries are my weakness. I still need His help.

Now at 69, I was thrown into the hands of the medical profession, while still at home before the operation while pacing the floor it dawned on me, Yes, Jesus is my primary physician. He is going to manage this whole thing I announced to my wife and friends.

Looking back I don't know if He managed the medical staff or not but I am sure He managed me.

After the surgeon told my wife the bad news she came home, got on the phone and called for prayer. A day or so later I started getting visits, cards, flowers, phone calls. In between these and the nurses and doctors I had a little time to meditate on the scriptures, which became life to me and then were reinforced and confirmed by the cards and visits, prayers and scripture reading of the visitors. In short, looking back, I now see that my primary physician brought my thoughts into His captivity (2 Cor. 10:5). I had no time to think of the bad news and that is where I choose to continue to live.

A nurse told my wife that the doctors were making notes on my charts about my positive disposition in light of the diagnosis. My last visit to the surgeon's office the surgeon's assistant said, "Bob, keep your positive disposition." I said, "With God's help I will." She said, "My children and I have you on our prayer list and we pray for you every night at bedtime." My wife complimented her and she said, "They learn this in school so we practice it at home." "Where do they go to school?" I asked. "St. Mary's," she answered.

My new MD, Dr. Mershon, wanted to see me after I was home a couple weeks and on this visit he said that he will stand by me on my decision, then he asked if he could pray for me. I said, "Please do." He asked for healing and said we will turn this over to the sovereignty of God. Sovereignty of God stood out to me and I thought yes, every thought captive to a sovereign God and none to cancer.

Am I healed? Do I still have cancer? Even though I have a new appreciation for the medical profession I am not going to ask them to open me up to see. Jesus is still my primary physician as well as Savior, Lord, Master, Good Shepherd.

On our twenty-third anniversary, six weeks before my forty-fourth birthday, we said goodbye to Dad. He passed peacefully in his sleep the morning of April 17, 1999. A few days later, I spoke at his funeral, an oddity now that I think about it, but honestly it was an honor and I wanted to do it. It wasn't difficult to find words to honor my dad. James Robert Gehman lived a full life and was ready to go, even though we all agreed, at the age of seventy, he died too young.

35 Uncle Amos' Tractors

A few years have passed since Dad died. Mother is remarried. After a steady stream of suitors – even in her seventies Mother still attracted men, who wined and dined her and let their intentions, some honorable and some not, be known – she found herself a good man, a fine widower from a solid Lancaster County Mennonite family. Of course she asked her son to perform the wedding ceremony. John and Fran flew to Pensacola for a simple ceremony on the beach, and a reception in our backyard.

Last August Beth and I flew to Lancaster to spend a long weekend with Mother and John in their home in Lititz. One evening we drove with Judy to visit Uncle Amos and Aunt Arlene in Bucks County, Pennsylvania. This quaint farmland area of bucolic rolling hills and woods has been their home for most of their lives. My uncle Amos is eighty-four years old, and Aunt Arlene, my Dad's older sister, is eighty-three. They have five children, who have given them fifteen grandchildren and seven great grandchildren. Four of their children, my cousins, still live nearby with their families. The fifth, Fred, is the only child who moved away. Fred is an investment banker in New York City, but even he, now in middle age and married with children, maintains strong ties to his roots.

Uncle Amos and Aunt Arlene greeted us from their front porch, standing side-by-side, as we drove up the gravel driveway through their beautifully manicured lawn, to a simple, but nicely decorated ranch house. Aunt Arlene, sweet and hospitable as always, invited us inside and promptly served us warm, freshly baked chocolate chip cookies, plus vanilla ice cream, and fresh cut watermelon slices. She still wears a head covering over her now gray hair. I don't remember, in my fifty-plus years, ever seeing her without it.

Three of their children, my cousins, dropped in to see us. Eleven years had passed since we were together, so it was great to see everyone again. For me the evening was a poignant punctuation of my roots. These people, my people, are not complicated. Country living and hard work define them, guided by a deep Anabaptist heritage, and an equally deep modesty. Bragging and flamboyant living is... shall we say... discouraged. A few youngsters like myself, and cousin Fred, perilously stretched this tradition of Mennonite reticence when we set out to conquer the world. I left after high school and moved to Asia. Dale and his Yamaha piano traveled with a rock band for a few years, a sad-happy-sad adventure that ended in California. The rest of the family stayed near the farm.

Uncle Amos and Aunt Arlene raised their five children on a 160-acre dairy farm, then sold the farm thirty years ago and bought a bus leasing business – running school buses, local commute buses, even tour buses that bring crowds of curious tourists to Lancaster from New York City. Oh, the irony. Some of the children work in the family business; others have businesses and jobs of their own. But all have stayed close to Mom and Dad.

Everyone gathered in the living room, about ten of us, to share family albums and cell phone pictures. The ladies eventually moved to the dining room table, while Uncle Amos, cousin Jerry and I sat at the kitchen bar. In front of me, above the kitchen cabinets on a long shelf stretching across the entire wall were a dozen antique toy tractors, all distinctively orange-colored. The toy tractors mingled with trophies on the long shelf. On the drive up Judy told me that Uncle Amos collected antique tractors. I knew this wall collection was NOT the tractors to which Judy referred.

I asked about his tractors.

Amos said, "Oh, I have a couple."

"Oh, really? What kind do you have?" I ventured.

"Well, actually, I have 26."

"Oh, really!" THIS was getting interesting. Uncle Amos has a hobby!

"What kind of tractors are they? Are they, like, uh, New Holland or John Deere?" I asked, trying to sound like I remembered SOMETHING about my Pennsylvania farm roots.

Aunt Arlene walked over to the kitchen. "Oh, they are ALL Allis Chalmers. We ONLY HAVE Allis Chalmers," she said, thus explaining the orange toy tractor collection. Aunt Arlene interjected the comment, in her characteristically quiet manner, as she scooped ice cream into bowls for the gang. The clarification was not sarcasm. This was an obvious defense of her husband's – maybe even the family's – passion for a specific tractor company.

One thing I know about men, we don't keep our hobbies to ourselves, locked up in the garage. We DO something with them. Uncle Amos would never brag, but I knew he had to be doing SOMETHING with all those tractors.

"Do you show any of your tractors?" I asked, wondering, besides farming, what else one could possibly DO with TWENTY SIX TRACTORS!

"Sometimes I take one to a tractor pull," Amos offered off-handedly. Now we were getting somewhere! "They are very specific about the rules in a tractor pull," he continued. "Each tractor must weigh-in within 500 pounds to qualify for the class. My tractor, the one I took to the Pull, is in the 6500 pound class." (brief pause.) "I beat everyone in that class."

"Wow," I said, genuinely impressed.

"Yeah, the man I pulled against came up to me afterwards and said, 'I can't believe you did that! Wait until next year!' He was kind of grinning and wasn't really serious though," Amos reflected, obviously proud of himself, but cagey about telling me. After a pause he offered, "I actually entered the 7000 pound class next, and won that one too."

"Really?" I said, again impressed.

Uncle Amos had a twinkle in his eye, but he was obviously a little embarrassed about the win. Familiar, but dusty, memories – not events, more like cultural paradigms – wafted through my thoughts. Was Uncle Amos boasting?

"Just good fun among friends, eh?" I asked.

Amos appreciated the spin. "Yeah, that's what it was."

Pointing to the toy tractor collection on the wall, I told Uncle Amos about a small cast-iron toy steam engine my Dad had given me as a boy. "I still have it and it is probably worth a lot of money today," I ventured.

Uncle Amos nodded and said, "Do you want to come out to the garage? I'd like to show you something."

"Sure!" I said enthusiastically.

We walked to the garage. There on the floor, between the car and pickup, was a child's pedal riding toy – a cast-iron replica of an orange Allis-Chalmers tricycle D-17 tractor, in like-new condition. Amos said, "I've had this for years. It's very rare and is worth over two thousand dollars now."

I got down on my knees and looked over the toy tractor. In the dim light of the garage it looked flawless.

"Would you like to see some of my tractors?"

"Yes, that would be great!" I said, trying to mimic Uncle Amos' modest tone.

Tractors! Who would have thought?

I love discovering a person's passion. Nothing makes conversation come alive more than asking a man about what he loves. My interest in Uncle Amos' tractors brought him to life and got him talking. He was delighted, in his characteristic understatement way, to share with an interested nephew his love for this icon of farm life.

We drove his golf cart out of the garage and across the lawn to the barn. In one side room he had stored something like eight or more old Allis-Chalmers tractors. In the main part of the barn, another ten were parked in neat rows on the dirt floor. One tractor dated back to 1937 he told me. Others were built in the 1950s and 60s. The one he used for tractor pull competitions was parked outside with a few more. It was a six-cylinder diesel Allis Chalmers D-19, built in the mid-1960s. To my amateur eyes, it didn't look more than two years old.

"That one," Amos said, pointing to the other end of the barn at an old D-17 with original but faded orange paint, "I bought for about five thousand dollars a few years ago. It is really in demand now, and people are asking twenty-five thousand dollars for tractors like it."

We walked over to it. Amos reached up, adjusted a couple of levers, grabbed another lever beside the steering wheel, and turned a key. The engine roared to life, filling the room with the loud, rumbling blat-blat-blat of a diesel engine. Thick smoke burst from the vertical exhaust pipe above my head. The stuffy barn air turned blue. Amos cranked the throttle a couple of times making the engine roar again, and then, he shut her down.

I'm sure he just couldn't help himself: A little display of tractor power to an admiring nephew.

We talked for a few more minutes about tractors, slid the barn doors shut, climbed into the golf cart and drove back to the house. An hour later, when we were leaving, and lingering in the doorway saying goodbye and exchanging hugs with everyone, I again thanked Uncle Amos for sharing his tractors with me. He took my hand firmly, leaned in, and with a twinkle in his eye said, "You know, when you're in that tractor pull and you're moving forward slowly, and you pull up beside the guy next to you and his tractor is stopped... and then you pull past him... there's nothing like that feeling."

Then Uncle Amos, still grasping my hand, said, "There's probably something wrong with that."

"Just good fun among friends." I replied smiling. He smiled back and nodded. Then we said our goodbyes.

As we drove away I pondered the well-lived life of my Uncle Amos, and longed for more of his kind of humility. Beating out a friend at a tractor pull! Is there something wrong with that? As we drove down those country roads on our way home, years of my cultural heritage welled up inside of me and I started to cry. No, Uncle Amos, there isn't ANYTHING wrong with that!

But there IS something wrong with the avarice and conceit that sometimes controls us, the stuff that drives us to run down our neighbor, and make winning the ONLY thing. There's is something wrong when we force our friends into the shadows, when Dads push their sons to win and belittle them when they don't, when executives offer multi-million dollar contracts to the up and coming, and the up and coming prostitute themselves to accept them, when billions are spent on sponsorships, product endorsements and advertising campaigns, not in pursuit of noble goals but for greed and vanity. There's something wrong when children go to bed hungry, and winners take all and losers get nothing.

So thank you, Uncle Amos ... for a gentle reminder about a more reasonable way to live.

Just good fun among friends? There's nothing wrong with that!

36 Return to White Picket Fences

John Whalen turned fifty-three this year. When we met and started our Asia adventure together, from that first meeting in New Delhi over a jar of peanut butter, a journey that has now spanned three decades, I was twenty-seven and he was twenty-two. Man do I feel old. I flew to Arizona for his fiftieth birthday a few years ago, a month-long conspiratorial plan between Maria and me. John's Mother and step-dad met me at the Tucson Airport and drove me back to Sierra Vista. When John walked into the house, I came out of the living room. He was blown away. We spent the next three days hiking and canoeing around a local hydro-dam, and trying to catch fish. Not much success with the fishing, but we enjoyed the togetherness.

A lot of time has passed since our first meeting. John married Maria in 1990, a beautiful Swedish missionary daughter. They met in Hua Hin in 1984, when Maria was only sixteen-years-old and John had just joined my team. He *was* the team. There was no one else. A couple of times a week, John jumped a song-tao (pickup truck taxi) and rode it to the other side of town to visit the Anderson family and their five kids, especially their oldest teenage daughter. He was a handful of years older than her, and had to wait for her to grow up and graduate from college. They were pen pal friends, no romance, for six years – all complete propriety and decorum – she in Sweden with her family, he in Asia with ours. Then, in December 1989, with a little push from me, and permission from her parents, he flew to Sweden to spend Christmas with the family and get an answer to a nagging question. On the last day, as he was leaving for the airport, father Bertil shook John's hand in the doorway and said, "Well, if you want her, you can have her."

They got married six months later. Some things are just worth waiting for. From my vantage point, watching a friend I loved dearly, patiently wait, year after lonely year, for the bride of his dreams, theirs was a romance and marriage made in heaven. John and Maria now have four children. Their oldest, Chris was born in Thailand, and is now studying at Auburn University. Last year, he and his girlfriend rode the Greyhound Bus to Pensacola to spend spring break with us, a home away from home for a couple of college kids. It was a badge of honor for us. John may come east this summer to spend another week with his Pensacola buddy, while Maria and the kids fly to Sweden to visit her family. Life and responsibilities don't allow for many of these reunions, but we treasure them when they happen.

Pastor Yoganathan and Sheila arrived at our home only two days after Chris and Katelyn left. They were traveling in the United States visiting friends and supporters, a lot of people we've known for many years. When we met Yoga and Sheila twenty-five years ago, their two children were babies. We were the first Americans they had ever known. Now their kids live in Australia, grown up and in successful careers, and Yoga and his wife are world travelers. Over the years I introduced Pastor Yoga to my American friends, church leaders and Christian businessmen, who had occasionally accompanied me to Sri Lanka. Introductions led to new connections; today Yoga's list of friends and partners is expansive. Every two years, when he and Sheila come to the United States, our home is one stop, a warm time of renewal and remembrances. Sheila insists we go to the beach and eat at

The Shrimp Basket. She loves their southern-style all-you-can-eat fried shrimp, new potatoes, hushpuppies and coleslaw. She always asks me about the latest computer gadgets too. Yoga is uninterested in digital technology, but indulges his wife's geeky passions. This year she bought an IPad. The internet and WIFI has found its way to Sri Lanka's hill country. Good thing. The ministry we started together two and a half decades ago has exploded. How things have changed.

Sri Lanka's civil war is going in the right direction and peace is in sight. Old resentments die slowly, so many years will pass before the Singhalese and Tamils forgive each other completely. It may never happen fully, not without God, the Great Forgiver. His grace is a powerful healer, so I have hope for this precious land. God has some good people in Sri Lanka. Their love for their country and their people is strong, they have faith and they aren't giving up. Dreams do come true. "Though it tarries, wait for it!"

In the meantime, Pastor Yoga, like me, ages and slows down... a little. He doesn't drive as crazy fast on the roads like he did in 1988. "I enjoy the journey now," he says. I can relate. When we were young we were ambitious to grab the future. Now we have hobbies. I surf... and write. Yoga raises chickens, not to eat them but for enjoyment, especially prize chickens. When they visited last time he purchased fertilized eggs from an online store (with Sheila's help, of course) and had the delicate little spheres delivered to Dallas. He timed the delivery to arrive just before they embarked on the final leg home. Yoga called me from Dallas. The eggs arrived safely. He carefully packed them – twenty-four eggs, each egg wrapped in soft tissue – in egg trays. He inserted the cartons into lead-lined X-ray proof bags (to preserve the embryos), and then packed the lot into the center of their suitcases.

When they arrived in Nuwara Eliya, he called me again: All the eggs arrived safely. He placed them into his automatic incubator. "The dormant eggs will come alive in the incubator," he said. "They'll hatch in twenty-one days." He's hoping for a whole new line of prize chickens, some to sell to collectors and others to keep for the simple pleasure of it.

Uncle Amos has his tractors, I have my writing and surfing, and Pastor Yoganathan has his chickens. Every man needs a hobby. The distraction keeps us young and healthy. In the pressure cooker of leadership and work, we need the diversion. Just good fun among friends.

A lot has happened this past year. Our oldest daughter Cori and her family are in transition with hopes from everyone that they will settle in this area. Jeremy and his family are in Germany, at Ramstein Air Force Base, for three years, a great experience for them, and another excuse for us to take European vacations. No one is complaining about that assignment! Kelly with her family just gave birth to Number Three, which means we now have nine grandkids. And Trevor married his dream gal. With all the changes, and the flow of grandchildren births, we abound with moments and memories. My Mother still chides me about denying her such experiences nearly forty years ago when we went "traipsing all over" the world. It's a topic of happy conversation now, no sour grapes. She enjoys our news from a distance, with regular phone calls and picture emails.

I recently posted on Facebook that I am proud of my kids. It's every parent's braggadocio, but I got many "Likes" and comments, a nice tribute. The pride extends to my grandkids too. I am unashamedly that water cooler windbag with a wallet full of family photos, all posted on Facebook these days. It's an infirmity from which I hope I never recover.

Mother and John sold their home in Lititz last year and moved to a retirement community near Lancaster. Brethren Village is nestled in old growth oak and poplar trees along Route 501. The architects and designers built the sprawling community on former farm and woodland, gently preserving the County's beloved green country ambiance. We drove up to help them with the move. Most of the heavy work was done before we arrived, so there was little to do, except, at

Mother's insistence, to pick through family memorabilia, odds and ends from a lifetime of collectables.

I found an old wire-bound wooden lattice egg crate. The side was stenciled with the words "Humpty-Dumpty" and the year "1903," faded but still visible. It belonged to Grandpa Gehman. Memories flooded into my soul when I picked it up. Grandpa collected eggs in that crate. And I helped him. I'm sure, if we could scrape samples from the faded surfaces, tests would find my DNA residue. I held the crate it my hands and let the nostalgia flow over me. When we said our goodbyes to Mother and John a few days later, I carried this piece of my own history back to Pensacola and put it in my office next to Grandpa Stoltzfus' Grandfather clock. Media like this, ancient but powerful, can convey more images and awaken more emotions than a Hollywood movie. I wish every family could hold such fondness and meaning in their own hands. Too many have been denied that wealth and those rich stories.

The nostalgia will be even sweeter when one day I pass the egg crate and the Grandfather clock to our children and grandchildren, with stories from these pages. They don't have the memories of this clock or crate, not like I do. But they'll have the stories. And, they will have their own stories to pass to their children. Yesterday, our oldest daughter Cori sent me a text with an attached picture of their third child, Chase, our eighth grandchild. Trevor's marriage promises a few more are coming, but I'm not making any demands. To use a good Bible cliché, our quiver is full and we are blessed.

Nostalgia is one of the most personal things in human existence. In the long list of human predilections, this one should be more indulged. The world needs more proud water cooler windbags like me, not to hear from them, but to be them. Too many people carry too many regrets from the choices they have made and what they have done to their families. I wish better things for them, like a wallet full of warm memories to brag about.

As a human commodity, nostalgia is too subtle to measure and too fleeting to gather into our hands. But it is as real as a wallet full of photographs, as tangible as a hug. It is in terribly short supply these days. Like an oak tree, nostalgia takes a lifetime to grow, and one bad decision to burn it to ashes. But when we nourish and protect it, its substance brings smiles to our faces, tears to our eyes, and a horde of loved ones gathered around us for the holidays. If life is about relationships, this is life. The quest for nostalgia builds our lives, raises our families, and over a lifetime enriches the future for our children's children.

The Bible speaks powerfully about the idea of nostalgia. The Pentateuch calls it "The Blessing" and envisions its influence going forward to the third and fourth generation. I've tried to live my life with The Blessing in mind. I've had to live carefully. You don't get it pursuing only your own goals. One must live to benefit others, especially one's family. That takes sacrifice. That means time, love, encouragement, guidance, and teaching children how to live. If I have done that right – and this is the real measure – they'll do the same for their kids, and pass that blessing forward. God knows, in our shortsighted, *me first, I'm worth it so get out of my way while I discover MY destiny* culture, humanity needs this longer view.

So, Beth and I carried an old wooden egg crate from one white picket fence home in Lancaster, Pennsylvania to another in Pensacola, Florida. Someday I will hand it off to our children. It's just a wooden egg crate. But, it is a symbol, in our family a weighty heirloom, much heavier than the three pounds it registers on a scale, a value measured by the people who owned it – Grandpa and Grandma Gehman, and others like them – who lived the example and passed on the legacy.

Hopefully, at some future moment when my two billion heartbeats are completed and the weight of my life is measured, the scales will speak well of James Douglas Gehman. Perhaps I am overly sentimental here. Maybe some of you are backing away from the water cooler. Frankly I am unapologetic. You would do well to measure the story that has your name on it. Good memories are in desperate short supply these days and too few people are making new ones. The world has more heartache and regret than it needs. The Blessing doesn't happen with quick fixes and Band Aid apologies. It is the fruit of a lifetime of consistency, of right choices, and living for others, a legacy of faithfulness that helps the next generation find their way down a smoother road, one that you paved. I was handed such a legacy and I've tried to lengthen and smooth the path.

So, maybe this old crate does have within its wood and wire some of Aaron F. and Katie Stoltzfus, and Eli H. and Mary Gehman, and James Robert and Fannie Arlene. Maybe their Amish legalism, Mennonite sensibility, and Anabaptist pride, if there is such a thing, has produced a better kind of life, not measured by competition, but by contentment and consistency that built good memories and few regrets, with more gains and less losses, and pride instead of shame.

Forgive the cliché, but in my experience on this planet, "It just doesn't get any better than this."

THE END

29415282R00226

Made in the USA
Charleston, SC
12 May 2014